GROWING UNUSUAL FRUIT

Alan F. Simmons

GROWING
UNUSUAL
FRUIT

DAVID & CHARLES
NEWTON ABBOT

ISBN 0 7153 5531 7

Set in 10/12 Plantin
and printed in Great Britain
by W J Holman Limited Dawlish Devon
for David & Charles (Publishers) Limited
South Devon House Newton Abbot Devon

Contents

LIST OF PLATES

Introduction

You will derive many pleasures from growing unusual fruits. Not only will you satisfy your creative instincts but you will be something of a pioneer—continuing the work of the plant hunters of times past and advancing the frontiers of fruit cultivation. Not only will you arouse the interest of friends and neighbours, but you will be growing pure, health-promoting fruits that can rarely be bought in the shops.

The difficulties immediately occur to most of us: climate, lack of space, lack of time, cost. Climate? This is certainly a challenge but remember that the tomato originated in South America and that the pineapple was being cultivated in England as recently as the seventeenth century. Today it is very much easier and cheaper, comparatively, to stimulate the climatic requirements of a plant—if necessary we have, for example, polythene, plastic piping and electricity. Space? Few of us have large country estates but not even a large garden is required to grow unusual fruits—pot culture works well. Time? Yes, but what hobby does not require time? As in all forms of gardening, some devotion will be required, but there is nothing wrong with that provided such devotion is not to the detriment of your wife—or husband! A pet is regarded as one of the family and your trees, bushes or plants are in much the same category. The cost? Well, as a matter of fact you can grow unusual fruits to suit your individual purse or pocket. In this book will be found something for everybody—whether you have a heated greenhouse or no greenhouse, a large garden or no garden. Some of the plants included are hard to come by; some you will have to search for in the catalogues of nurserymen and seedsmen; some you can grow from seed after you have eaten the fruit; some may be found growing wild. And there is nothing wrong with that. All plants, in the beginning, were uncultivated, so if you have a fancy for a 'wild' fruit take some seed or a cutting of it, grow it, nurture it, enjoy it.

Introduction

Much of the material here should be useful to gardeners in temperate climates generally, especially to those in Britain, Europe and the United States. American readers will find that some of the fruits dealt with are not so unusual to them, whilst others—the alpine strawberry, for instance—are common on the European continent but interestingly rare in the States.

The fruits are listed in alphabetical order under the most common name, and any alternative name is also given. Set notes under each heading summarize for speedy reference the main details concerning the fruit.

Akebia fruit

Classification   : *Akebia trifoliata* (syn. *A. lobata*); *A. quinata*.
Physiology   : Semi-hardy plant climbing up to 10ft.
Origin   : China; Korea; Japan.
History   : Introduced to Kew 1837, now occasionally seen out of doors in southern England. Sometimes grown as an ornamental in southern USA.
Recommended site : Sun lounge; sheltered porch.
Culinary uses   : When ripe eaten raw as a dessert.

There are two species of cultivated akebia—*A. trifoliata* (sometimes classified as *A. lobata*) and *A. quinata*. The akebia belongs to the family Lardzibalaceae which is a family of climbers producing (usually) edible pod-like fruits. The difference between the two akebias is in the leaflets—*trifoliata* has leaves of three leaflets and *quinata* leaves of five leaflets—and also in the size of the fruits, which will be described presently.

The akebias are twiners. That is to say they climb like runner beans, by entwining themselves around a support. They are very strong climbers and will soon be up any slender support within their reach. They are also fairly hardy plants and although they are deciduous they may, in a well-sheltered position, keep their leaves on during the winter.

Like most twiners they like a little bit of shade. They also like a good loamy soil but are not particular whether it is acid or alkaline. The only pruning necessary is the thinning out of any crowded shoots and the shortening of straggling stems in the winter. Thus the plants

9

themselves are easily grown. Propagation is also fairly easy. This can be by layering in autumn and then cutting the rootlet from its parent in the spring; or by rooting cuttings in the summer, either under a cloche or cold frame; or by sowing ripe seed and allowing it to remain in a cold frame over winter to germinate the following spring.

Fruit cultivation, however, is somewhat more difficult. The flowers, which blossom during April and exhale a delightful fragrance, are on racemes, both females and males occurring together, but the females, larger than the males, are more distinctive and easily recognized. The females too are usually nearer the stem of the plant whilst the males are further out on the raceme.

Although the plants flower steadily it is difficult to get them to fruit heavily in northern latitudes. For one thing the flowers, appearing as they do in April, are easily killed off by frost unless they are in a very sheltered position; for another, there are not many insects about at that time of year. It seems, too, that chilling can take place even when temperatures are above freezing. To aid fruiting, therefore, they need to be in a reasonably warm atmosphere. Syringeing the flowers with tepid water will help fertilization, and hand-pollination of the flowers is also desirable.

But if you want a highly flavoured fruit then the akebia is not for you. Its value is in the novelty of its shape and colour. The fruit of the *Akebia trifoliata* grows up to 5in long, is sausage-shaped and pale violet or purple in colour. In late summer when the fruit is really ripe the jackets burst open showing jet black seeds in a white, fleshy, pulpy, but insipid fruit. *Akebia quinata* has egg-shaped fruits up to 3in long.

In the sun lounge, kept under control and trained up ornamental trellis work, akebia should give considerable interest—particularly when your friends can pick and eat a sausage.

Almond

Classification	:	*Prunus amygdalus.*
Physiology	:	Small deciduous tree growing 10-20ft tall.
Origin	:	Persia; Afghanistan.
History	:	Believed to have been introduced into Europe by the Greeks and Romans. Grown commercially in Mediterranean area and in California. Grown in England hitherto only as an ornamental tree.
Recommended site	:	Outdoors—well sheltered from cold winds, in garden position or in pot.
Culinary uses	:	The sweet almond nut is used in confectionery or for dessert.

The almond tree belongs to the large and commercially important *Prunus* (plum, cherry, peach, apricot) genus. It is most closely related to the peach. When young the almond tree is very erect but as it ages it begins to spread. Yet, even so, it never becomes a large tree and many gardens can accommodate it.

Commercial growing in Europe is fairly extensive in the Mediterranean area. In the British Isles the nut usually matures only in southern England consequently it is grown generally as an ornamental. In the United States commercial growing is confined mainly to California but there is a form, possibly a hybrid with the peach, which will mature as far north as Illinois and Pennsylvania. It is, however, considered to be an inferior form as it possesses a hard shell and poor flavour.

Almond

The almond is not particularly choosy about soil, except that it does like a little lime. Most garden soils if well drained are suitable for almonds but if the soil is infertile, or of a very sandy texture, as much organic manure or humus as possible should be dug into the root area before planting. Provided the soil is prepared in this way little future manuring should be required. On neutral or acid soils annual dressings of lime are required. It is also worthwhile to give the soil a dressing of compost over an area equivalent to the spread of the tree about every third year if you can manage it. If any nitrogen deficiency occurs the leaves will become pale and undersized; the remedy lies in sprinkling organic fertilizer such as dried blood or hoof and horn meal around the tree.

Special care is needed in choosing a site for the tree outdoors. To obtain maximum cropping it needs to be sheltered from very cold north and east winds and at the same time it needs to receive as much sun as is available. The ideal position is, of course, on a southern slope which permits cold air to drain away and so minimizes the frost danger—most certainly the tree should not be planted in a frost pocket. If it is grown in a pot, it can spend part of its time indoors—and it is nice to have indoors when in blossom.

It is quite possible to raise a baby almond tree from a stone—if you do not mind waiting at least five years before it starts producing almonds. The stones should be sown about 3in deep in open ground in October and by the following spring there should be evidence of germination.

In the spring when the tree is a year old pruning must be carried out with the aim of building up a robust body or framework for fruit bearing. It should be cut down to a height of 18-24in so that it forms a single short stem or leg. The cut should be made close above a bud and the top two or three buds will then make new leaders during the coming season. The next year the young tree will have three or four leaders, and each one of these, again in the spring, should be cut back to about a third of its length. This cut must be made at a point where there are outward pointing buds on opposite sides of the shoot, and it will have the effect of doubling the leaders. In the third spring the leaders should be cut back by half—again at the outward growing buds. By the fourth year the tree can be regarded as established and should be a goblet-shaped bush with its centre as open as possible.

Once you have established the young tree's body shape you should prune only those branches which are not growing from the top or are only growing weakly, and these should cut back to the next strong side shoot. If any buds along the middle of a branch have not commenced growing cut back to the first outward-growing shoot but do not touch those branches which are growing strongly.

Almonds should never be pruned until after the blossom has set in May. The reason for this is so that cuts can be made where the new buds are seen to be growing. Also when the tree starts cropping it is possible to relate the severity of the pruning to the size of the current anticipated crop. Foliage area should always be related to the crop (or vice versa, which is one of the aims of thinning out fruit).

There is a disease which affects almond trees and this is commonly known as die-back, so named because it first causes the blossom to wilt, and this affects the spurs, then the twigs, and finally the branches die. The only thing to do is to cut out the dead branch or twig. When this disease is seen, even if it should develop after the spring pruning, it should be cut out completely; cut well back into living wood, so that no sign of the characteristic brown stain remains.

When dormant the almond tree is almost as hardy as the plum, but in southern England fruiting is sometimes affected because blossom appears at any time from the end of February to the end of March, when there is not only danger of frost but few pollinating insects are about. Because of this scarcity of insects it is worthwhile to hand-pollinate with a camel-hair brush.

When ready for harvesting, the fruits begin to fall from the tree and the outer husk to split. A common method of harvesting almonds is to brush them off the tree with a broom. The nuts should be removed from the outer husk and be thoroughly dried before storing otherwise they will go mouldy.

There are two kinds of almond—the sweet and the bitter. *Prunus amygdalus amora* is the bitter almond tree. Bitter almonds contain a minute quantity of hydrocyanic or prussic acid which could, as you possibly know, be dangerous if taken in large enough quantity. The bitter almond, however, has a much stronger flavour and for this reason is often used in marzipan and for almond flavourings, but it should never be eaten in quantity for dessert.

The sweet almond nut needs no description. It is worth mentioning

Almond

perhaps that in some countries, where they are grown commercially, the nuts are eaten green, though at that stage they do not seem to have much flavour.

The two varieties that are usually used for sweet almond growing are *P. amygdalus macrocarpa*, which has pale pink flowers and large nuts, and *P. amygdalus praecox*, which also has pale pink flowers but blooms two weeks earlier than *macrocarpa*.

Almond growing has never been attempted commercially in southern Britain despite the fact that the tree is found in many gardens, where in early spring the pale pink blossom appearing before the leaves gives much joy and pleasure. Its value as an ornamental tree is undisputed—but why not have an almond tree that will provide some nuts as well? Remember, though, it is the sweet one that you want!

Alpine strawberry

Classification	:	*Fragaria vesca sempervirens.*
Physiology	:	Hardy perennial plant growing 6-8in tall.
Origin	:	Mountains of northern Italy.
History	:	Grown for a long time on the Continent; now becoming more widely known in Britain; rare in North America.
Recommended site	:	Outdoors in partial shade. Indoors as a pot plant.
Culinary uses	:	Eaten as fresh fruit dessert. Also good for jam making.

The strawberry genus consists of numerous species and the common or garden strawberry is the result of hybridization between certain of these species. The European wild strawberry is *Fragaria vesca* and the Alpine strawberry is said to be a variety of this but it is quite likely that there has at some time been hybridization with other species by continental growers. Because of its rapidly increasing popularity in Britain, it may in a few years be incorrect to refer to it as unusual. It is still comparatively rare in North America, where it certainly needs pioneering.

The Alpine strawberry will grow in most soils but it must be emphasized that it flourishes best in rich humus. As in the case of the ordinary garden strawberry you cannot overfeed it with organic manure. Although the plants will do quite well in full sun provided that the soil is not allowed to dry out, they do really prefer partial shade. An important difference between them and garden strawberries

15

Alpine strawberry

is that they do not make runners. They are upright fellows and as they should be divided or replaced at the end of each season they can be planted close together in the rows. Plant them, say, about 9in apart in the rows but keep the rows about 18in apart so that air can circulate freely. A free circulation helps to lessen the incidence of mildew in wet seasons, but this occurs less frequently in alpine than in garden strawberries.

Another way to grow the plant is in a 6in pot. Pot the plants up in November and leave them outside; bring them into the house just after Christmas when you have got rid of the decorations and guests. This way you should be getting fruit by the end of May, if not before. Outdoors they will fruit from June until the first frosts and, believe it or not, the birds do not touch them.

Although they do not grow runners they do develop crowns and they can be easily propagated by separation of these crowns. The one danger here is the possibility of virus disease; Alpine strawberries have not yet been bred for virus resistance like garden strawberries, and although plants grown from seed are perfectly free from the disease they can, as they continue to grow, become infected.

Growing from seed is fairly easy if you make allowance for rather erratic germination. Sow the seed in early spring and as soon as the seedlings are big enough to handle plant them out into a nursery bed made rich in humus. Unless you want fruit later in the same year, pinch out any flowers that may appear so that the young seedlings, thriving in their rich humus bed, will grow up into big sturdy plants. By the autumn they may have two or three crowns and these can be separated to double or treble your number of plants.

Cultivation is very much the same as for garden strawberries, but if you want the fruit to be larger than normal pick out all the flowers on each truss except for one or two. Also give the plants a good watering with liquid manure, or water in dried blood around them.

Alpine strawberries should be looked upon as a delicacy. Washed and sprinkled with sugar several hours before they are eaten, so that they are almost swimming in their own juice, their flavour will be tasted to the full. In contrast to garden strawberries they have a very high pectin content and are, therefore, better for jam making.

In Britain the best varieties are:

ALEXANDRIA—a very good cropper; the red berries are large for an Alpine.

BARON SOLEMACHER—another large, red berried variety.

HARSLAND ALPINE—red berries and a good cropper.

YELLOW ALPINE—decidedly different with its yellow berries. Something to put on the table when you want to impress. Or serve them mixed with the red. Delightful!

B

Appleberry

Classification	:	*Billardiera longiflora.*
Physiology	:	Evergreen half-hardy plant climbing to 5ft.
Origin	:	Australia; Tasmania.
History	:	Introduced to Britain in 1810 and planted outdoors in mild areas. Sometimes grown as an ornamental in southern USA.
Recommended site	:	Sun lounge; cold greenhouse; south wall in mild areas.
Culinary uses	:	Eaten raw as dessert.

Billardiera is a very small genus of evergreen twiners originating from Tasmania and Australia. It is fairly hardy and has been planted in the milder areas of the British Isles, such as Cornwall, Devon and southern Ireland; it has also fruited at Inverewe on the Scottish west coast. In cool temperate climates, however, it is generally only suitable for the greenhouse. It will climb up trellis work etc without any hesitation but is not a rapid grower. It is unlikely, for instance, to climb over a wall more than 5ft high to trespass in your neighbour's garden.

Propagation is by seed, which should be sown in a temperature of 55°F (13°C), or by cuttings of half-ripe wood taken in summer and inserted in a sandy soil at about the same temperature. It should be planted out in its permanent location in April and although its best place outdoors is in front of a south-facing wall where it will get plenty of sunshine, it does, like most of the twiners, like to have its feet shaded. It prefers an acid soil but will make do, if need be, with an alkaline one. The only pruning it requires in subsequent years is the removal of dead wood and all weak shoots, and this should be done in April.

Because it flowers in July there is no frost problem. The bell-like flowers are long and yellowish, but changing to purple. In October, in the right habitat, it gives a good harvest of fruit. The appleberry, however, does not resemble an apple. It is an oblong berry fruit an inch or so long, and quite agreeable in taste. *B. longiflora* gives shining dark blue berries, and *B. longiflora fructo albo* has white berries. As these are comparatively small plants both varieties could be grown to give blue and white fruits together.

Applerose

(WOLLY DOD'S ROSE)

Classification	:	*Rosa pomifera.*
Physiology	:	Shrub growing 6-8ft tall.
Origin	:	Central Europe.
History	:	Rose species have been known and cultivated for centuries. Today they are grown in every continent of the world.
Recommended site	:	Outdoors.
Culinary uses	:	Fruit, heps or hips, used for preserves, wine, etc.

The *Rosa* genus is very large but its species, with their broadly similar characteristics, are well known. The cultivated rose, although common, is greatly honoured. Through the centuries and in many civilizations, including Christian and Moslem, it has featured in history, legend and mythology, symbolizing purity, romance and love. But as it is not usually grown for its fruit, I make no apology for including it here.

A great deal has been written about the cultivation of the rose in general and there is no need to go into this subject. The applerose, however, needs specific mention. It is a most outstanding and handsome shrub. Being tolerant of almost any soil it can be accommodated in any garden, but it does like a sunny place, not too exposed, and of course not too near trees or shrubs whose roots will rob it of nourishment.

Propagation can be by division of clumps, or by suckers, layers or cuttings. A good rose hedge can be obtained by taking hard wood cuttings in early winter after the leaves have fallen, and burying three-quarters of their length very firmly in the ground 6-9 inches apart. They should be well firmed again after any frost that may loosen the soil.

When the applerose is grown as an ordinary shrub or bush the only pruning necessary is to keep it in shape and to remove old and dead branches. Little else needs to be said about its cultivation.

Its flowers are carmine in bud, opening to clear pink. In the autumn the fruits are very distinctive—up to an inch in diameter, crimson and covered with bristles—in fact, more like large red gooseberries than apples.

The rose fruit, hep or hip, is known mainly for its medicinal usefulness as a rich source of vitamin C in rose hip syrup. Latterly, however, there has been a boom in amateur wine making, and for this the usefulness of the hip is second only to that of the grape. It can also be used to make a very pleasant rose and apple jelly. In the Balkans and Arabian countries the essential oil of the rose is used extensively for flavouring desserts but, alas, this use seems to have been almost forgotten elsewhere.

Because of the size of its fruits *Rosa pomifera* has been chosen for mention here, but American commercial growers favour another species, *Rosa rugosa*, whose large succulent fruits contain a very high percentage of ascorbic acid. It is said to have sometimes as much as twenty-five times the amount of vitamin C as citrus juice. The *rugosa* species is also especially good for hedge making. It forms a stout shrub with thick and very prickly branches. Its flowers are large, solitary and heavily scented; its fruits are large and tomato-like. There are several varieties and hybrids of *rugosa*, giving a good range of flower colour. So here we have a choice of two good species for wine making, jelly making or love making!

Apricot

Classification	:	*Prunus armenaica.*
Physiology	:	Small deciduous tree growing up to 20ft.
Origin	:	Western Asia.
History	:	A gardener in the service of Henry VII introduced it to England. In the early part of the eighteenth century it was taken to North America, where it was first grown in southern California.
Recommended site	:	Outdoors in sheltered position. Cold greenhouse; pot cultivation.
Culinary uses	:	Unsurpassable for preserves; also for dessert.

There are three species of the great fruit-producing genus *Prunus* which give what are generally recognized as apricots: *Prunus armenaica* (common apricot); *P. mume* (Japanese apricot); *P. dasycarpa* (black apricot). The Japanese apricot is not of particular interest because its fruits are small and of very poor quality. Pride of place must, without any reservation, go to the common apricot.

Because it bears the name *armenica* it has been believed that it originated in Armenia but this is now in doubt. It grows naturally throughout a very wide area, from western Asia as far east as Peking, and the Chinese are believed to have cultivated it 3,000 years before the birth of Christ. Alexander the Great brought the apricot from Asia to Greece and from there it was taken to Italy. A gardener in the service of Henry VII introduced it to England. In the early part of the eighteenth century it was taken to North America, where it was first grown in southern California. Commercial cultivation is still confined mainly to the Pacific coast. In Europe cultivation is extensive in the Mediterranean area.

In the nineteenth century the cultivation of the apricot reached the height of its popularity in Britain. Its culture was mainly confined to house walls and for a time it seems to have done quite well. Then its popularity waned. Why did it suddenly lose favour? Perhaps there was some bad luck with the weather—a severe winter, a wet cold summer—creating the idea that the English climate is not really suitable for its cultivation. In fact, although the apricot does not like excessively wet conditions it is hardy in north temperate zones. One of its real troubles is that as it normally blossoms in late March there is always the danger of frost damage. Frost protection must, therefore, always be considered. Another suggested reason for its decline in favour is that it is susceptible to the disease known as die-back. Now, when wall-trained trees become affected with die-back whole branches have to be cut out, and this not only means a loss of crop but because it is not always possible to have a newly grown branch in reserve the symmetry of the tree is spoilt. Fortunately, new varieties are now available which seem to be less prone to the disease.

In the south and especially the south-east of England it is quite possible to grow the apricot as a bush in the open. It hardly needs to be mentioned, though, that if planting in the open a frosty hole or dell should be avoided—no plant likes that anyway. A slope which allows the frost to drain away is ideal.

The apricot in one respect is like a blackcurrant—it needs continuously to make new growth—and it therefore requires a good friable loam with the subsoil well drained, and it loves lime. Where the plum flourishes there also the apricot will grow well.

The tree or bush should be planted between about the middle of September and the end of November. In preparing the site a hole should be dug 2ft deep and if the subsoil appears damp and sticky it is a good idea to put some brick rubble in the bottom of the hole to improve the drainage. One thing the apricot does not like is heavy wet soil. If the soil lacks lime a few lumps of chalk can be added to the brick rubble.

Usually the apricot tree is grown on plum stock but if you want to

Apricot

grow your own apricot tree, and you are a really patient person and do not mind waiting, there is intense satisfaction to be gained from growing your tree from seed. Well-formed and fully ripe fruits should be chosen, the stones taken from these and buried in the ground until February when they should be uncovered, the outer shell chipped and then replanted 2in deep and 8in apart in a warm bed of sandy soil. In the autumn cover the bed with about 6in of leaves or straw or similar litter. When the seedlings have made a year's growth lift them from their bed, shorten their tap roots and either plant them in pots or place them against a wall and train them as you desire.

If propagation is to be by budding from a proved and chosen tree the buds should be inserted in the main stem of the stock fairly close to the ground. Mussel and St Julien plum rootstock are the best for smaller trees, but it may be that more vigorous trees are required as a further combative measure against die-back and some commercial growers have, in fact, used peach rootstock.

The apricot tree is very ornamental: in the spring its delicate pink flowers give a touch of beauty to this world. In a normal season it produces a mass of blossom but some of this consists of infertile flowers. The tree itself is self-fertile and because it produces more than enough blossom the infertile flowers need cause no worry. At times the tree will set such a large number of fruits that thinning will be necessary. When the young fruit has reached the size of marbles thin them out 3-4in apart, otherwise you will lose weight in the ultimate crop and the individual fruit will be of poor quality.

The fruit forms on both new wood and old spurs and you should therefore try to maintain a proportion of both, remembering that to obtain fruit on the growth of the previous year it must be well-ripened wood. The best quality fruit grows on the old spurs but the growth of young wood is desirable and should be encouraged because apart from normal growth it is always desirable to have a reserve of new wood to replace any of the old affected by die-back (see under Almond).

Although the tree can be grown as a bush or standard in the open in the south and south-east of England there are some parts of the country where the only outdoor place for it is against a wall. Make sure that the wall is of good height and breadth and facing south or west; on an east-facing wall the early morning sun can do severe damage to blossom still touched with frost. The general rules are that in southern England the wall can face west providing there is no danger from gales; in the midlands it should face south; in northern England only sheltered corners should be chosen; and in Scotland the apricot should be grown only under glass.

In the United States, though the commercial cultivation of the apricot is confined mainly to the Pacific coast and to certain areas between the Sierra Nevada and the Rocky Mountains, there is no reason why amateurs should not grow it elsewhere if the general principles here outlined are followed.

In general, pruning should be in May when die-back, if it has occurred, will be apparent. All dead wood should be cut out back to the third side shoot, which will be 2-3in long, but cut further if necessary. All inward growing branches, and any rubbing against each other, should be removed. From the second year after the tree has been planted the branches should be headed back—this helps to strengthen the wood and also encourages fruit spurs to develop. For the bush tree grown in the open the pruning should also aim at the formation of an open cup-shaped bush.

Pruning of the wall-trained tree should be on the same lines. Also any young shoots which grow from the front of the branches should be removed: these can usually be pinched out with the finger and thumb. Weakly shoots on the sides of the branches should also be removed. The young shoots left should then be examined and the strongest ones selected to form future branches; they should be laid and fixed between the older branches. The other young shoots should be shortened back to the fourth leaf and any subsequent growth from them shortened back to one leaf to form fruiting spurs. When the old, dead and exhausted branches are removed the young ones previously laid in will replace them. The judicious removal of old wood encourages the tree to produce new shoots.

From May onwards the apricot must have plenty of water. A mulch of manure or compost will help to retain moisture and during hot, dry weather it must be watered. Spraying the foliage with water in the evenings is also beneficial but this should not be done when the fruit is ripening. The roots can also be fed with liquid manure.

For trees kept in pots and grown indoors, and for trees grown in the greenhouse, the soil should be thoroughly soaked in February and

25

Apricot

given a mulch of manure or compost. The temperature should rise to 55°F (13° C) in February and to 65°F (18°C) during the summer. They should be given ventilaton and their foliage sprayed with water daily. At the end of the season give them as much ventilation as possible to encourage them to become completely dormant and so rest. The potted tree can, of course, be carried outdoors to encourage this.

The fruit has to be picked when it is fully ripe and if it can be taken whilst still touched with dew it is fit for a queen (or a king). The apricot begins to get soft some time before it is fully ripe, but if you pick it as soon as it is soft it never ripens to its full flavour and lusciousness.

VARIETIES AVAILABLE

If you are able to grow several varieties fruiting can cover a period from early July until September but much will depend on local climatic conditions. The best known varieties in Britain at the present time are:

FROGMORE EARLY—small fruit, juicy. July.

NEW LARGE EARLY—large fruit, good flavour. End of July.

FARMINGDALE—medium-sized fruit, good flavour, moderately juicy. End of July. This is an American variety, of vigorous growth and said to be less prone to die-back.

ALFRED—very similar to the above and also less prone to die-back.

ROYAL—large fruit, rich flavour. Less prone to die-back than most.

BREDA—small fruit, very rich flavour, juicy. Early August. A very old hardy variety, probably one of the first ever to have been grown in this country.

EARLY MOORPARK—fruit of medium size, good flavour and juicy. Mid-August.

KAISHA—medium-sized fruit, good flavour and sweet. Mid-August. Very good cropper and of moderate growth.

HEMSKIRK—large fruit, juicy and good flavour. Mid-August. Very hardy and a heavy cropper.

MOORPARK—large fruit, of excellent flavour. Early September. Prone to die-back.

BLACK APRICOT
(Prunus dasycarpa)

This apricot is mainly cultivated in China, Kashmir and Afghanistan. The tree itself is more upright and a little taller than the common apricot. The flowers are also large but the fruit is smaller, almost black in colour, and smooth skinned and plum-like. The flesh is soft, sub-acid and juicy but the flavour is said not to equal that of the common apricot. It seems to have a close relationship with the plum and its fruits can easily be mistaken for very dark plums. The tree is much hardier than the common apricot—as hardy in fact as the apple —and can therefore be grown in colder regions than its relation. It comes very true to seed.

In this brief survey of the apricot a good deal has been written about the difficulties of growing it, but it is hoped that in bringing these problems to the notice of the reader and at the same time showing that they are not *too* serious it will stimulate new interest and serve as a challenge to enterprising growers in both North America and Europe.

Avocado pear

Classification   : *Persea americana* (syn. *P. gratis-sima*).
Physiology   : Vigorous tree growing up to 60ft.
Origin   : Central and South America.
History   : Cultivated centuries ago by natives of Central and South America but only comparatively recently introduced to North America and even more recently to the Mediterranean area.
Recommended site : Heated greenhouse.
Culinary uses   : Versatile as dessert or savoury.

There are about fifty different species of *Persea* but apart from *americana* their fruiting quality is poor as they produce only small fruit. *Persea schiedeana* does, however, bear large fruit and is said to have a very pleasant flavour, but it has a stringy flesh and is watery. It is eaten by the people of southern Mexico and other countries of central America where it has its home.

The native Indians of South America were great ones for fruit and they cultivated the avocado in their fruit gardens long before the arrival of the Europeans. They just planted an avocado stone and up grew a tree. Despite the existence of this very important fruit tree comparatively close to the United States of America it is only in about the last fifty years that it has taken up residence there. Today it is grown in Florida and California. Now, at last, it appears to be moving to the Mediterranean region.

In a soil and climate which is to its liking it is a strong-growing

28

tree and in its native habitat, which is humid forest, it will grow up to 60ft. Growth tends to be from the ends of branches rather than from sprouting buds or older wood. This results in spreading trees, with branches that are often bent down under their own weight.

Although the tree is evergreen it tends to behave as though it were deciduous and it is not unusual for it to lose all its leaves from the previous season's growth at the beginning of a fresh flush of growth. Another characteristic is that the tree forms no visible hair roots; when you take it from a pot to transplant it, its roots appear almost freakish because of this. It seems that absorption is through a corky tissue at the tips of the many secondary branch roots.

The avocado tree will make do with all kinds of soil but it cannot survive in soil which is waterlogged or badly drained; nor, on the other hand, can it survive severe drought. When you give this tree a home in your greenhouse provide it with a soil it will really like— equal parts of loam, peat and sand. It can be planted in a large tub or pot. Summer temperatures should be 75-85°F (24-29°C) and winter temperatures 55-65°F (13-18°C). The atmosphere should be humid during summer and, because of its desire for moisture, it needs to be sprayed daily and watered plentifully, but in winter only very moderate watering will be required.

Leafy cuttings of some avocado trees may root, but this is not the best means of propagation. Grafting or budding can be carried out— Mexican varieties being used as rootstock for the better types. Seed can also be propagated easily in a temperature of 85°F (29°C). It is said that seedlings cannot be depended on to bear desirable fruit; this is usually true, but in those countries where the avocado has been grown for centuries the tree has always been propagated from seed.

Seeds can be stored for several months in dry peat at a temperature of 41°F (5°C) provided they are not permitted to dry out, but best results follow if they are planted as soon as they are taken from the fruit. They germinate better if a thin section is cut from the apex and the base of the seeds and the seed coats are removed. This is more easily done if the seed is first wetted and then dried rapidly in warmth. It should be put in the soil with its base downwards and covered by not more than an inch of soil. The base is usually the broadest part and is that part farthest from the stem of the fruit— this needs to be mentioned because the shape of the avocado does vary.

Avocado pear

As the seedling grows it is necessary to shorten it so that it makes growth in the lower branches—otherwise it will grow up very lanky. Pruning in general should be for the convenience of its keeper. If it is growing too tall it should be shortened so that it forms spreading branches, and if, on the other hand, it sprawls about all over the place then prune back the troublesome branches to upward growing laterals.

The avocado tree in suitable conditions produces an enormous number of flowers. As many as 1,000 may appear on a branch no more than a foot long and yet only one fruit may set per 5,000 flowers. The reason for this extremely low proportion is not yet fully understood: but because hand-pollination is hardly feasible reliance must be on insects and self-pollination.

Nowadays the avocado pear is widely available and so well known that a description of it is unnecessary. It is said to be a highly nutritious fruit, having almost twice the energy value of the banana, very rich in protein, oil, calcium, iron, phosphorus and vitamins but low in carbohydrates. In Mexico and Central American countries it is used as a meat substitute. Of its oil 93 per cent is entirely digestible and is similar in composition to olive oil; it is pleasant in taste, excellent for salad dressings, and is also used in cosmetics. The flavour is nutty and slightly herby, and it can, therefore, be eaten with various accompaniments, sweet or savoury; you can use it, for example, in a fruit or vegetable salad or you can eat it with just salt and pepper.

When the fruit is harvested it is clipped or cut off; pulling would leave a wound where rot might start.

Three forms of avocado are generally recognized:

MEXICAN—believed by some to be a distinct species (*Persea drymifolia*). It is the hardiest and most promising for cultivation in cold climates. The fruit is small, weighing no more than 3-8oz, is thin skinned and has a very rich flavour.

GUATEMALAN—native to the highlands of Central America. It is not so resistant to frost as Mexican. The fruit is characterized by a thick woody skin and can be up to 2lb in weight.

WEST INDIAN—although this is tropical in origin it is grown widely in Florida. It is the least hardy of the three forms. The fruit has a leathery skin but is large and of excellent flavour.

A good deal of natural crossing has taken place between the three forms. These mixed marriages have resulted in numerous types or varieties, some of which are now very important in the commercial world.

Commercial growers are already producing this fruit in the south of France. As its cultivation has spread from tropic to sub-tropic and now to the milder temperate zone, it obviously does not demand a tropical climate. In the temperate zone generally it should be possible to grow the avocado in a greenhouse which is given heat only during the winter months. The only problem is its size, but it grafts easily and so if a dwarf rootstock can be found this is the answer. Due to the ready and natural hybridization which has already taken place, there are good opportunities for extending the climatic frontiers of this very nutritious fruit. The small but hardy Mexican form seems to offer most scope for this.

Banana

(CAVENDISH BANANA; CANARY BANANA)

Classification	:	*Musa cavendishii*.
Physiology	:	Large perennial plant growing to about 8ft with a 5ft spread of leaves.
Origin	:	Believed to be south-east India.
History	:	Cultivation is of great antiquity. Cave paintings in India, possibly dating from about 500 BC, depict the banana. Now widely grown in tropics and also sub-tropics.
Recommended site	:	Warm greenhouse—in the border or large pot.
Culinary uses	:	Good for all dessert purposes.

The banana was one of the first fruits gathered and cultivated by man. There are several species of *Musa* which bear edible fruits (some of the fruits—plantains, for instance—need to be cooked before becoming edible) but here we will only concern ourselves with the Cavendish or Canary banana. This is considered by some to be a dwarf form of the sweet banana, *Musa sapientum*, but generally it is accepted as a separate species—*Musa cavendishii*. The other species, although of great importance to plant breeders and commercial growers, can be ignored by the amateur because of their large growth.

The origin of *Musa cavendishii*, or Canary banana, is not definitely known but it is now grown extensively in the Canary Islands, Florida, Australia and Israel. Although it is a dwarf amongst its numerous relations it is, even so, a good-sized plant. It may grow up to about 8ft and have leaves 4ft long and 1ft wide. Its 'trunk', 1ft in diameter

I (left) Typical avocado fruit. It should be clipped off at harvesting to avoid causing a wound; (right) pot-grown banana. As the fruit develops, the bud, pointing downwards, produces only male and useless flowers

II (left) Mountain cranberry. The red acid berries make a good jelly, and the plant itself is most attractive in the rockery; (right) rare blueberry (vaccinium cylindraceum). Although the 'commercial' blueberries give a larger fruit, this and many other vaccinium species provide worthwhile edible berries at its base when fully mature, is in fact a leaf sheath. At the top of this trunk or leaf sheath a rosette of leaves spreads out, perhaps as many as fifteen of them. Each new leaf grows rolled up in the sheath and when it emerges at the top it unrolls as it continues to grow. This description may give the impression that this 'little' chap is difficult. Actually this is not so, provided you have the space to allow it to develop properly. What you need is a hot-house at least 8 x 8ft with 10ft headroom.

Although it thrives naturally in deep, loose, well-drained soil in humid tropical climates, it is adaptable to cultivation in a large greenhouse—where minimum temperatures of 65°F (18°C) are attainable. It can be set in the greenhouse border in at least 2ft of rich soil with good drainage, or in a large pot or tub not less than 2ft in diameter.

Propagation can be from seed but vegetative propagation is far easier and in any case fruits of the cultivated banana are usually seedless. As the banana plant grows it develops into a stool or head of buds which in turn develop into shoots or suckers. These buds or suckers can be cut out with a portion of the rhizome and allowed to grow on and provide further plants. They should be potted in small pots and then, after a few months, put into large pots or tubs. If seed is used for propagation then this should be from fruit that is mature but not over-ripe or rotting. The seeds should not be soaked in water to clean them as this lessens the chance of gemination.

The growing plants should have full exposure to sunlight and much will depend on temperature. When, for example, temperatures are 65°F (18°C) by night and about 80°F (27°C) by day, fruit may be obtained in about 16 months from the time of setting out the sucker. If the minimum temperature can be above 75°F (24°C) so much the better. If the temperatures are right the first crop will be within 10 to 15 months and production will be more or less continuous.

When a good temperature is maintained and there is steady growth frequent 'pruning' is necessary to remove the surplus suckers and to prevent crowding in the clump. This 'pruning' means, in practice, regulating the number of suckers you are permitting to fruit and this must be governed by soil and temperature. At the beginning only one sucker at a time should be allowed to grow and bear fruit. Later on when the first fruit has been borne you can, if you are able to provide very good conditions, try allowing a second sucker to grow

c

Banana

whilst one is reaching maturity. If you do this the growing suckers should, as far as possible, be on opposite sides of the clump.

The plant should be kept well watered because the large leaves transpire very large quantities of moisture but, as already mentioned, let it have as much sunshine as possible. It will also derive much benefit from a feed of liquid manure about once a week, especially when high temperatures are maintained. On hot days let it have plenty of fresh air provided this does not cause the temperature to fall to any large extent.

The flowers appear at the top of the trunk or leaf sheath. The bud, containing many flowers, turns downwards on emerging and the base of the flower cluster is then at the top. The female flowers set and develop into fruit without pollination. As the fruits develop, the flower bud, still pointing downwards, continues to produce male flowers, and as these males are useless and yet no doubt using food, this part of the plant can now be cut off. Cut it at about 8-10in from the fruit cluster. Each bunch of fruit is comprised of several 'hands', which in turn are comprised of 'fingers' or bananas. Usually the more hands there are to a bunch the more fingers there are to a hand and this, to a large extent, is governed by the variety and vigour of the plant.

If there is an unfortunate fall in the temperature during the ripening period then the taste of the fruit may be impaired. If, for example, the temperature drops to 50°F (10°C) when the fruit is nearly ready to be harvested then quality will be much reduced. On the other hand bananas can be harvested when still green. The greener they are the longer they will take to ripen but they should be harvested before they become soft, and then ripened in a warm room. When it has finished fruiting the stem or trunk will die off and should be cut out. If conditions are good you will have another already growing to take its place.

The banana as a fruit needs no description nor do its many varied dessert uses. Its nutritional value is also well known. It is rich in vitamins A and C as well as in the B complex. When it is fully ripe, which is when the skin has just begun to turn brown, it is richer in sugar than most other fruits. Only the avocado, tamarind and breadfruit are said to be higher in energy value.

There are several varieties of the Cavendish banana and three, of particular interest are:

LADY FINGER—a pleasant flavoured, small banana about 4-6in long.
RED FIG—the fruit of this is about 3in long and stubby. Skin is reddish bronze and the flesh pinkish. It has a good flavour.
SILK FIG—this variety is said to have an aroma resembling that of an apple.

Barbados cherry

(ACEROLAS)

Classification	:	*Malpighia glabra.*
Physiology	:	Erect evergreen shrub or small tree growing to 15ft.
Origin	:	Tropical America.
History	:	Cultivated in warm countries for its fruit. Introduced to Britain in the early eighteenth century. Commercial cultivation in Puerto Rica but very little in USA.
Recommended site	:	Warm greenhouse—pot or border.
Culinary uses	:	General uses, but especially for jellies and juice.

A number of *Malpighia* species are cultivated for their fruits but the one principally grown is *Malpighia glabra.* In Puerto Rica, where it is cultivated commercially, several varieties are available. It was introduced to Britain early in the eighteenth century since when it has been grown in stove-houses or warm greenhouses more as an ornamental flowering shrub than as a bearer of fruit. In USA, even in California, it is not grown to any extent. Although it will grow to 15ft in its natural habitat it can, as a pot shrub, be kept to 8ft.

Propagation is usually from cuttings taken from half-ripened wood in summer. These are inserted in a sandy soil in a propagating frame with bottom heat. The plant can be grown on either as a pot shrub or in the border of a warm greenhouse. When grown in a pot it should be given equal parts of sandy loam and fibrous peat which should be well drained.

The temperature during winter will need to be no less than 55°F (13°C), and during summer it can rise to 75°F (24°C). When grown in a pot it should be watered freely during spring and summer, but only moderately during the colder months of the year. Repotting, when necessary, should be done in spring or autumn.

Its flowers are pinkish white and are produced from March onwards. The fruits which follow are cherry-like. When ripe they are bright red, thin skinned, juicy and very rich in vitamin C. They also contain carbohydrates, calcium and iron. The fruits have a sharp, acid flavour and are especially useful for jellies and juices, and for mixing with other fruits.

Barberry

Classification	:	*Berberis vulgaris*; and other *Berberis* species.
Physiology	:	Deciduous spiny shrub growing 8-10ft tall—some species evergreen or semi-evergreen.
Origin	:	Barbary coast, now naturalized in much of Europe, including Britain, and in eastern states of USA.
History	:	At one time cultivated in Britain for its fruit but today in disuse. Taken to USA by early settlers and now grown in some states as an ornamental.
Recommended site	:	Outdoors.
Culinary uses	:	Used principally for preserves.

The genus *Berberis* includes many species—some wild, some cultivated—which provide edible fruit. The genus itself belongs to the family Berberidaceae to which the genus *Mahonia,* also a producer of similar edible fruit, belongs.

The name *Berberis* of course is associated with the name of a race of people, the Berbers, who inhabit the northern coastal area of North Africa, the Barbary coast. It is, therefore, quite possible that it was the Arabs who first made use of this fruit in their sherbets. At one time the shrubs were commonly grown in Britain for their fruit. Cultivation may have been discouraged by wheat farmers because the common barberry (*B. vulgaris*) is a host plant, or carrier, for rust fungus, which although not affecting the barberry itself does affect wheat.

The evergreen species, however, also bear edible fruit and are not host carriers of this disease. The common barberry was taken to North America by the early pioneers and is now naturalized in the eastern states where, as in Britain, it is grown as an ornamental.

It is a most attractive shrub, particularly in the spring when its yellow flowers hang in drooping racemes or pendants. The stamens possess the pecular characteristic of moving at the slightest touch, so striking the stigma and causing fertilization and, usually, a very heavy crop of berries.

The barberry offers no difficulties in cultivation: it will grow in sunshine or shade and make do with any soil providing it is not water-logged. Planting should be carried out in autumn or winter. No special requirements are called for, but to ensure a good crop of berries old, exhausted stems should be removed at ground-level. Weakly and straggling branches should be removed and vigorous ones cut back. Suckers should also be removed. The deciduous species should be pruned in January or February and the evergreen ones in April. Propagation can be by seed after stratification, the seeds being sown in the open ground. Alternatively, existing shrubs can provide suckers or cuttings. One or two shrubs are ample for the normal household.

The common barberry is the best for fruit production. After flowering it carries oblong ovoid-shaped berries which, as they ripen, turn to a brilliant scarlet colour. These berries are too acid to be eaten raw but they make a delicious jelly. The berries can be pickled in vinegar when green and they then make an excellent appetiser to be served wiith cold meats. They can also be used for sauces, tarts and pies and are often preserved in sugar or syrup. There is a seedless variety, *Berberis vulgaris* var. *asperma* (now very scarce) which was used for a famous conserve made in Rouen. In some countries they are used as a substitute for lemon juice in the preparation of cooling drinks, and for flavouring ices, sherbets and punches. In India they are cured to make barberry raisins.

The seed of the common barberry is very variable and seedlings may produce red, black or even yellow berries.

OTHER BARBERRY SPECIES

MAGELLAN BARBERRY (*Berberis buxifolia*) South America—

Barberry

large purple-black, well-flavoured berries. Used for a popular preserve in Chile.

HIMALAYAN BARBERRY (*Berberis angulosa*) Himalayas—very large berries.

PEPAL BARBERRY (*Berberis aristata*) India—purple berries which in India are dried like raisins and used for dessert.

RAISIN BARBERRY (*Berberis asiatica*) India—said to make the best Indian raisins.

DARWIN BARBERRY (*Berberis darwinia*) Chile—a very good ornamental but also produces edible berries.

MEXICAN BARBERRY (*Berberis haematocarpa*) New Mexico, Arizona—bright, blood-red berries which are pleasantly acid in taste.

The hardy and productive barberry with its useful and pleasant fruit deserves a bigger place in fruit growing. Indeed it is a fruit well worth improving and has much potential.

Bilberry

(BLAEBERRY; WHINBERRY; WHORTLEBERRY)

Classification	:	*Vaccinium myrtillus.*
Physiology	:	Small deciduous shrub growing 6-18in tall.
Origin	:	Northern Europe (native of Britain).
History	:	Fruit for a long time esteemed by country folk but little attempt made to cultivate this particular species.
Recommended site	:	Outdoors—peaty soil.
Culinary uses	:	Good for jellies, tarts or eating with cream.

There are about 300 species belonging to the genus *Vaccinium* and many of them produce edible fruit. They grow mainly in the northern hemisphere, south of the Arctic region, and on mountains in the tropics. In the United States, where the fruit is much appreciated, the species have, for pomological purposes, been divided into blueberries and cranberries. The blueberries are those species bearing blue-black berries and having the sweeter taste, the cranberries are those bearing red berries more acid in taste. In this book the *Vaccinium* species will be dealt with under three headings: Bilberry (native to Britain), Blueberry and Cranberry.

Different names are used for the bilberry in different parts of Britain, among them blaeberry, whinberry, whortleberry, and this in itself reveals a long history of use in different regions. There was a time not so far back when it was common practice for the berries or whorts, as they are often called, to be gathered and taken into the markets where they were readily bought by the townsfolk. Although

41

Bilberry

today this still happens in some areas, in parts of Devon for instance, imported fruit is cheap and time a scarce commodity so that this wild native fruit is almost as forgotten as the muffin man.

The habitat of this little plant is moist peaty woodland and moorland. It grows no higher than 18in and is extremely hardy, but although quite happy on some of the highest and bleakest mountains it does not always thrive when brought to sheltered gardens in the south. This failure to thrive is due to man-made conditions. It is known for instance that many plants cannot obtain nourishment from the soil if a certain fungus (mycorrhiza) is not present. The bilberry grows where this organism is abundant, amidst the rotting vegetable waste of woodland and moorland. It cannot, therefore, be expected to thrive in man-made soil sterility. Nor can it tolerate lime; the soil must be acid. Therefore, in order to cultivate the bilberry, and for that matter any of the *Vaccinium* species, a moist peaty soil enriched with leaf mould or other humus must be provided.

If you are able to provide these soil conditions bilberries require no special cultivation—apart from planting them 2ft apart either way and keeping them free from weeds. Propagation is by seed, which should be sown in sandy peat in the spring. The best temperature for germination is 55-65°F (13-18°C). An alternative to propagation by seed is by layering the shoots.

Bilberries are partially self-sterile and it is, therefore, necessary to grow more than one plant so that cross-pollination occurs. The flowers are small, pinkish or flesh coloured, and urn-shaped, appearing from April to June. They are usually produced singly on drooping stalks from the leaf axils. The berries which follow ripen from July to August and are up to half an inch in diameter, globular, purplish or black and covered with a blue bloom. They are juicy, slightly acid and agreeable to the taste; they can be eaten with cream, made into very good jelly, or can be used with other fruit in tarts.

GREAT BILBERRY or BOG WHORTLEBERRY
(Vaccinium uliginosum)

This species grows in mountain bogs in north Britain. It requires moister conditions for cultivation than *Vaccinium myrtillus*, and its berries are smaller. It can be grown successfully in a bog garden or on marshy land.

42

Blueberry

Classification	:	*Vaccinium* species.
Physiology	:	Shrub, sometimes evergreen, growing from 2in to 20ft.
Origin	:	Mainly North America.
History	:	The early pioneers of North America quickly appreciated the many edible berries found growing wild. The blueberry is one that has been developed by selection, breeding and cultivation.
Recommended site	:	Outdoors—peaty soil.
Culinary uses	:	Good for jellies, tarts, eating with cream or for wine making.

There are scores of *Vaccinium* species native to North America and known as blueberries (see Bilberry). There has been considerable selection and cultivation of the species in the United States, resulting in many varieties being grown there. The blueberry bushes produce larger and better flavoured berries than the European bilberry, and whereas the berries of the bilberry are produced singly those of the blueberry are usually produced in clusters. For Americans the blueberry is far from being unusual but it is little known in Europe. It is only in recent years that the amateur grower in Britain has begun to take an interest in them and there is still little choice of variety.

In the United States the blueberry is often catalogued as High Bush or Low Bush, depending on its height. But there are other important differences: some blueberries grow in swamp, others on dry land, and yet others on rocky mountains; some are evergreen or ornamental, and

Blueberry

others are only semi-hardy. The fruit grower needs to consider all these characteristics in making his choice of bush. Some of the principal species of the above forms will be dealt with in a moment, but first let us look at their cultivation in general.

The blueberries are essentially heath shrubs and although they are not difficult to grow they will only thrive in an acid soil, in which root fungus or mycorrhiza is able to exist. Also, although most of the blueberries require a moist soil they do not like it to be perpetually waterlogged.

Blueberries tend to be self-sterile and it is therefore desirable to plant more than one bush so that there can be cross-pollination. No special pruning is necessary except to keep the bush tidy—removing branches that grow too high or slump over and spoil the compact shape of the bush. Remember when pruning that the berries are produced on the previous year's wood so that if you butcher the bush you will get no fruit that year.

Propagation of selected varieties should be by cuttings or by layering. Hard-wood cuttings have been found best in the High Bush blueberry and soft wood cuttings for the Rabbit Eye blueberry. It is also possible to propagate by sowing the seed in sandy peat in the spring, but this should not be done for a named variety. When seed is sown it is necessary to prevent evaporation and keep the soil moist: pots or trays should be covered or shaded.

THE PRINCIPAL SPECIES

HIGH BUSH OR SWAMP BLUEBERRY (*Vaccinium corymbosum*) 6-12ft. This species is an inhabitant of bogs and moist woodland, and is widely cultivated in the eastern part of the United States. It tends to be variable in form so that it is quite possible that natural hybridization with other species has taken place. Although it requires moisture during most of the year it prefers a dry period during late summer and autumn whilst it is forming its roots. The flowers appear in May and the berries ripen during September. These berries are about half an inch in diameter, are blue-black with a bloom, and are borne on the ends of branches of the previous year's growth.

The bush can also be considered an ornamental shrub—its stems and branches are red and its leaves are flame-coloured in the autumn.

It is a pleasant enough bush to have in the garden. Varieties advertised by nurserymen in Britain are Jersey, Robel and Pioneer. Plant the bushes 5 x 8ft apart.

BLACK HIGH BUSH BLUEBERRY (*Vaccinium atrococcum*)
Grows to 12ft. Another inhabitant of swamps and bogs. In fact it is similar to the preceding species and readily hybridizes with it. Its fruit, however, is black and much smaller but with more flavour. Plant 5 x 8ft apart.

SOUTHERN HIGH BUSH BLUEBERRY (*Vaccinium virgatum*)
2-10ft. This grows in the southern part of the United States. Berries are black with no bloom and not so well flavoured as the two preceding species. It does not, however, grow quite so tall. Plant 5 x 8ft apart.

RABBIT EYE BLUEBERRY (*Vaccinium ashei*)
8-20ft. A tall growing species which inhabits swamps and barren pine land. Fruit is black and well flavoured. Plant 8 x 12ft apart.

LOW BUSH BLUEBERRY OR SWEET BLUEBERRY
(*Vaccinium pennsylvanicum*)
6in-2ft tall. This small shrub grows in shady places or on mountains in pine woodland or heath, sometimes existing where the soil is no more than a couple of inches deep. It is a little harder to domesticate than the High Bush blueberries but it should be remembered that its real home is amongst fallen and slow-decaying pine needles. Plant the bushes 2 x 2ft apart.

The fruit of the Low Bush blueberry ripens about a month earlier than that of the High Bush variety. The berries are large, bluish black, sometimes red, with or without bloom. They are sweet with a very slight honey taste but are soft and easily bruised.

Two other forms of the same species are of interest: *V. pennsylvanicum angustifolium* (dwarf mountain blueberry), which is a very small shrub growing no more than 1ft high, and *V. pennsylvanicum nigrum*, which produces black berries.

CANADIAN BLUEBERRY (*Vaccinium canadensis*)
Grows 1-2ft. This is a many-branched, erect-growing shrub, found in heath and pinewood. It needs similar conditions to the Low Bush

Blueberry

blueberry but its asset is great productiveness and lateness of fruit. The berries, blue with a heavy bloom, are more acid than is usual for a blueberry and have an agreeable piquancy. Bushes should be planted 2 x 2ft apart.

DRY-LAND BLUEBERRY (*Vaccinium vacillans*)

6in to 3ft, erect and wide branched. The habitat of this species is in sandy and rocky places in north-east America. It is better able to stand up to dry conditions than most of the blueberries. Its berries are produced in dense clusters at the end of the previous year's wood, which is usually 2-4in long and leafless, and therefore it is very easy to strip the bush. The berries are sweet, large and blue with a heavy bloom. Plant the bushes 3 x 3ft apart.

WESTERN BLUEBERRY (*Vaccinium ovatum*)

6-15ft. This is evergreen and can, therefore, be considered not only as a fruit bush but also as an ornamental. It grows in the coastal regions of western North America. The berries are black or slightly blue. Plant the bushes 5 x 8ft apart.

HAIRY BLUEBERRY (*Vaccinium hirsutum*)

Grows to 2ft and spreads by underground rhizomes and by producing suckers. It comes from the mountains of North Carolina and likes a moist and sunny position. Its interest is in its overall hairiness, especially on the berries. These are blue-black and sweet.

GEORGIA BLUEBERRY (*Vaccinium melanocarpum*)

Grows 3-6ft tall. This medium-sized shrub needs fairly moist conditions. The berries are purple. Plant 3 x 5ft apart.

MOUNTAIN BLUEBERRY (*Vaccinium membranaceum*)

3-6ft tall. A native of the Sierra and Cascade mountains, from northern Oregon to British Columbia. It is a very drought-resistant species and does not object to rocky soil. Its berries are borne singly and are coloured deep maroon to black. Plant 3 x 5ft apart.

DWARF BLUEBERRY (*Vaccinium caepitosum*)

4-10in. Grows from Labrador to Alaska and southwards on mountain summits. Despite its smaller size (sometimes only 2in high) it carries berries a quarter of an inch in diameter. The berries are black with a blue bloom and sweet. This can be planted in a rock garden.

Brambleberry

(BLACKBERRY; DEWBERRY)

Classification	:	*Rubus* species.
Physiology	:	Deciduous or evergreen shrubs; thorny, prickly, although sometimes unarmed. Blackberries—semi-erect, or arching stems. Dewberries—prostrate or trailing stems.
Origin	:	Europe, North America, temperate Asia.
History	:	From ancient times the brambleberry has been gathered from the wild. In Europe and America it is still so gathered but today it is often cultivated in our gardens. Today there are American and Oriental species and hybrids to choose from—some common, some unusual.
Recommended site	:	Outdoors—against fence or trained over pergola.
Culinary uses	:	Unsurpassed for jellies, jams, pies etc, and to eat from the hand.

The genus *Rubus* is confusing both to the botanist and the pomologist. There are well over 400 species in the genus and innumerable forms are under cultivation. Much of the confusion is created by the fact that hybridization takes place naturally between the species, and their own natural 'promiscuity' is added to by artificial hybridization by man. When we discuss this genus we are, therefore, dealing with a 'thorny' subject.

47

Brambleberry

It is not possible in a book of this nature to dig too deeply into the details of this genus, nor for that matter is it desirable. All that the fruit grower needs is a broad classification of fruiting and growth characteristics. For the pomologist the usual classification is threefold: raspberries, blackberries and dewberries. But this still leaves a group of small-growing herbaceous brambles, mainly oriental in origin, and also a few other distinctive species not usually grown in the fruit garden.

It is very easy to distinguish the raspberries from the blackberries and the dewberries. The raspberry fruit, when ripe, comes away easily from the flower receptacle or remnant, whereas the blackberry and dewberry fruit adheres to it. Raspberries, then, will be dealt with under a separate heading, and so also will the small-growing species and the other distinctive species (see Wineberry, Cloudberry, Raspberry-Strawberry).

It is not so easy to distinguish between blackberries and dewberries. Dewberries have a trailing growth habit and because of this they might be said to be nothing more than trailing blackberries. This, however, is not quite the case, for they fruit earlier than blackberries and are also considered to have a better flavour. In fact, as some blackberries also trail it is the difference in time of fruiting that is an important point of classification.

If one classifies by growth habit, which is a useful method for the fruit grower because he needs to know *how* a plant grows just as much as *where* it grows, blackberries can take the following first three forms and dewberries the last form:

1. Stems sub-erect, propagating themselves by suckers.
2. Stems growing in a high-arching curve, often propagating themselves by the tips of their stems which take root.
3. Stems generally growing in a low-arching curve, forming rootlets where they touch the earth.
4. Stems low-arched or prostrate, propagating themselves by rooting at the tips of their stems.

As has already been mentioned fruit growers have hybridized between these different forms. The Americans, especially, have utilized their native dewberries and blackberries and some of the European species and, as a result, have produced varieties which bear really large and luscious berries. Many of the hybrid berries now available

48

III Oregon blackberry (p50). *A prolific bearer. Note that this blackberry is completely thornless*

IV (above) *Chinese gooseberries, or Kiwi fruit. They can be cut crosswise into round translucent slices to decorate trifles etc; (below) custard apple, a typical shape. This fruit is symmetrical because all the pistils in the flower cone were fertilised*

in Britain originated in America.

Blackberries and dewberries are easy to grow. When cultivated, their berries are much larger and juicier than the ones gathered in the wild. Nor need they be untidy, scrambling wild things; they can be made quite pleasing and decorative garden subjects when trained to cover a fence or to form a fence along wires or, most pleasing of all, trained over pergolas. If they are grown against a fence they should be planted 1ft away from it and at least 12ft apart from each other. Only six to a dozen shoots should be allowed to grow from the roots. As the stems grow up train them along the fence, and during summer allow an equal number of new stems to grow as replacements. After fruiting, the old stems should be cut out and the new ones put in their place for fruiting in the following year. Do not let the stems get tangled and out of control and do not let side shoots grow too long and make a nuisance of themselves.

Unless they are a tender species it does not matter if they occupy a frosty site because normally they do not flower until July. Avoid a gravelly, dry soil; blackberries prefer deep, moist, rich loam. If you have observed the size of the wild blackberry after a wet summer you will have no doubt about their need for moisture. In excessively dry weather it will be necessary to water your blackberry shrub, but remember that though they like a moist soil they should not be waterlogged.

Dewberries can be grown in the same way as blackberries, that is against a fence or trained over a pergola. They can also be conveniently trained to a system of wires. Posts should be firmly set 5ft above ground level and stout wires should be stretched along the posts at varying heights of 3ft, 4ft and 5ft. The wires should be really taut. The plants should be set at 8-10ft apart. As the stems grow from the roots they should, during the first year, be tied up to the wires. Then, when the leaves have fallen, they should be spread out in the form of a fan, six stems to the plant, three each way and each one set along a wire. The centre of the fan should be kept as open as possible. In the following year these stems will bear fruit whilst the six strongest new stems can be tied together into the open centre of the fan. As soon as the fruit has been harvested the old stems should be cut out as near the soil as possible and the new stems spread out along the wires in replacement. This

49

D

Brambleberry

method of growing can, of course, also be used for the arching and prostrate forms of blackberries.

The propagation of blackberries and dewberries can be by tip layering in June or July. Blackberries can also be propagated by suckers.

Deep cultivation should be avoided because rooting is shallow and can be easily damaged. Perennial weeds must, however, be kept in check and for this reason it is better to see that the soil is free from such nuisances before planting takes place. It is beneficial to give a good mulch in summer to retain moisture. Feeding with fish or meat and bonemeal is also beneficial. Where there is lime in the soil the plants may suffer from iron deficiency and where this becomes apparent (by paleness or yellowing of the leaves) give a dressing of chelated iron. Finally, see that they are protected from strong winds by making sure that the stems, which are brittle, are tied to their wires or their other means of support.

There is a thornless species of blackberry (*Rubus millspaughii*), and many of the thorny species have thornless forms so that today many of the cultivated plants available are thornless. The following list of species is far from being complete but it includes the most important, most useful and the most unusual. Blackberries are listed first, then dewberries, followed by the very useful hybrids.

BLACKBERRY SPECIES

OREGON EVERGREEN (*Rubus laciniatus*)
   A native of Europe and a very vigorous and productive plant. It seldom fails to produce a large crop of fruit in late summer and early autumn. The berries are jet black when ripe—large and juicy.

HIMALAYAN GIANT (*Rubus prucerus*)
   Thought to have originated in central Europe, very vigorous and a good cropper. The fruits are black, ripening in August and September.

MOUNTAIN BLACKBERRY (*Rubus allegheniensis*)
   A mountain blackberry from North America. It grows to a medium height, 3-6ft. The berries are generally small, oblong or conical, and usually twice as long as they are wide. The slender berries are

50

more solid and less juicy than those of most other species but have a peculiar pleasant flavour and are sometimes spicy. Another point of interest is that amber-coloured berries, which sometimes occur in other species, occur quite frequently.

CANADIAN BLACKBERRY (*Rubus canadensis*)
Another mountain species mainly from Canada. This has tall, rather weak and usually thornless stems, erect or recurving. The fruits are sub-globose to short cylindric in shape and consist of large, juicy, somewhat acid drupelets.

DEWBERRY SPECIES

FIELD DEWBERRY (*Rubus procumbens*)
This is a native of the United States of America. Its woody stems, several feet long, become prostrate in natural growth. This species can tolerate much drier soil conditions than most. It has a good constitution and is the parent of many well-tried American dewberries. The fruits are jet black, large, sweet and juicy.

SOUTHERN DEWBERRY (*Rubus trivialis*)
The common dewberry of the southern United States. Its stems grow to a very long length and are trailing, hence its other name— the running blackberry. Although its fruits are usually excellent they can sometimes be dry and seedy.

WESTERN DEWBERRY (*Rubus vitifolius*)
An inhabitant of California, growing especially beside streams and in other moist places, and one of the most important of the dewberry species. Pure-bred varieties are cultivated, and the species has been used for hybridizing with other species. The loganberry is held by some to be a red-fruited variety of this species, although when it was discovered growing wild by Judge Logan in California in 1881 it was considered to be a natural hybrid between a dewberry and a raspberry.
The species is characterized by slender stems, usually trailing though sometimes erect. The fruit is black, oblong, of medium size, sweet and pleasant.

Brambleberry

HYBRIDS

KING'S ACE BERRY (blackberry x raspberry)

This is a moderate grower producing stems 5ft or so long. As it is not so rampant as many of the brambles it is suitable for the smaller garden. It can be adapted for growing against fences or can be trained to stakes like raspberries. It should however be pruned and propagated like a blackberry.

The flowers are self-fertile. The large fruit is produced in clusters and has a sweet, refreshing flavour and is excellent for dessert, jam making or for pies. The berries come away easily from the flower receptacle like a raspberry.

VEITCHBERRY (blackberry x raspberry)

A strong semi-erect grower which can be trained against fences or to stakes and trellises in the open. It should not be pruned in the first year but subsequently should be pruned like a blackberry. The fruits ripen after the raspberries have finished and before the blackberries begin, and it is therefore a useful plant for the fruit garden. When ripe the fruits are a deep mulberry colour and twice the size of the ordinary blackberry; they are sweet and possess the flavour of both parents.

LAXTONBERRY (loganberry x red raspberry)

The average height of this hybrid is 6-8ft, and having much the growth habit of the loganberry it is suitable for growing against fences or training up arches or stout poles. It should be trained and pruned in the same way as a blackberry. Unfortunately its blossoms are not wholly self-fertile so that it must be planted close to a loganberry or raspberry. The berry is very much like the loganberry in colour and flavour but it separates from the flower receptacle like a raspberry.

LOWBERRY (blackberry x dewberry)

Sometimes called the black loganberry, its parents being a blackberry from Texas and the western dewberry. Its trailing stems can reach a length of up to 20ft. The stems are stout and grow erect for several feet before they begin to trail. In a very mild locality the leaves are semi-evergreen. The blossoms are self-sterile and a pollinator is needed—either a blackberry or loganberry.

It is noted for its very large black berries which are less acid than those of the loganberry and possess the flavour of the blackberry. The berries make an excellent dessert fruit.

PHENOMENAL BERRY (dewberry x red raspberry)

Its parents are said to be the western dewberry and an American red raspberry. It is similar to the loganberry but perhaps a little hardier. Its berries are larger, brighter in colour and ripen a little later than the loganberry. They are excellent for jam and stewing.

YOUNGBERRY (dewberry x dewberry)

A hybrid within the dewberry species, its parents being a western dewberry and a southern dewberry. In the States it is extensively culti- vated and is known there as the Young Dewberry. The stems are fairly vigorous, have few thorns and have the dewberry trailing habit. The berries are very large and of good flavour. As they ripen they turn from deep red to purplish black.

NECTARBERRY (youngberry parentage)

The nectarberry is said to have originated from the seed of the youngberry and it is not therefore possible to name the other parent. It is a hardy fellow and like the dewberry in growth but its berries are different. They ripen later than either the youngberry or the boysen- berry and are a deep wine colour. They have few seeds and little core.

BOYSENBERRY (blackberry x dewberry x raspberry)

This hybrid is said to have originated from California in 1930. It is usually declared to be better than the youngberry. It can stand fairly dry conditions and yet give a good crop of very large berries. The stems grow very vigorously each year and the long fruit spurs grow well out from the stems, thus making fruitpicking easier. The berries turn from red to purplish black when ripe.

Brazilian cherry

(PITANGA CHERRY; SURINAM CHERRY)

Classification	:	*Eugenia uniflora*.
Physiology	:	Small ornamental, evergreen tree or shrub.
Origin	:	Brazil.
History	:	Taken from South America to India by the Portuguese. Now cultivated also in Florida and California. Grown in the Mediterranean area as an ornamental.
Recommended site		Warm greenhouse—pot shrub.
Culinary uses	:	For jellies, syrups and wine.

The genus *Eugenia*, comprising 1,000-1,500 species, offers a very large number of edible fruits. One species (*Eugenia aromatica*) provides us with cloves, although these are not fruits but are unopened flower buds which have been dried. One of the most promising species for fruit cultivation is *Eugenia uniflora*.

Originating in Brazil, it is today found in many warm countries, particularly in India where it was taken by the Portuguese and where it is cultivated for its fruit. Fruit cultivation has also taken place in Florida and California, though only on a small scale. Very often it is grown as a small ornamental bush and in this form is sometimes seen in the Mediterranean area.

In Brazil it usually grows along the banks of streams, and under favourable conditions it can become rampant and grow to a height of 25ft. When cultivated it has shown itself tolerant of heavy pruning and because of this is sometimes grown as a hedge. Its evergreen leaves, 1-2in long, offer a pungent agreeable odour when crushed. Because of this aroma the leaves are sometimes scattered on the floors of Brazilian homes.

Propagation is usually from seed—most of the fruiting bushes being seedlings. It can also be propagated from cuttings made from mature wood in the summer, and put in a propagating frame in a temperature of up to 75°F (24°C).

The Brazilian cherry bush should be potted in a soil of 2 parts sandy loam plus 1 part leafmould and sand. It does not object to some lime in the soil. Although it comes from the tropics it can withstand a temperature of 28°F (−2°C), but it really needs to be kept in a greenhouse where the winter temperature does not fall much below 50°F (10°C). The climate in its natural habitat is warm and moist and during a warm summer the Brazilian cherry needs frequent watering and syringeing. As it withstands heavy pruning it can, therefore, be kept very conveniently as a pot shrub, but remember that if it is clipped back too severely it will not produce so heavily.

In Brazil it may flower twice in the year but in northern latitudes flowering takes place in the spring. The creamy white four-petalled flowers are solitary or clustered and are borne in the axils of the leaves. They are about half an inch wide and slightly fragrant. Many flowers are produced and the shrub is particularly attractive if at the same time it is revealing dainty, copper-coloured young leaves.

In the warmth of the tropics fruit is borne in the third and fourth year, and under favourable conditions a good strain will produce prolifically. The fruits hang singly or in clusters on long stems. They vary in shape, size, colour and flavour. Usually, however, they are oblate in shape and deeply eight-ribbed. They are, on average, a little less than one inch in diameter and have one large spherical seed or two smaller hemispherical ones. As the fruits ripen they change from light green to yellow to light scarlet, dark crimson or nearly black. The colour of the flesh is soft, juicy and of sub-acid flavour. Those with the darkest colour are said to be the most acid.

The fruit should never be eaten until fully ripe, when the skin is thin, the flesh very tender and the aromatic flavour rather pleasant —in under-ripe fruit it is usually too strong. Jelly made from the fruit, pitanga jelly as it is usually called, rivals guava jelly. Syrups and wines are said to have medicinal value.

SOME OTHER EUGENIA SPECIES

ROSE APPLE (*Eugenia jambos*)

A native of Asian tropical areas from India to Burma, now naturalized in many warm countries. It grows 20-30ft tall in its natural habitat and is a broad-topped tree. Has handsome, short-stalked, pointed, elliptic leaves up to 8in long and 2in wide. Fragrant greenishwhite flowers up to 3in across with numerous long stamens usually occur in small terminal groups. The fruits, about 2in in diameter, are pale yellow to pinkish white in colour, apple-shaped and with the odour and flavour of the rose but not very juicy. (Seeds show a tendency to be polyembryonic—see Lime.)

MALAYA APPLE (*Eugenia malaccensis*)

Native of Malaya. In its natural habitat this tree will grow 30-50ft. It is very ornamental. Leaves are 8-14in long. Flowers are purplish red, 2in wide and form clusters. Fruits are 2-3in long, red, pink or whitish in colour, pear-shaped and with an apple-like flavour. They are eaten raw, cooked, preserved, or are made into wine, but they have not much flavour.

JAVA PLUM (*Eugenia curanii*)

Native of Indonesia. Grows to 80ft in its natural habitat. Has elliptic leaves up to 1ft long. Flowers are produced in panicles. It is often cultivated for its dark red to black fruits which are about three-quarters of an inch in diameter and have an acid flavour. They are eaten raw, made into jelly or wine.

WATER BERRY (*Eugenia cordatum*)

Native of South Africa where it grows to 60ft. It has four-angled twigs and blue-green leathery leaves. Creamy white flowers are produced in terminal clusters. Fruits are purple-black, about 1in long and pleasantly flavoured.

Buffalo berry

(NEBRASKA CURRANT)

Classification	:	*Sheperdia argentea.*
Physiology	:	Deciduous, spiny shrub 6-18ft tall.
Origin	:	North America.
History	:	Fruit first used by North American Indians, then by the early pioneers, since when attempts have been made, principally in USA, to grow plants for commercial use.
Recommended site	:	Outdoors.
Culinary uses	:	Very good for sauces, jellies and conserves.

The buffalo berry belongs to the Elaeagnaceae family and is, therefore, related to the goumi and sea buckthorn. It is a native of the Great Plains and flourishes from Manitoba and Saskatchewan southwards to Kansas, New Mexico and Nebraska, growing especially along the banks of streams. The Red Indians supplemented their diet with the berries, which perhaps were as numerous as the buffalo once were. As the pioneers and settlers moved into the great virgin lands they readily made use of the wild berries, finding that they made a good relish to eat with buffalo meat—hence the name. The berries are, however, somewhat difficult to harvest because they are small, no bigger than currants, and the shrubs are thorny. This, no doubt, has discouraged commercial cultivation.

It is one of the hardiest of the wild fruits and under ideal conditions will grow as high as 20ft, although it can be kept smaller under cultivation. It is a very erect shrub with whitish, thorny branches and

Buffalo berry

small silvery leaves. Blossom time is March and the flowers are small, yellowish in colour, and in dense clusters at the nodes of the branches. Because the shrubs are dioecius (ie bearing flowers of one sex only) it is necessary to have a male and female plant together. Experience has shown it is sufficient to have one male to each five or six females. The males are distinguished by their dense clusters of plumpish buds, whilst the females have loose clumps of slimmer, pointed buds.

The buffalo berry is adaptable and will grow in dry rocky soil if it has to. But it should be remembered that in its natural habitat it does prefer moist river banks and so will do best in good moist soil. Planting time is during autumn or winter.

Propagation is by seed, which should be sown in the autumn, half an inch deep in a well-prepared bed outdoors. Alternatively cuttings, which should be from hard ripe wood, can be taken in October. They should be about 12in long. A slit should be made in the soil with a spade and the cuttings inserted at least 8in deep and 1ft apart in this slit. A year later they can be dug up, when they will be found to have formed roots and can be planted where required. They can be used to make a good hedge. Little pruning is required except to keep the shrub under control. Once established, the buffalo berry does not take very well to being transplanted.

This shrub can normally be relied on to produce a good crop of oval scarlet berries, which hang in clusters much like red currants. In the wild the crop is prolific and the berries remain on the bushes well into winter. There is some variability in the produce: some bushes may bear golden-yellow berries, or berries varying greatly in size, season and quality. This variability shows that they have a potential for improvement. Harvesting can be left very late, provided the birds are kept off. It is said that a touch of frost sweetens the berries and makes them very pleasant to eat—their flavour has something of both the grape and redcurrant. They have a single, slender seed, are especially good for jellies, and when dried they retain their sprightly flavour and can be used in puddings like dried currants, or served with syrup to make a nice dessert. As already mentioned, the fruits also make an excellent relish to be had with meat.

There is one other species which is of interest. This is the Canadian buffalo berry (*Sheperdia canadensis*), a much smaller shrub which produces orange-coloured berries.

Cape gooseberry

(GROUND CHERRY)

Classification	:	*Physalis* species.
Physiology	:	Perennial and annual plants growing from 1-3ft tall.
Origin	:	South America.
History	:	Cape gooseberries have been in cultivation for at least 200 years and although today grown commercially throughout the warm countries of the world little attempt has been made to improve them.
Recommended site	:	Outdoors—warm bed. Frame, cloche or greenhouse cultivation. Ring cultivation. Pot cultivation.
Culinary uses	:	Can be eaten raw; stewed and used for pie fillings; can be made into preserves.

Species of the genus *Physalis* give useful fruits which are generally called Cape gooseberries or ground cherries. Although there is some difference in the growth habit of the three species described below the fruits are very similar and can be dealt with here under the one general heading.

Like the tomato to which they are related (family Solanaceae) they originated in South America and from thence they have travelled to many of the warmer countries of the world. The true Cape gooseberry (*Physalis peruviana*) is the one that has been mostly cultivated for its fruit and is now naturalized in South Africa, but even this has never reached the economic and commercial importance of the tomato.

It is true that Cape gooseberries or ground cherries are not what one would call luscious fruits but, even so, they are quite agreeable and have a flavour all their own. They also have versatility—they can be eaten raw with either a fruit or vegetable salad; they are delicious stewed, with a dash of orange or lemon juice, and they make excellent preserves and pie fillings. Moreover, the fruits of all three species are ready wrapped, so to speak, with a parchment-like husk, so that if they are dry when harvested they can be stored for some weeks while at the same time continuing to ripen. In this way they provide a supply of home-grown fruit after most other fruits have been harvested.

Although they are only semi-hardy they are not difficult to grow. If they are grown outdoors they must be planted out and the fruit harvested entirely within that period of the year which is free from frost. They will grow in any soil but do best in a rich loam.

GROUND CHERRY (*Physalis pruinosa*)

The ground cherry, a half-hardy annual, is a many branched shrublet growing, usually, not much more than 18-24in tall. In its growth habit it tends to resemble a dwarf outdoor bush tomato, and it can be allowed to grow its own way and take its own form.

The plants should be propagated from seed sown about the middle of March. It takes, on average, about 10 weeks before the young plants are fit to plant outdoors, but the earlier they can be hardened off and planted outside (remember the danger from late frost) the longer they will have to ripen their fruits.

The seed should be sown in trays filled to about half an inch from the top with the seed compost. This should then be pressed down lightly and the seeds sown about one inch apart. The seed should then be covered to a depth of about one-sixteenth of an inch. The compost should be thoroughly moist and covered with paper so that the moisture is retained. The temperature in which the seed tray is placed should not be less than 65°F (18°C), and the seed will then germinate in 7-10 days.

If only a few seedlings, sufficient for family use, are required, these could be grown in a pot on a window-sill in a warm room. It is, however, better to sow more seed than the number of plants you require, so that the weakest as well as any that are malformed can be discarded. Also some seedlings may be lost through damping-off, and it is a good idea to have a few young plants in reserve just in case the first of the plants to go outside are lost through frost or some other unexpected cause.

As soon as the first seedlings push their 'baby' leaves (cotyledons) through the soil the paper covering should be removed. They can then be left to grow in the seed tray for about a month but the soil must not be allowed to dry out. The next step is to set them out individually in 3in pots (polythene pots are excellent for this). After they are potted they should be thoroughly watered so that the soil around their roots is soaked. John Innes Compost No 2 is ideal for the young seedlings.

From the beginning of May the plants should be gradually hardened off. A cold frame is ideal for this if available, otherwise some other provisional means of protection must be devised or a well-sheltered spot chosen. By mid-May the process should be completed but extra care must be taken during the second and third weeks of May as this is a danger period for late frosts.

It is better for them to be planted out into soil which has been well manured for a previous crop; to manure the soil immediately before planting results in lank growth and a delay in fruiting. They should be set in rows 3ft apart and with a space of 2ft between the plants, in the sunniest bed available. They can also be grown in a cold frame or under cloches. Each plant should be given a good watering at planting time but after this they will not need anything unless there is exceptionally dry weather.

Flowering begins by the end of June and continues until the first frost, though only the earlier flowers give fruit that can take advantage of the sun. In very dry weather the first flowers may not set, but a light watering at this time, preferably in the form of a light spray over the heads of the plants, will help. Normally ground cherries are prolific bearers of fruit. When the fruit has set the calyx of the flower develops into a small green husk which, as the fruit ripens, turns first yellowish and finally a grey-brown colour. The fruit often drops to the ground before it is ripe, but is in no way spoilt, and can be harvested from the ground and stored in a warm temperature where it will continue to ripen.

The parchment husks or wrappings are easily opened between the fingers to reveal the fruit, which may vary in size from one-eighth of an inch to half an inch in diameter. When these fruits are ripe they are deep yellow in colour. They have a distinctive sweetish flavour but blend well with other fruits. They can be stewed and make a good filling for tarts and pies; green and less-ripe fruit can be used in this way. They also make a good jam.

JAMBERBERRY OR TOMATILLO (*Physalis ixocarpa*)

Jamberberry is another half-hardy annual but tends to grow slightly taller than ground cherry. The seed should be sown and the seedlings treated in the same way as for ground cherry. Outdoors they can be planted the same distance apart in the rows but each plant should be given a cane about 3ft high to which, as it grows, it can be carefully tied, to avoid loosening by strong winds. As they grow it may be advantageous to pinch out a lateral growing shoot here and there so that a better formed, more erect plant is obtained.

By the end of August the aim should be to ripen the growing fruit before the onset of frost. Existing flowers can be pinched out and the growing apex of the plant removed. If cloches are available the plants can be untied from their canes and laid out on the ground so that cloches can be placed over them.

Jamberberry can also be grown by the method of ring cultivation, which encourages the formation of two distinct root systems: the 'food' roots are encouraged to grow in a bottomless container containing a soil or compost, and the 'water' roots grow down through the bottomless container into wet gravel, clinker or vermiculite. The gravel, clinker or similar medium is kept constantly moist whilst the compost in the container is kept dry. With good feeding and attention it is possible to obtain a good yield of fruit by this method. In the greenhouse a shallow trench to a depth of 4–6in is made and lined with thin polythene sheets so that it is isolated from the surrounding earth. It is then filled with well-weathered cinders or gravel, etc. If ring cultivation is to be practised outdoors a trough made of bricks or boards can be devised. Whether it is a trench or trough, it must be wide enough to take the compost containers which should be of 9in diameter and spaced 2ft apart. John Innes Potting Compost No 3 is suitable for the containers.

Once the plants are in the containers the trough should be kept well watered from thence onwards but the compost in the containers is left unwatered unless the plants show signs of distress. The aim is to encourage the water roots to penetrate down through the bottomless container until they reach the moisture provided in the trough. Feeding, in the form of liquid manure, begins when the first fruit has formed and this should only be given to the food roots which have remained in the *container,* and at weekly intervals. This method of cultivation not only allows the plant to take as much water as it requires without interfering with its food intake, but it also permits cultivation where there is soil sickness or where there is no soil at all, as in a yard or patio.

If the plants are to be grown in a greenhouse border it should be remembered that they are related to the tomato. Therefore, if tomatoes have been grown previously in the border it is necessary either to replace the old soil with new or to sterilize it.

Jamberberry flowers similarly to ground cherry. Like ground cherry its fruit varies in size, but is larger—from a quarter of an inch to one inch in diameter. Unlike ground cherry, whose fruit is much smaller than its husk, the jamberberry fruit when mature completely fills its skin-like husk which sometimes bursts revealing the pale yellow globular fruit. As a consequence the slightly sticky fruit and covering do not separate easily. However, after a slight soaking in water the outer covering is quickly removed. The fruit can be used in exactly the same way as ground cherry.

PERUVIAN CHERRY (*Physalis peruviana*)

This is the true Cape gooseberry, which is grown commercially throughout the warm countries of the world. It is a perennial, but being tender and susceptible to frost it needs protection during the winter. It can be propagated from cuttings which should be inserted singly in pots of light sandy soil in a temperature of 65-75°F (18-24°C) from March to April. If seed is sown in March and a temperature of not less than 70°F (21°C) is maintained it should be possible to harvest the first fruits by late summer. If possible the temperature should be not less than 55°F (13°C) at night and during spring and summer it can be allowed to go up to 80°F (27°C). Spraying the plants in summer helps to set the fruit (if temperatures are high avoid excessive humidity) and gently tapping the plants releases some of

63

Cape gooseberry

the pollen. Adequate ventilation should be given.

Peruvian cherry can be grown in the greenhouse border in the same way as the annual plants previously described and if it is a lean-to house the shoots can be trained up the wall at the back. It can also be grown in 6in pots and the shoots trained up sticks. A good compost for them is John Innes No 3. During April to September they should be freely watered, and from May to September given a feed of weak liquid manure once or twice a week. During autumn and winter they should be watered only moderately. Repot them in February or March.

Healthy plants can be kept to the required size by judicious pruning when necessary, provided this is not overdone. A lateral shoot can be pinched out, preferably when it first appears. The plant can be kept to the height required by removing the top of the leading stem at the topmost laterals. For convenience of handling some of the long and lanky stems can be completely cut out when repotting. In adequate temperature new growth will soon commence.

If a greenhouse is not available potted plants can be sunk into a warm bed outdoors and treated in the same way as the annuals but must be brought into a well lighted shed during the period of frosts. If the temperatures are not persistently below 45°F (7°C) the plants will stand the winter. If they are grown outdoors during the spring and summer months and the seed is sown late it will, however, not be possible to gather fruit during the first year.

The fruit when ripe is a deep gold and in shape and size it resembles a cherry. Its husk is much larger than the fruit which, however, can be up to three-quarters of an inch in diameter. The husk, like that of ground cherry, easily breaks to release its fruit. In a dry condition and in their husks they will keep for months.

The fruit is a little more sub-acid than either ground cherry or jamberry, but when fully ripe it is delicious and rich in vitamins.

Carambola

Classification	:	*Averrhoa carambola.*
Physiology	:	Small tropical tree growing to 30ft.
Origin	:	Probably Indonesia.
History	:	Now widely distributed throughout tropical countries and grown as a dooryard or garden tree.
Recommended site	:	Warm greenhouse.
Culinary uses	:	Eaten fresh; used for jams, jellies, preserves and refreshing drinks.

The carambola is a member of the same family as the wood sorrel (Oxalidaceae) but unlike the wood sorrel it is a native of the tropics. In many parts of Asia and South America the tree has been domesticated and seedlings are grown to provide fruit for home consumption, but little pomological study or commercial cultivation appears to have been undertaken.

It is a comparatively small tree and, although it may grow to a height of 30ft it tends to begin bearing while it is still small. Because of this it is thought that it may be a useful subject for hot-house cultivation and a few of its general characteristics are here briefly described.

The tree grows best in warm humid tropical areas and young trees are known to be injured by temperatures just above freezing point. Therefore it is necessary to maintain a reasonably high temperature in the hot-house throughout the year. Possibly, as the tree gets older, it may be found that spells of lower temperature will be tolerated.

The majority of the trees at present being grown in the tropics are seedlings. Once a tree is producing good fruit, however, it is better

65

E

Carambola

to propagate from it by layering or inarching on seedlings because, under satisfactory conditions, these will commence bearing in 10 months as compared to 5 years needed for seedlings. Under natural conditions flowers and fruit are produced continuously, with peak periods influenced by weather factors such as rainfall and humidity. The flowers are borne in clusters in the axils of the leaves.

The fruit when ripe is golden yellow in colour and has a waxy and attractive appearance. Some varieties, however, remain green when ripe. In shape it is ovoid or oblong, 3-5in long, and with three to five longitudinal and prominent ribs. The flesh is tender and pulpy; some varieties are sweet in taste and others are acid or tart. It can be eaten fresh and it is said to be high in vitamins A and C. The acid varieties can be used for jams and jellies or for making refreshing drinks.

Another species known as bilimbi (*Averrhoa bilimbi*) produces small fruit which is more acid and is used for pickling, preserving and eating fresh.

Casimiroa

(WHITE SAPOTE)

Classification	:	*Casimiroa edulis.*
Physiology	:	Evergreen tree growing to 30ft.
Origin	:	Central America.
History	:	Taken from its natural home it has been introduced to Florida and California, where several varieties are now in cultivation.
Recommended site	:	Warm greenhouse—pot cultivation.
Culinary uses	:	Used fresh for dessert.

The name by which this fruit is most frequently known, white sapote, is misleading because it is in no way related to the sapotes. Possibly it has acquired this name because of a similarity in leaf and in the shape and size of the fruit. Casimiroa, to give it its proper name, belongs to the family Rutaceae and is a near relation to the famous *Citrus* species. Yet, despite this relationship, it does not hybridize nor show any grafting compatibility with them.

It is a native of Mexico and Central America and there has been some cultivation of it in the hills of those parts. It is also today under some cultivation in Florida and California where several varieties are grown. As a fruit it is not known in European countries and there is little point in listing these varieties.

The tree is a strong growing evergreen with bright green palmate leaves. Because of its relationship to the *Citrus* species it appears to be suitable for pot cultivation. It is ornamental and worth having about the place. The flowers it produces are pale green and occur in panicles, which are borne terminally on either short shoots or on long

67

Casimiroa

shoots, or in the axils of mature leaves, or around the bases of shoots a year or more old. There may be 15 to 100 flowers in each panicle.

A good open loamy soil suits the tree best, and in fact it is not very tolerant of wet, poorly aerated soil conditions. It is about as frost resistant as the lemon tree but from the end of March until October the average temperature should be about 65°F (18°C). On warm days it can stand outside in a sheltered position, providing the temperature does not fall below 57°F (14°C).

Propagation can be from seed, which germinates quite easily. The seedlings should be cut back to about 2ft to encourage branching and in subsequent years the branches must be shortened to encourage laterals. If this is not done the tree tends to have long, straggling branches, but severe pruning should be avoided.

Under suitable conditions fruit produced from spring flowers will ripen from the end of September until November. When ripe the fruit will drop, but if it is picked several weeks before this time it develops almost to its full flavour. If, on the other hand, it is picked only a few days before it is ready to fall it becomes soft in a very short time. Casimiroa fruit is from 3-4in in diameter and resembles the Japanese quince in shape. The colour of the thin but inedible skin is green in some varieties, yellow or golden in others, sometimes with a streak of bright orange or yellow. The flesh or pulp is tender, with the texture of butter, sweet in taste but with a slight resinous or bitter flavour. It carries from two to five large seeds.

The fruit is rich in vitamin C and vitamin A. It is nearly as rich in carbohydrate and protein as the banana. In fact only the banana, date and fig possess more food value, pound for pound, than casimiroa. It is used for dessert and can be eaten with cream and sugar, having, it is said, a richer flavour and better texture than the banana similarly prepared.

Checkerberry

(BOXBERRY; PARTRIDGE BERRY; TEA BERRY)

Classification	:	*Gaultheria procumbens*.
Physiology	:	Evergreen shrub of tufted habit, spreading by means of underground suckers. Height 2-6in.
Origin	:	North America.
History	:	Introduced to England in 1762 but not usually cultivated for its fruit either in Europe or USA.
Recommended site	:	Outdoors—peaty, moist places, in partial shade.
Culinary uses	:	Eaten from the hand; used for flavouring; medicinal uses.

Gaultheria is a fairly large genus, most common in North America but also native to China, Japan, the Himalayas and Australasia. There are no species native to Europe. Several of the species produce edible fruit and checkerberry is one of them. Checkerberry, however, is not cultivated for its fruit, even in North America. It was introduced to Britain in 1762, since when it has been grown as an ornamental. It is known by various names other than checkerberry: partridge berry because the berries are very much relished by partridges; tea berry because it is possible to make a tea from its leaves; and wintergreen berry because of the essential oil of that name which is extracted from its leaves. In the garden it is usually grown as an ornamental ground-cover plant and for this purpose it is well suited.

It is a tufted creeping evergreen shrub with underground runners or suckers. From the underground growth it sends up slender stems

Checkerberry

2-6in. high. These stems are leafless except at their top where about four glossy leaves are clustered. The young leaves are a light, yellowish green, but as they mature they become a glossy dark green and are rather rigid or stiff. In the autumn the leaves assume a bronze colour, so that the plant is decorative at all times.

The white, pinkish flowers occur in July and August and appear singly in the leaf axils. The flowers are followed by berries which become bright red and, birds permitting, hang on the stems all winter. These berries are globose, about three-quarters of an inch in diameter, possessing the spicy aromatic flavour of wintergreen and much relished by partridge and grouse. They are pleasant to eat just as they are or they can be used for flavouring. They are said to possess tonic properties and, of course, the medicinal value of wintergreen oil is fairly well known. The berries might also be used to make a liqueur; it is said that a very pleasant and refreshing tea can be made by steeping the leaves of the plant in boiling water for a few minutes.

Checkerberry is not difficult to grow provided the soil is peaty, sandy and moist. Partial shade suits it best, and if desired it can be grown under the cover of other lime-hating shrubs. Its propagation can be by seed, which should be sown in the autumn either in a cold frame or outdoors in sandy, peaty soil; by cuttings taken in April; or by root offsets removed in the spring.

OTHER SPECIES PRODUCING EDIBLE FRUIT

MIQUEL BERRY (*Gaultheria miquelima*)

This is from Japan. It is evergreen, grows from 8-12in, flowers in June and is very attractive both for its flowers and berries. White flowers are produced, one to six in number, on drooping racemes. The berries are three-eighths of an inch in diameter, globose, pink or white, and edible.

MOUNTAIN CHECKERBERRY (*Gualtheria ovatifolia*)

From north-west America. This is a low evergreen shrub of spreading or trailing habit but with erect branches and grows from 8-12in. The flowers appear in the leaf axils and are produced singly. The berries are a quarter of an inch in diameter, scarlet in colour and exceptionally spicy.

SHALLON BERRY (*Gualtheria shallon*)

Also a native of north-west America. This distinctive species was introduced to England in 1826 by the botanist David Douglas who, with the help of the Hudson Bay Company, had been travelling and plant hunting in North America. In 1825, when he first saw it, he wrote, 'the fruit is abundant and very good, so I hope it will, ere long, find a place in the fruit garden as well as the ornamental border'. His hope has not yet been fulfilled. After almost 150 years it still has not found a place in our fruit gardens, although within a dozen years of its introduction into England it was being planted in Scotland as cover for game. It is now naturalized in many parts of Britain.

Shallon is an evergreen shrub which grows from 2-6ft tall, spreading by underground suckers and forming a dense thicket with its many stems. Because its young stems and branches are bristly and a reddish colour it is of ornamental value. Pinkish-white flowers, more noticeable than those of the other species, are produced during May and June. Racemes up to 5in long are produced at the end of the previous year's shoots as well as in the axils of some of the terminal leaves.

It can be cultivated in any moist, shady place provided the soil is lime free. It will, in fact, grow on very poor soil and if soil conditions are very good it can get out of control due to the spread of its underground roots or suckers. Propagation can be by seed and also by the division of the roots. If propagation is to be by division it is preferable to plant the pieces in a warm bed as they do not always commence growth readily in an open bed. Pruning should be restricted to keeping the bush neat and at a convenient size. If too much of the previous year's growth is removed the subsequent harvest will be lessened.

The fruit is a dark purple, hairy berry about three-eighths of an inch in width and with numerous very small seeds. It is juicy and pleasant in taste. In the days of Douglas the North American Indians made cake from the dried fruit.

Chequers

(SERVICE BERRY)

Classification	:	*Sorbus torminalis.*
Physiology		Small, deciduous, round-headed tree growing to 30ft.
Origin	:	Europe, including southern England.
History	:	Fruit at one time sold in the markets of Britain—fruit of other species still used in some European countries—but tree never cultivated for its fruit.
Recommended site	:	Outdoors as an ornamental.
Culinary uses	:	Used like the medlar for dessert or for jellies and conserves.

About 100 species comprise the genus *Sorbus* and these, roughly, can be divided into the whitebeams or service trees and the mountain ash or rowans (see also Rowanberry). Some whitebeams and service trees are planted as ornamentals but they are not generally known as bearers of edible fruit. Indeed, the chequers tree (the wild service tree) is not well known, let alone its fruit. Even as a wild tree it is comparatively rare in Britain, except in Kent and Sussex; in the Weald of Kent it may be seen in woodland or hedgerow. There was a time when its fruit was gathered and sold in the markets. Today this is no longer so and it is just another of those local fruits discarded with the advent of cheaply imported foreign fruits.

The tree is small, round-headed, and usually does not grow to more than 30ft. In young trees the bark is smooth and grey but as it ages the bark becomes darker and splits or cracks into small squares. In general it is similar to the whitebeam but as its leaves are not unlike those of the maple it is sometimes called the maple service tree. Despite its size it is at all times an eye-catching tree. In spring and summer its large leaves are a shining green. In autumn those same large leaves turn red and yellow. In winter the twigs are a greenish brown and large, green buds are very prominent. Whitish flowers appear in May and June and are produced on numerous stems growing from the tips of the shoots. Flowers carry both pistils and stamens, and pollination causes no problems.

Propagation of the tree is very easy from seed but it may take up to two years for the seed to germinate. Cuttings can also be set, or it can be grafted or budded on to the mountain ash or rowan. They thrive best on clay soil. Young trees should be planted in autumn; no pruning is necessary except for the removal of dead wood and for keeping the tree to a convenient size.

The fruit is a pome like the apple or pear and is two-chambered and two-seeded. The case is brittle and usualy egg-shaped, though sometimes it is broader than it is long. It is about the size of a small cherry. When ripe it is brown and chequered, or speckled, with spots of a lighter colour. The flesh is soft and fairly sweet and is rich in vitamin C. It can be eaten like the medlar and used for jellies and conserves.

KINDRED SPECIES

SERVICE BERRY (*Sorbus domestica*)

The tree which bears this fruit is commonly known as the true service tree and it is another native of Europe. It is slow growing and attains a great age and size (60-80ft). It was recorded as a fruit tree as far back as 1883, the gardener of HRH Duchess of Albany referring to the fruit as 'being in season for dessert.' Although it is not now cultivated for its fruit in Britain it is so cultivated in some countries of southern Europe.

The tree is easily grown on well-drained soil in an open situation. No special pruning is necessary and it can be propagated by the same methods as the chequers tree. Its leaves are of the mountain ash or rowan type, being about 10in long and with about thirteen leaflets. Blossom time is May and the flowers are white.

There are two different forms of the fruit: one is apple-shaped and

73

about 1¼in in diameter; the other pear-shaped and much smaller. Both kinds are red-brown in colour and much spotted. When the fruit is still green it is exceptionally bitter and inedible; in fact, it should only be eaten when it is past maturity, like the medlar, or after it has been touched by frost.

In France the fruit is used for making perry or is dried like prunes.

FONTAINBLEU (*Sorbus latifolia*)

This is a small tree which is found growing wild in some parts of southern and western England. The fruit is russet yellow with conspicuous black dots, and about half an inch in diameter.

WHITEBEAM (*Sorbus aria*)

The whitebeam is indigenous to the chalky downs of southern England but is most common on the Chiltern hills. It is a shrub or small tree but can reach a height of 50ft. The bright green of the upper side of the leaf contrasts with the white felt-like underside and makes it an eye-catching tree.

Its whitish flowers are produced in May and June. The fruit is about the size of a small cherry but is egg-shaped. When ripe it is brown and speckled with red spots.

Cherry plum

(MYROBALAN)

Classification	:	*Prunus cerasifera*
Physiology	:	Deciduous, round-headed tree, growing to about 25ft.
Origin	:	Caucasus.
History	:	It has been little cultivated for its fruit although this is of good quality. It has, however, been widely grown as a rootstock for other plums, especially in USA.
Recommended site	:	Outdoors.
Culinary uses	:	Eaten fresh; used for pies, tarts, jam etc.

The cherry and the plum, both members of the genus *Prunus*, are common enough fruits, but the cherry plum is not so well known. The tree originated, as far as is known, in the Caucasus but is now to be found in the temperate and sub-tropical regions of the world. It is often known as the myrobalan but why it should have acquired this name is not known; the true myrobalan is a fruit of the East Indies and is not, in any case, one of the *Prunus* species.

The cherry plum is usually grown as a rootstock for other plums and also, sometimes, as a hedge tree. Yet it is a fruit tree in its own right and will grow up to about 25ft, taking a round-headed shape but with slender upright branches. It flowers before the blackthorn or sloe and with its mass of pure white flowers it is the prettiest of all the plum trees. The flowers appearing on the previous year's growth are produced singly, but sometimes there are two or three together.

75

Cherry plum

They also occur in clusters on short stems produced during the current year.

In general, its cultivation is the same as for other plum trees. It is easy enough to grow but, like all the stone fruits, prefers a chalky soil. When planting, therefore, it may be advisable to add brick mortar or chalk lumps to the soil. Little pruning is required beyond the removal of unwanted branches, and this should be carried out in the spring when the sap is rising. It is permissible to do this even when the tree is in flower. Propagation can be from cuttings or from the seed (small plum stones). When seed is used it should be placed in pots containing sand, which should then be buried in the open ground and left during the winter. Lift them in spring and plant in individual pots or the open ground.

In appearance the fruit is cherry-like but larger, of about 1in diameter, round, smooth and red. The skin is thin and tender, the flesh soft, juicy, sweet and pleasantly flavoured.

The one disadvantage with the cherry plum is that although it blossoms well it does not produce its fruits in great quantity. Little research into the reason for this appears to have been undertaken. To encourage this likeable tree to bear more heavily would be a challenging and rewarding task.

Chinese gooseberry

(KIWI FRUIT)

Classification	:	*Actinidia sinensis* and other species.
Physiology	:	Hardy, deciduous plant climbing up to 30ft.
Origin	:	China.
History	:	Introduced into England over a century ago but seldom grown for its fruit. Now grown commercially in New Zealand.
Recommended site	:	Outdoors — on pergolas, arches, trelliswork or walls.
Culinary uses	:	Used for dessert.

The true Chinese gooseberry, *Actinidia sinensis,* is a plant native to China. It was first brought to Britain from Hupeh province in 1900, but it is still not commonly known. Its fruit is, perhaps, a little better known than the plant itself. In Britain this fruit is generally imported from New Zealand, hence its other name—kiwi fruit.

The Chinese gooseberry, like all the other species of the genus, is a twiner. That is to say it climbs by entwining itself around whatever slender support comes within its reach. It is vigorous and hardy in character and deciduous by habit. Given the opportunity, it will grow up to 30ft. It has large heart-shaped leaves, is ornamental and will be a credit to any pergola, arch, trellis or wall.

It is not particular about the soil in which it is grown although it does prefer loam. Sun or shade it will tolerate, but warm sun is required to ripen and flavour its fruit. Once growing it requires little cultivation. It can be propagated by seed (which should be sown in

77

pots in April), by cuttings of half-ripened shoots inserted in a sandy compost in a cold frame, or by layering of stems in the autumn. It is normally unisexual, so a male must always be planted close to a female if the creamy-white flowers are to develop into Chinese gooseberries.

When the fruit is ripe, it is dark reddish brown in colour, covered with red bristles, and is the size of a walnut or small pullet's egg but shaped like a large gooseberry and with something of a gooseberry flavour. The thin woody shell is easily peeled from the berries which can then be used in various ways for dessert purposes. Thin green translucent slices can be used to good purpose as decoration for trifles, whipped cream dishes etc.

OTHER SPECIES OF INTEREST

SIBERIAN GOOSEBERRY (*Actinidia arguta*)

From the Amur region, East Siberia. A very vigorous climber which is well suited to climbing up trees. It is one of the species with hermaphrodite flowers which can fertilize themselves. The flowers are small and white, but distinctive because they appear in groups of three and have an attractive fragrance. The fruits are greenish yellow berries about 1in long. They have little flavour.

CHINESE EGG GOOSEBERRY (*Actinidia coriacea*)

From west Szechwan. Another vigorous climber growing up to 25ft. Its small flowers are produced in groups of three to five during June and July. It is unisexual. It produces small egg-shaped fruits three-quarters of an inch in diameter, which are brownish with white dots and very juicy.

MANCHURIAN GOOSEBERRY (*Actinidia kolomikta*)

From Manchuria. This one is not quite so vigorous as the others and grows to about 10ft only. Bamboo canes are needed to support its stems. The plant is, for some reason, very much liked by all breeds of cat, therefore when young it must be protected. It is otherwise quite hardy. It is unisexual. The fruit is yellowish in colour.

PURPLE CHINESE GOOSEBERRY (*Actinidia purpurea*)

From Yunnan and west Szechwan. This species does not exceed 25ft in height. It has distinctive oval leaves which may be 5in long. It is unisexual. The fruit is purple and 1in long.

Cloudberry

(AVRONS; MAROSHKA)

Classification	:	*Rubus chamaemorus.*
Physiology		Herbaceous creeping plant, with erect stems up to 10in high.
Origin	:	Northern Europe.
History	:	Its fruit has always been much prized by the inhabitants of northern regions. Grows wild in northern England and Scotland but has never been commercially cultivated in Britain. It has been slightly cultivated in USSR.
Recommended site	:	Cool boggy places; rock gardens; peat gardens.
Culinary uses	:	Eaten fresh as dessert; stewed; preserves.

The cloudberry belongs to the same genus us the brambleberries and raspberries but because it is a very distinct species it is dealt with here under its own heading. It is native to cold, moist, alpine and lonely places of northern lands: in Scotland it is known as avrons, in Norway as moltebeere and in northern Russia as maroshka. Yet, outside the Soviet Union little seems to have been done to cultivate and improve it.

If it is to be cultivated, and it deserves to be, its characteristics and requirements have to be noted. First, it is a spreading plant with long underground rhizomes from which it sends up erect stems 4–10in in height. These stems are without prickles and bear solitary large white flowers from June to July. The flowers are dioecious (either

79

Cloudberry

all male or all female) but pollination should occur naturally without any problems.

The propagation of cloudberry can be by seed but the easiest way is by separation and planting of parts of the underground rhizomes. Because of these long underground rhizomes and the plant's preference for peaty, boggy or at least moist conditions it does not seem to be suitable for small gardens. For those, however, who can provide its requirements and are not afraid to have a 'wild' plant in their garden there are rewards.

The fruits are composed of a few large globular drupes which change from red, to orange, to amber as they ripen. When fully ripe they are very juicy and pleasant, and have the colour, flavour and fragrance of apricots. The fruit can be stewed and used in jams and jellies, but is delicious straight from the plant and makes an excellent dessert.

Coffee bean

Classification : *Coffea arabica.*
Physiology : Small evergreen tree growing 14-30ft.
Origin : Probably Ethiopia.
History : First cultivated in Arabia. Culinary use introduced into Europe by Arabs. Dutch began cultivating it in Dutch East Indies at end of seventeenth century. Plants from the hot-houses of Louis XV of France helped establish coffee growing in South America.
Recommended site : Warm greenhouse.
Culinary uses : Coffee bean when roasted and ground used as beverage or in confectionery.

There are about sixty species of the genus *Coffea* but *Coffea arabica* is the species generally grown for the well-known coffee bean.

It is believed that the tree originated in Ethiopia and it has also been suggested that it was the province of Kaffa in Ethiopia that gave it its name. The first Arab record of its use dates from the fifteenth century. It was first cultivated in Arabia and it was the Arabs who introduced the culinary use of the bean into Europe. From Arabia its cultivation spread to Ceylon and the Dutch took it to the Dutch East Indies at the end of the seventeenth century. Early in the eighteenth century a young French naval officer, Gabriel Mathieu de Clieu, learning of the successful cultivation of the tree by the Dutch, determined to pioneer its cultivation in Martinique. He appealed to Louis XV of France and succeeded in obtaining plants from the king's own

Coffee bean

hot-houses. These plants not only thrived in Martinique after a long and near-calamitous sea journey but were the ancestors of many of those grown in South America today.

The coffee tree is grown principally in Brazil and Columbia. Other growing regions are the West Indies, Indonesia and more recently Mexico and East Africa. All these regions, of course, have tropical climates but even so coffee is grown at considerable variations in altitude (sometimes up to 6,000ft) which means some variation in the temperatures. In fact that grown at a higher altitude is milder and has a better flavour than coffee grown at a low altitude, so it seems that the lower temperature actually produces a better quality coffee.

However, the coffee tree is not, at present, suitable for outdoor growing in northern climates and so it must be located in the warm greenhouse. It is, though, more resistant to frost than other tropical fruit plants (eg the banana) but if frost does injure it then it has less ability than some to produce new shoots. Another thing about it is that it is more tolerant of cool summers than of very high temperatures. The ideal temperature seems to be 65-70°F (18-21°C) although greater variation will be tolerated—65-85°F (18-29°C)—provided these temperatures do not fluctuate suddenly.

In commercial plantations it is often grown in the shade of larger trees although at high altitudes good-quality coffee is grown without shade. But the ideal for warm greenhouse cultivation should be a filtered or diffused light with the sun on it for only part of the day. As the tree gets older it can stand more sunshine and it does, of course, need some sun or warmth to ripen its fruit. It should be remembered that it is a native of shady tropical rain forests and for this reason likes warm, moist conditions. It should be watered plentifully during spring and early summer but sparingly during winter. The aim should be to keep it moist at all times except when it is resting. The soil should always be well drained, and at no time should it be allowed to get excessively wet or boggy. If possible water from below. If the water supply is frequent and adequate it will put up with a shallow soil, so it should make a good pot subject in the greenhouse. If it does not get the water it wants, however, its roots will very quickly penetrate to a great depth. In coffee plantations there is some variation in the soil but the best soil for building up a healthy tree in a greenhouse is two parts good loam, one part peat and one part sand.

Trees vary considerably in their height. Some grow no more than 14ft; others will top 30ft. They will, however, tolerate very close pruning, so their height can be easily controlled. They can also be grown as many-branched bushes or shrubs. But before you start pruning or propagating it is essential to know the peculiar growth characteristics of the coffee tree. A central stem or leader is always strongly dominant and the primary lateral branches grow in pairs opposite each other and horizontally from this central stem. The primary laterals may branch to give secondary laterals and these again branch to give tertiary laterals. All these lateral branches—primary, secondary and tertiary—are spread out on more or less the same plane and at right angles to the central stem. No upright branches grow from these horizontal laterals, but only from the central stem; if this central stem is cut back or bent over then upright branches are more likely to grow, and from them again horizontal laterals will grow in the same way as they do from the central stem.

Cuttings must always be taken from the central stem or upright branches. If taken from the laterals they will root but grow horizontally close to or along the ground. Propagation can, then, be by leafy cuttings taken from an upright branch, but it is also quite satisfactory to raise young seedlings from seed. The seeds should be sown half an inch deep in sandy soil during March, in a temperature of 85°F (29°C).

Two methods of pruning lend themselves to the requirements of greenhouse cultivation. The first is known as single-stem pruning. By this method all upright branches are removed while they are very small and the central stem has its apex cut out when it is about 4ft high. This causes the primary laterals to branch. The secondary laterals should be thinned so that only one is left at each node. At the first node with two laterals one of them is cut out. At the next node the lateral on the opposite side is this time cut out. The tertiary laterals may be dealt with in the same way and may be made to alternate along the secondary laterals. Primary laterals can be cut back to prevent over-bearing of fruit; this also helps to stimulate growth and branching of upper laterals on a young tree.

The other method of pruning is known as multiple-stem pruning. The growing apex of a young tree is cut off at about 18in. A pair of upright branches will start from below this. Later, one of these has its growing tip removed so that this in turn branches, giving two more upright stems. There are now three upright stems and when these become too tall all the laterals up to several feet from the ground are removed. This causes new uprights to form on the main stem. The three old stems can then be cut out.

Although it is a small tree it grows rapidly and begins to fruit when still comparatively young. When it is only 3 years old it will begin to bear fruit and may bear a good crop by the time it is 4 and be in full bearing by the age of 5 years. It will then go on providing its fruit for almost 50 years. It should, however, be mentioned that self-pollination seldom occurs and that this task is usually done by insects.

The tree has large, evergreen glossy leaves and in blossom it is a beautiful thing. The fragrant, strikingly beautiful white flowers are produced in dense clusters set beside each pair of dark green, wax-like leaves along the horizontal laterals. Unfortunately the flowers last for only a very short time. But if the moisture supply is good and the temperature is not too low both flowering and ripening of fruit may be at irregular periods during the year. When the flowers fall they are followed by clusters of green cherry-like fruit which change through various shades of green and golden brown until, when they are fully ripe, they are a bright red. Each fruit contains two beans.

There are two fairly well-known varieties of coffee tree, Kent and Jackson, but there is little point in discussing varieties because although there has been hybridization between some of the *Coffea* species most commercial trees are seedlings and, in any case, no variety has yet been developed to suit cool temperate climates.

It may well be that the coffee tree will tolerate conditions more adverse than has been supposed possible, and the time may come when it will be possible for many of us in Europe and in corresponding climates in North America to grow our own coffee beans as well as roast and grind them.

Cornelian cherry

Classification	:	*Cornus mas.*
Physiology	:	Deciduous small tree or shrub growing up to 25ft.
Origin	:	Europe.
History	:	Cultivated in Europe for centuries. Introduced into Britain during the sixteenth century and cultivated both for its fruit and as an ornamental. Grown today in cool temperate regions, including USA, as an ornamental.
Recommended site	:	Outdoors—sheltered position.
Culinary uses	:	Used for preserves, tarts, etc.

The genus *Cornus* provides several ornamental evergreen and deciduous trees as well as herbaceous plants, but the interest here is in its fruits and the principal species as far as this is concerned is *Cornus mas*. It is itself a good ornamental, and goes under the common name of Cornelian cherry. It was known in ancient times, certainly to the Greeks. Its wood is exceedingly hard—it is said to have been used for the Trojan horse! Its bark produces the red dye traditionally used for the red Turkish fez.

It was introduced into Britain about the middle of the sixteenth century, and was cultivated in fruit gardens for its fruits, called cornet plums, which by the seventeenth century were very popular. The fruit was seldom eaten straight from the tree but was used to make tarts and similar confections. At one time it was not uncommon for it to be kept in brine and used like olives. Its popularity declined, and now this fruit is practically unknown.

Cornelian cherry is a slow-growing, long-lived tree or shrub, with a rather spreading, open habit. In February it carries yellow blossom on grey naked branches and rivals witchhazel in appearance. The starry flowers are produced in short-stalked umbels at the joints and terminals of the previous year's growth. Each umbel is about three-quarters of an inch across.

There is another species, *Cornus sanguinea,* which is called the female cornel because it starts to produce female flowers at an early age. Unfortunately its fruits are not palatable. *Cornus mas,* on the other hand, is the male cornel and is so called because it produces male flowers only in its early life and may be 10-15 years old before female flowers are produced. Propagation should, therefore, be by cuttings from mature trees, and these root reasonably well. It can be grown from seed, but if this is done germination may not take place until the following year and then there is possibly a long wait for the female flowers.

However, its use as an ornamental tree compensates for its slowness in fruit bearing. It should be given a well-chosen site, sheltered and moist, so that, like the almond, it can show off its beauty in late February.

Pruning should be confined to removing dead and untidy growth. New wood should be encouraged because it is upon this that flowers and fruit will be borne the following year. The fruit is a bright red oblong-elliptic drupe about five-eighths of an inch long and about half an inch wide. It is like a small plum. When first picked its flesh is rather austere but after keeping it becomes pleasantly acid. The preserve it makes is one of the best.

DWARF CORNELIAN CHERRY
(*Cornus suecica*)

This is the one other species of the genus which is of interest because of its fruit. By nature it is a sub-arctic and alpine plant. It is native to the moors, heaths and mountains of northern Europe (including Scotland, although rare).

It is an herbaceous creeping plant with underground rhizomes. Erect stems, growing about 6in high, are produced annually. For this

86

plant you need moist, acid, sandy, peaty soil. It can be grown as a carpet plant under acid-loving shrubs. Propagation is preferably by division but propagation by seed is possible. Very small dark purple flowers are produced during July and August in terminal umbels, followed by red berries one-fifth of an inch in diameter.

It used to be said by Scottish Highlanders that the berries create appetite and the plant was, therefore, known as 'Lus-a-chraois' which, in Gaelic, means plant of gluttony.

Cranberry

(AMERICAN CRANBERRY)

Classification	:	*Vaccinium macrocarpon* (*V. oxycoccos macrocarpus*).
Physiology	:	Creeping, evergreen, peat-loving undershrub.
Origin	:	North America; north Asia.
History	:	Early American settlers quickly utilized this berry fruit. The plant has since undergone selective breeding and the fruit is now grown on a commercial scale in Massachusetts, New Jersey, Wisconsin, and coastal areas of Washington and Oregon, but rarely by the amateur.
Recommended site	:	Outdoors in moist, peaty bed.
Culinary uses	:	Renowned for sauce; good for tarts and other kindred uses.

The cranberry belongs to the same genus as the bilberry and blueberry (see under these separate headings). Many of the *Vaccinium* species are natives of North America and early settlers there very quickly made use of the berries so abundantly provided. Since then there has been a steady development and cultivation of the cranberry, and today it is finding its way, frozen and canned, into the supermarkets of Europe.

But this imported fruit now being brought to the housewife's attention is really no new fruit at all. In fact, in the last century it was being imported into Britain from Russia and Scandinavia and was especially used for tarts. It is strange, therefore, that only comparatively recently have the British begun to take an interest in growing this fruit themselves.

The plant generally chosen for cultivation is the American cranberry (*Vaccinium macrocarpon*), a small prostrate creeper with thin wiry stems and small box-like leaves. It is another of those heath plants and as such is a lime hater—or peat lover. To cultivate it successfully it is necessary to give it a moist position and peaty soil. If such conditions are not naturally available the next best thing is to prepare a bed specially for it. Dig out the soil of an area of a convenient size to a depth of 2ft, half fill it with stones and cover these with peat and leaf mould. The area you dig out (it can be a trench) can be based on the number of plants you intend to have, each plant being 2ft from its neighbours.

Planting should preferably be carried out in early autumn and, if available, a thin layer of sand can be put over the bed. Immediately after planting the whole bed should be flooded, if possible with rain water or water free of chalk. No more water should then be given until the following summer when the bed should be again flooded from time to time. Just as it is necessary to simulate tropical conditions for tropical plants so with the cranberry it is desirable to simulate the seasonal wet, peat-bog conditions of mountain and moorland. If such conditions are provided the cranberry requires no other attention apart from keeping it free of weeds.

The propagation of this small undershrub can either be by division or by layering of the stems in summer. Propagation by seed is also possible but the American cranberry of today, it must be remembered, is the product of selection and breeding so that today's plants are cultivars.

The pink flowers of the American cranberry appear in clusters during the summer and are followed by oval-shaped scarlet berries, normally twice the size of currants, which are ready for picking in September. Cranberries have a palatable acid flavour and ought to be used in the kitchen more often than they are. Not only do they make a good sauce but they are excellent for tarts, cranberry and apple pie, cranberry cake, etc.

There is also another American species which is of some interest. This is the Southern cranberry (*Vaccinium erythrocarpum*) which

Cranberry

grows on the mountains from Virginia to Georgia. Its berries are dark red and have a very good flavour.

CRANBERRIES NATIVE TO BRITAIN

SMALL CRANBERRY or MARSH WHORTLEBERRY
(*Vaccinium oxycoccos*)

The small cranberry is a native of northern Europe as well as of north Asia and America. In Britain its habitat is peat bogs, principally in the north. It is a very low straggling perennial with prostrate wiry stems which root at intervals. Pink flowers, appearing solitarily from June to August, are followed by dark red berries. Apart from its smaller berries it is not dissimilar to the American cranberry.

MOUNTAIN CRANBERRY, COWBERRY or
RED WHORTLEBERRY (*Vaccinium vitis-idaea*)

This is a native of northern Europe, and in Britain it is usually found on mountainous moorland. It is a creeping dwarf evergreen shrub. Its flowers, appearing in June and July, are white or pink and are grouped in clusters at the terminals. It is an attractive shrub and is useful as a carpeting plant and for peat pockets in rockeries.

The berries are red and acid and make a very good jelly. In the Scottish Highlands venison is not venison unless there is cranberry jelly to accompany it. Large quantities of this particular cranberry used to be imported into Britain from Sweden.

Crowberry

(BLACK CROWBERRY)

Classification	:	*Empetrum nigrum*.
Physiology	:	Low evergreen undershrub, 1ft high.
Origin	:	Northern Europe.
History	:	Never cultivated but fruit was eaten in arctic regions as a preventive of scurvy.
Recommended site:	:	Moist, shady places—under other shrubs or on rock gardens.
Culinary uses	:	Eaten from the hand; medicinal; as a beverage.

There are only a few species of *Empetrum*. An inhabitant of the sub-Arctic and the higher regions of the northern hemisphere, *Empetrum nigrum* grows naturally in the acid moorlands and mountain parts of northern Britain.

It is a low, procumbent or prostrate undershrub growing about 1ft high. With its many spreading, procumbent stems which are well clad with small, but numerous and overlapping, evergreen heath-like leaves it forms a low dense mass of green in summer and winter. Apart from the fact that it is another of those lime haters it is quite easy to grow. If possible, plant it in the spring in a peaty soil in a position which is shady and moist. Propagation should be from cuttings and these should be inserted in sandy peat in a cold frame during the summer.

The fruit, borne in small clusters, ripens in the autumn and it is then a black, globular drupe three-sixteenths of an inch in diameter, carrying within it six to nine seeds. Its taste is slightly acid—to some

Crowberry

it has a taste of turpentine. In the extreme northern regions it was eaten because it was said to have medicinal properties. The fruit can be eaten raw or made into a beverage with sour milk, but it is not to everybody's taste.

Its flowers are mostly unisexual, with each sex on different plants. However, pollination is by the wind and causes little trouble. The pinkish purple flowers are produced during March and appear solitarily or in small groups in the axils of the upper leaves near the tips of the previous year's shoots. The flowers are very small and with the exception of their stamens (there are three in the male flower) are not very noticeable.

SIMILAR FRUITS

MOUNTAIN CROWBERRY (*Empetrum hermaphroditiem*)—bisexual but in other respects similar to black crowberry.

PURPLE CROWBERRY (*Empetrum nigrum* var. *purpureum*)—bears reddish purple berries.

SOUTH AMERICAN CROWBERRY (*Empetrum rubra*)—a native of the southern part of South America. It grows 6-18in high and bears red berries.

Custard apple

Classification	:	*Annona* species.
Physiology	:	Shrubs or small trees, semi-deciduous or evergreen, growing 15-25ft.
Origin	:	Tropical South America.
History	:	There is archaeological evidence of the existence of cherimoya-type fruit in prehistoric South America. From its original home it spread to Africa and India, later to the Mediterranean area and to Australia. Under commercial cultivation in all these areas.
Recommended site	:	Warm greenhouse—pot cultivation.
Culinary uses	:	For dessert or mixing with ice cream and cool drinks.

There are a few species of the genus *Annona* which bear edible fruit; they are generally called custard apples—though their fruits are often known by other names. These different fruits (sharifa, cherimoya, guanábana, llama) will be dealt with, each in a separate section under this general heading of Custard apple.

They all originated in the tropics or near-tropics of South America and were known to ancient civilizations of that continent. Terra cotta vases in the shape of the cherimoya have been dug up from prehistoric graves in Peru. From South America the fruits were taken to Mexico and the West Indies—it is not known when—and on to Africa and India. Now, today, some of them, principally the cherimoya, are grown in southern Spain, Israel and Australia. But generally they have never been grown on a large scale commercially; their supply to markets has usually been from garden or dooryard-type cultivation, although recently hybrid fruits grown commercially have been exported by Israel.

They were introduced into Britain as far back as the end of the last century, but little, so far, has been attempted with them. They do, of course, require a warm greenhouse, and as they are comparatively small trees, and can be kept as small as the peach tree with far less pruning, it would seem that they are suited to pot cultivation.

SHARIFA, or SUGAR APPLE (*Annona squamosa*)

The sharifa is very widely grown in India, where it has a long history. It is mentioned in the Hindu Sanskrit and because of this it is quite widely believed that India is its home. Bearing in mind, however, that the other *Annona* species originated in South America and were taken at some time to other lands, there seems to be no reason to doubt that this was what happened with the sharifa.

When growing naturally it forms a bushy shrub 15-20ft high and carrying a large number of branches. It is semi-deciduous, and normally it sheds its leaves immediately after its fruit has ripened and goes into a period of dormancy lasting about 2 months. Although it is a slow-growing shrub its normal life span is about 15-20 years.

The soil it likes is sandy to medium loam. It can stand drought but its roots suffer if the soil is waterlogged or if there is stagnation of the soil. It is essential, therefore, to ensure proper drainage by putting crocks in the bottom of the pots. The best time to pot it up is in the spring.

The sharifa thrives in a fairly hot, dry temperature and is very sensitive to frost; young plants can be killed at 30°F (−1°C). The minimum temperature should be 80°F (27°C) in summer and 65°F (18°C) in winter. During the summer it is advisable to shade it from direct sunshine.

Propagation by seed should preferably be from fresh seeds, and germination can be assisted by soaking them in water for 3 days. Although the tree is slow growing, it may as a seedling grow 1ft within a year at the beginning. It does not like being transplanted and should always be repotted with care, with as little disturbance of the roots as possible. Under ideal conditions a seedling may come into bearing after 4 years. Some seedlings are more productive than others and there is variation in the quality and size of the fruit. When, therefore, a tree proves to be good it should be propagated by budding in the same way as for citrus fruits. A budded tree should come into bearing when it is 4 years old.

As the tree grows, the aim of pruning should be to make a well shaped tree with well-spread branches. Light pruning of the old wood will induce new growth so that better branching will result. When pruning it should be remembered that fruit is borne on both old and new wood.

Flowering should start in late spring and continue for a month or so. The flowers are produced singly or in clusters of two to four. Only a very small percentage will set and produce fruit. One reason for this is because the stamens and pistils mature at different times. Within 3 days of the opening of the flowers the petals drop off if fertilization has occurred. When it has not occurred the whole of the flower, including the ovaries, drops. Because the stamen and pistils mature at different times a flower seldom fertilizes its own eggs. The correct temperature or humidity might possibly cause the pistils to remain receptive until the pollen is shed but no information concerning this is available and it is, therefore, necessary to assist fertilization by hand pollination. Flowers can be gathered in a paper bag and then when the pollen is shed it can be put on the pistils of newly opened flowers with a small camel-hair brush. Only a few flowers will need to be fertilized to get a satisfactory crop but usually there are not enough flowers ready for fertilization in any one day.

During the flowering period humidity should be increased by syringeing daily as this also assists fruit setting. Under normal conditions the period from flowering to harvesting is about 4 months. The tree should be kept well watered during the fruiting period as this improves the size and quality of the fruit; an occasional feed of liquid manure is also beneficial.

The fruit is heart shaped or conical, 2-3in in diameter, and its layers of outer carpels are yellowish green when it is ripe. As the fruits mature the carpels may be separate so that the white flesh below can be seen, but they should be picked before they reach this stage and placed in a warm room where they will ripen in 2 or 3 days. Immature fruits will not ripen to a good flavour once they have been picked if the temperature is lower than 55-65°F (13-18°C). The flesh of the fruit

Custard apple

is custard-like, sweet and slightly acid. It is sweeter than the cherimoyer but does not possess the same piquancy.

Usually the fruit does not ripen all at one time so it may be possible to prolong the harvesting period. When all the fruit has ripened the plant sheds its leaves and enters into a period of dormancy, but if it has been neglected in some way dormancy may commence before the fruit has ripened. When this happens the fruit will turn brown and will be of no use whatsoever.

CHERIMOYER (*Annona cherimola*)

It is thought that this tree originated in the Andes, between southern Ecuador and Peru. From its original habitat it has spread throughout the world and is now cultivated commercially in Mexico, Chile, Argentina, southern Spain, Australia, and in Israel where it has been profitably hybridized with the sharifa.

In the near-tropics and sub-tropics it appears to produce better fruit than in the true tropics. In the true tropics fruit grown at an altitude of 3,500-7,500ft has a better taste than fruit grown in the lowlands. Thus it can be said that successful growing of this fruit requires a relatively dry climate of temperate heat. Even so, although it is the hardiest of the custard apples, temperatures below 27°F (−3°C) cause severe damage. Winter temperatures must, therefore, always be mild, and never drop below freezing.

The cherimoyer grows vigorously when young but tends to decline in growth early in life. It can take several forms—it can be small and erect, it can be bushy, or it can be straggling. Generally, in its normal habitat, it grows from 15-25ft high. Its leaves, which are its great attraction, are light green, velvety, large, oval-shaped and abundant.

The soil it likes is a rich loam. Like the sharifa it can be grown in a pot and its general cultivation is the same. Summer temperatures should be between 70 and 85°F (21-29°C) and winter temperatures should not be below 60°F (16°C) except for a short chilling period to encourage complete dormancy. Any pruning that is necessary should be done when the leaves have dropped and before the new ones appear. It should be pruned to establish a convenient form. Severe pruning may reduce flowering and fruiting but moderate annual pruning does not usually prevent new shoots from flowering and it promotes larger fruit.

Propagation can be from seeds covered to a depth of not more than three-quarters of an inch. In a warm temperature they will germinate in a few weeks. They should be kept moist but not watered too copiously.

The cherimoyer grafts fairly easily and the sharifa provides a good stock when a dwarf tree is required. Budding should be carried out at the beginning of the growing season. The chosen stock plants should be three-eighths to half an inch thick. The budwood should be well matured, not green, and if possible wood from which the leaves have dropped.

Cherimoyer flowers somewhat later than sharifa, the fruit ripens later, and its period of dormancy is consequently later. The fragrant flowers are about 1in long, they are borne singly or perhaps two or three together. As is the case with the other custard apple species the stamens and pistils are crowded together in the fleshy receptacle. Three outer petals extend about 1in below a band of stamens and a cone of pistils. As the pollen is usually not shed until the day after the pistils have become receptive some of the pistils may not be fertilized. This not only means that the tree may bear few fruits but that where fruit does form this may be deformed or be unsymmetrical in shape because some of the pistils in the flower cone were not fertilized.

Because of this behaviour, it is necessary to pollinate by hand when the pistils have become receptive to pollination. The time is judged by the opening of the three outer petals which have until then been nearly closed together. The petals should be carefully held apart with one hand and with the pollen on a small camel hair brush this is stroked back and forth over the pistils so that they all receive it. The flowers will not all be ready for pollination at once, and it is not desirable that they should be because if too many fruits are set at the same time the flowering season will be shortened. A flower at the base of a long shoot usually produces large fruit.

Cherimoyer fruit can weigh anything from a few ounces to a few pounds and they can ripen from 5 to 8 months after the flowers have been pollinated. The ripe fruit is heart-shaped or conical in form and is pale yellowish green. On some the skin is smooth, on others it is covered with small conical protuberances. The skin is thin, and the fruit is therefore easily bruised.

The time to harvest the fruit is when it has turned from brownish

97

G

Custard apple

green to yellowish green. It can then be kept up to about a week at a temperature of 65°F (18°C). The flavour is said to be impaired if the temperature during this period is lower than 60°F (16°C) but when fully ripe the fruit is pleasanter if it is cooled to 45°F (7°C) before eating.

Its flesh is white, with a buttery texture and moderately juicy. It contains ten or fifteen brown seeds about the size and shape of beans (sharifa has about sixty such seeds). The flesh of a good cherimoyer has an agreeable blend of mild acidity and sweetness—it is said by some to resemble a pineapple and banana—and has a richness all its own. A good cherimoyer is essentially a dessert fruit. On the other hand the flesh can be coarse and have an unattractive taste. At its best it is the choicest of the custard apple fruit.

GUANABANA or SOUR SOP (*Annona muricata*)

This tree is very commonly grown in gardens in the West Indies and its fruit is seen in the markets of South America. It is an evergreen, upright in character, somewhat smaller than the two previous species, and bears the largest of the custard apple fruit. The guanábana's leaves are a glossy green and as it is not normally dormant it is at all times attractive and should make a good indoor pot tree provided there is space to accommodate it.

Generally its cultivation and propagation are the same as for the preceding species but it is much less resistant to cool weather. Although it is not a heavy bearer, fruit may ripen on the same tree during most of the year if a good temperature can be maintained—there can be flowers and mature fruit on the tree at one and the same time. The flowers, incidentally, are borne mainly on old wood.

The fruit is 6-9in long, green in colour, ovoid or heart-shaped and on its surface there are soft spines. The flesh is white and juicy, pulpy in texture, with soft cotton-like strands that contain many seeds. The taste is pleasantly sub-acid and has a slight mango-like flavour.

In Cuba guanábana juice is used to make a very popular and refreshing drink. It makes an excellent sherbert and can be used in ice cream or mixed with milk. The pulp is good for jellies and preserves, containing three or four times as much acid as the sharifa.

LLAMA (*Annona diversifolia*)

Llama grows on the foothills of mountains in Mexico, Guatemala and Salvador but is seldom found above 2,000ft. In its natural habitat it can grow to 25ft, but it is slightly smaller than cherimoyer and, like all the custard apples, it can with judicious pruning be kept to a convenient height, size and shape. Left to grow naturally it is sometimes slender in habit, the trunk of a mature tree being no more than 10in in diameter; but it can be erect, or it can be spreading.

Cultural and pruning requirements and propagation are the same as for the other custard apples. Temperatures can be as for sharifa —ie 70-80°F (21-27°C) in summer and not less than 60°F (15°C) in winter—but in fact this custard apple thrives in the tropical lowlands. Its altitude limit is 2,000ft, which shows that it resents cool winds. For several consecutive months of the year llama happily enjoys a hot dry climate but this is followed by plentiful rainfall during the rest of the year.

The flowers are maroon coloured and need to be pollinated in the same manner as for the other custard apples. The fruit is conical, ovoid or round, with a rough surface. The largest of these fruits may weigh up to 1½lb. The colour varies from pale green to magenta pink, with a thick white bloom over the surface. In the pale green varieties the flesh is white and the flavour sweet, like that of the sharifa; in the pink varieties the flesh is pinkish, is more acid and not unlike that of the cherimoyer. The seeds are as numerous as in the cherimoyer but are larger in size.

The fruits can be used for dessert—eaten with cream, layered in trifles or mixed with ice cream. They can also be used for jellies and preserves.

Custard banana

(POOR MAN'S BANANA)

Classification	:	*Asiminia triloba*.
Physiology	:	Hardy deciduous small tree or shrub growing 10-20ft tall.
Origin	:	South-eastern USA.
History	:	Fruit for long eaten in USA but seldom grown commercially.
Recommended site	:	Outdoors—sunny position; pot cultivation.
Culinary uses	:	Used solely for dessert.

The genus *Asiminia* belongs to the Annonaceae family and is, therefore, related to the genus *Annona* (custard apples). The only species of interest is *Asiminia triloba*, a low tree or shrub which grows wild in south-eastern USA.

In all probability the Indians of North America ate and enjoyed this fruit many long years before the coming of the white man, but since then the greatest popularity of the fruit has been with American boys who have hunted for the choicest of these custard bananas. Little if anything appears to have been done to grow the fruit commercially.

In the wilds the shrubs are conspicuous because of their very large leaves—sometimes 12in long and 6in wide—and their attractive flowers and fruits. The flowers are produced either singly or in clusters of two or three and are about 2in in diameter. The petals are at first green but become dark red and then purple. It is a hardy deciduous tree or shrub but, unfortunately, it seldom fruits in Britain. However, remembering the character of its relations the custard apples, this failure to set fruit might be overcome by following the same

100

practice of pollinating the flowers. Some study and experiment is required on the matter of pollination and setting of fruit.

The shrub will grow in any soil but should be planted in a warm sunny position. It could also be a subject for pot cultivation and by this method some control would be possible at vital times of flowering and fruit setting and when there is inclement weather.

It should be propagated by seed in the spring in a warm temperature so that it is already growing well before the commencement of winter. No special pruning is required except, in its early life, to form a bush or shrub of convenient size and shape, and later on to keep it healthy and to maintain a convenient size.

The fruits which mature in autumn are from 3-5in long, about half as thick as they are long, and cylindrical in shape. When they are fully grown they are green with a heavy bloom, but before they become ripe the pulp is greenish-white at the centre and at this time has a rather offensive fetid odour and taste. As the fruits ripen the skins become brownish-black and the pulp changes to creamy white or yellow (resembling custard in texture and colour) and is succulent, sweet and rich. A thoroughly ripe fruit is very rich—too rich for some people until the taste for it is acquired. The flavour has some resemblance to banana and is improved when the fruit has lightly been touched by frost. Its one disadvantage as a dessert fruit is that it has very large seeds. These are about an inch long and half an inch broad and are embedded in the pulp. However, the seeds in properly ripened fruit easily separate from the custard-like pulp.

There are two natural varieties which are found growing wild. The difference is solely in the fruit; in one the pulp is an orange-yellow colour and in the other it is a pale creamy white. The one with the yellow pulp is sweet and delectable but the one which is creamy white is bitter and has a fetid odour which it keeps until it decays; neither sunshine or frost can make it desirable. American boys long ago knew of this difference but botanists have not, so far, separated and named these two distinct varieties.

Desert plum

(AUSTRALIAN NATIVE NECTARINE)

Classification	:	*Owenia acidula*.
Physiology	:	Small, ornamental tree, growing to 20ft.
Origin	:	Australia.
History	:	Fruits eaten by Aborigines and early Australian colonists to quench thirst. Rare in cultivation.
Recommended site	:	Greenhouse—pot tree.
Culinary uses	:	Possibly for drinks, juice or jellies.

This small tree is a native of the western plains of New South Wales and Queensland. It is considered to be one of the most handsome of the trees of the Australian interior—erect in habit and usually with a very shapely, round-headed, leafy top. It carries pendulous branches with pinnate foliage—and from nine to nearly thirty leaflets, 1-1½in long. Flowers are small, white, and borne in clusters in the axils of the leaves.

Propagation is usually from seed but germination is not always successful. Although it produces root suckers these are difficult to transplant. In its natural habitat it will grow on sands, loams, clay-loams and clay—no one kind of soil seeming to suit it especially. In temperate rain climates it needs to be grown in a greenhouse and pot cultivation is recommended.

Both the Aborigines and the early Australian colonists made use of the fruit to relieve thirst and enable them to endure the inconvenience of lack of water for many hours. It is natural, therefore, that the fruit should have been given numerous, almost affectionate, names such as

102

'emu apple', 'mooley apple', 'rancooran', 'warrongan', 'bulloo', 'dilly boolen'.

The fruit is bluish black and about the size of a small nectarine. The pulp is a rich crimson colour not unlike that of a prickly pear. Contained in the pulp is a large rough stone which the Aborigines used for making bracelets and anklets. (No doubt many an Aborigine girl, because of an insatiable appetite for jewellery, gave many an Aborigine boy a nasty tummyache.) It is in fact a very acid fruit and it could possibly be used for drinks, juices or jellies.

Elderberry

Classification	:	*Sambucus nigra.*
Physiology	:	Deciduous shrub or small tree.
Origin	:	Europe, western Asia.
History	:	Known in ancient times; formerly cultivated in Britain for making wine.
Recommended site	:	Outdoors.
Culinary uses	:	Used for wines, pies, jams, jellies etc; medicinal.

The genus *Sambucus* belongs to the Caprifoliaceae family which includes the genus *Viburnum,* another provider of edible berries (see Guelderberry). *Sambucus nigra,* the common elderberry, is native to temperate Europe and is a shrub or small tree, some varieties of which may grow to 30ft. It is, however, very variable and many of the cultivated varieties are less tall and not so vigorous in growth.

The tree was known in early times and it may well be that the Romans introduced it into Britain along with the grape vine. In the middle of the nineteenth century the tree was still being planted extensively in Kent for the dual purpose of serving as an orchard hedge or shelter tree while also providing fruit. At that time the fruit was carted up to London in large quantities for wine making.

Its cultivation is very easy and it requires little attention. A moist loamy soil in semi-shade will give the best results but the tree thrives in a wide range of soils and climate. Propagation is also easy, and can be by seed or by 9-12in hardwood cuttings inserted in the open ground in the autumn or early winter.

It can be grown to form a hedge, which is cut back as required, or as a small shrub, which should be pruned during the winter or before new growth has commenced and then, by the application of nitrogenous fertilizer, encouraged to make new growth in the spring. This is required because flowers and berries are produced on the new growth.

Its numerous small creamy white flowers appear in June on five-stemmed umbellate cymes forming thick clusters. The fruit it produces are globose, purple-black lustrous berries about a quarter to half an inch in diameter, very juicy and said to be rich in iron. Although country folk still use the berries principally for wine making they can, in fact, be used for other purposes. Like blackberries they can be mixed with apples to make excellent pies, jellies and jams with a very attractive, rich, red colouring. They have long been known for their medicinal properties. The seventeenth-century English writer John Evelyn, who devoted much time to gardening, said of it, 'If the medicinal properties of the leaves, bark, berries etc, were thoroughly known I cannot tell what our countryman could ail for what he would not find a remedy, from every hedge, either for sickness or wounds.'

The elderberry is in fact a neglected fruit which is capable of improvement by selection and cultivation. For further encouragement there is an old proverb which says that he who cultivates the elderberry will die in his own bed.

OTHER SPECIES AND VARIETIES

YELLOW ELDERBERRY (*Sambucus nigra fructo-lutea*)
   This is a variety of *Sambucus nigra* and is similar to it in all respects except that it bears yellow berries.

RED ELDERBERRY (*Sambucus racemosa*)
   A native of Europe, western Asia, Siberia and North America, growing 8-10ft tall. It has been cultivated in Britain since the sixteenth century and as a shrub it is one of the most attractive of the elder species. It prefers cool, moist conditions and grows well in Scotland.
   The flowers appear in April in terminal pyramidal panicles. The berries ripen in June and July and are scarlet. Unfortunately, for reasons which do not appear to have been studied, it does not bear its fruit with much abundance in Britain.

Elderberry

AMERICAN ELDERBERRY (*Sambucus canadensis*)
A native of North America, found especially in Nova Scotia and the Rocky Mountains. It grows about 10-12ft. Flowers appear in July in convex umbels 4-8in across. The berries are purple-black like those of *S. nigra* but are larger, sweeter, richer, better flavoured and more abundant.
One variety of this species bears cherry-red berries.

WESTERN ELDERBERRY (*Sambucus caerula*)
Another native of North America and very similar to *S. canadensis* but larger. Its berries also are larger, bluish black with a heavy bloom, and have a distinctive flavour.

GOLDEN ELDERBERRY (*Sambucus pubens zanthocarpa*)
This is a North American shrub very similar to the red elderberry (*S. racemosa*) but it bears golden-yellow berries.

WHITE ELDERBERRY (*Sambucus pubens leucocarpa*)
As for the previous entry, but this variety has white berries.

CALIFORNIAN ELDERBERRY (*Sambucus callicarpa*)
A native of California growing to only 6ft and bearing scarlet berries.

BLUE ELDERBERRY (*Sambucus glauca*)
In California this tree grows from 15-30ft; in climates similar to that of Britain it can be grown as a shrub 5-10ft tall.
Yellow-white flowers appear in June in flat umbels 6-7in wide. The berries are sweetish, juicy and bluish black, covered with a pale blue bloom which gives them a distinctive hue.

Eve's date

(DATE FRUIT)

Classification	:	*Yucca baccata.*
Physiology	:	Evergreen succulent shrub with spiky, sword-shaped leaves growing to a length of 3ft.
Origin	:	Mexico.
History	:	One of the first plants brought to Europe from the New World.
Recommended site	:	Greenhouse and/or a sunny position.
Culinary uses	:	Can be eaten fresh.

The *Yucca* species, numbering about thirty, are members of the lily family, and originated in Central America, Mexico and southern USA. Some of these species were amongst the first plants to be brought from the American to the European content where, provided the climate is not excessively wet, they flourish quite well.

Yucca baccata is a semi-desert species which grows naturally from Colorado to western Nevada and from Mexico to Texas. Its leaves, up to 3ft long, are stiff and sharp pointed and, growing as they do from its base, they make it an almost stemless plant. The plant or shrub, whichever you prefer to call it, is quite hardy, but being a succulent and native to arid conditions it detests stagnating water and excessive rain.

Because of this detestation of wet conditions it is suitable for growing in a pot or tub and can spend its time in a cold greenhouse or other well-lighted, airy, indoor position during the coldest and wettest part of the year. When placed outdoors during May it should be allowed to occupy a sunny position and the pot which contains it

107

should be buried up to the rim. By spending half their time indoors and half in the garden they serve the dual purpose of providing indoor decoration during winter and giving a sub-tropical touch to the garden during summer.

A compost of two parts sandy loam to one part leaf mould plus a little sand suits it best. The potting should be done in March and it should then be freely watered from April to September but given very little for the rest of the year. Repotting will only be necessary when it becomes pot-bound.

Propagation can be from suckers in March or April; by cuttings of roots inserted in sand in spring in a temperature of 55°F (13°C), and by seed. Germination of the seed, however, requires a warm temperature. The seed should be soaked for 24 hours before sowing, and after sowing should be shaded from the light. Germination normally takes from 4-6 weeks.

Its numerous flowers are produced in panicles from its leafy centre and are creamy white, bell-shaped, pendulous and about 2in across. In their natural habitat the *Yucca* are pollinated entirely by the *tegeticula*—a genus of moths in which each species is adapted to the pollination of a separate species of *Yucca*. No other insect is able to pollinate this genus. The *tegeticula* emerge when the flowers open— usually at night. The female moth makes a small ball of pollen and flies with this to another flower where she lays four or five eggs in the pistil. After she has laid the eggs she seals the hole she has made with the small ball of pollen. When the eggs hatch the larvae feed on the seed of the plant—each one requiring from the plant about 20 seeds for its food. The plant, however, produces somewhere about 200 seeds so that after the larvae have taken their food requirements sufficient seed is still left for the plant to reproduce itself. Unfortunately the *tegeticula* does not live in temperate climates and so it is necessary to pollinate the flowers by hand.

The fruit is a seed pod, 3-6in long, and in shape like a short, stubby banana or cucumber. When ripe it is a dark purple and when eaten fresh it is said to have an aromatic, sweet taste but with a slight bitterness.

Feijoa

(PINEAPPLE GUAVA)

Classification	:	*Feijoa sellowiana.*
Physiology	:	Small, shrubby, evergreen tree.
Origin	:	Paraguay; Uruguay; southern Brazil; northern Argentine.
History	:	Discovered in South America in 1819, now grown in many sub-tropical areas but not extensively cultivated.
Recommended site	:	Indoors as pot plant. Outdoors but only in sunny sheltered position.
Culinary uses	:	Eaten fresh as dessert. Also used for marmalade and jellies.

The feijoa fruit is sometimes called pineapple guava but neither the fruit nor the tree in any way resembles the guava. *Sellowiana* is the only known species of the genus *Feijoa*. It was discovered by the German explorer Sellow in 1819 and it has since then become established in many sub-tropical areas, including California, New Zealand and the South of France. Although grown for its fruit it is not extensively cultivated, but cultivars or varieties are now grown in those areas just mentioned. In Britain it is sometimes grown as an ornamental tree though not for its fruit, and indeed it is only in very hot summers that its fruit will ripen outdoors. However, it deserves consideration for at least the following reasons: by nature it is a small tree so that it is useful for pot cultivation; its flowers are extremely distinctive; the petals of the flowers are edible and can be used with salad.

The tree has a bushy habit and by pruning it can be kept to a reasonable size. It is an evergreen with leaves about 2in long, glossy

109

and dark green on the upper surface but silver-grey and felt-like on the lower. The twigs and branches are rather brittle but are not broken by the weight of its fruit.

It will grow in any ordinary soil but prefers it to be light and loamy. It has been known to withstand a temperature as low as 12°F (−11°C), but if grown outside it should be planted in a very sheltered position or against a south-facing wall. If it is to produce fruit in climates similar to that of Britain it should be grown as a pot plant in a temperate greenhouse. It can be propagated from seed sown in sandy soil during February or March in a temperature of 55-60°F (13-16°C). Germination takes about 2-3 weeks. It can also be propagated from leafy cuttings taken during June and July, better results being obtained when gentle bottom heat can be provided. The aim of pruning must be to keep the tree a convenient size but also to encourage new growth; it is on the current year's growth that flowers are borne.

Flowers are normally produced from June to July and appear solitarily in the lowermost leaf axils. Usually each new shoot carries from two to four very pretty and distinctive flowers. They consist of four thick petals, purplish on the inner side and white on the outer with numerous dark-red stamens forming a tuft extending beyond the petals. They are somewhat similar to fuschia flowers. The 'beauty' of these flowers is that if you tire of them and you are too impatient to await their fruit you can eat them with salad.

The feijoa can begin bearing when 3 or 4 years old. When grown outdoors in warmer countries bees appear to be the pollinating agents and usually there is a good set of fruit. In a greenhouse hand-pollination will probably be necessary. Ripening can take 4-6 months depending on temperature. Unlike other fruits (with the exception of the apple) the feijoa develops a richer flavour at lower temperatures.

The fruit is an attractive, waxy, dark green or yellowish-green berry, either oblong or perfectly round. It varies in size even on the same tree—some of the fruit may be 2-3in long and some less than 1in. When ripe it falls to the ground and should be gathered and used at once because the centre part begins to deteriorate and turn brown within a few days. The whole of the fruit is edible except for a very thin outer part of the skin; its sugar content may be about 6 per cent, and with its tart but pleasant myrtle-like flavour it makes good marmalades and jellies.

Fig

Classification	:	*Ficus carica*.
Physiology	:	Deciduous, sub-tropical tree or bush. Up to 20ft tall.
Origin	:	Western Asia, possibly Arabia.
History	:	One of the first fruits used by man. Now widely cultivated in Mediterranean area. When it was first introduced to Britain is not known. Grown in gardens throughout southern USA but commercial cultivation confined mainly to California and Texas.
Recommended site	:	Pot cultivation. Outdoors—sunny, sheltered position. Greenhouse— heated or unheated.
Culinary uses	:	For dessert—fresh or dried; or cooked as a sweet.

The borderline between unusual and common fruit is often blurred or ill-defined: the fig is on this borderline. To some growers this fruit is quite well known. But for the many who still think of it as being a foreigner it is included here.

In warm countries four kinds of fig tree are usually grown but in cooler climates one only when fruit is required. The reason for this is as follows. The fruit of the fig tree is peculiar in that it is an inflorescence or a collection of many flowers which form *within* the skin of the fruit itself. Pollination of these flowers can only take place through a small opening at the apex of the fruit and only *blastophaga* (fig wasp) can get into this opening and carry out the necessary process. Unless

111

this *blastophaga* entry is made the seeds and the fruit (with the important exception of one kind of fig tree) cannot develop. Unless the flowers are pollinated the fruits shrivel and drop when about 1in in diameter.

The four kinds of fig tree are: Smyrna, White San Pedro, Adriatic (the common fig) and Caprifig (the wild fig). Smyrna provides the best quality fruit but it produces female flowers which must be pollinated. When fecundity is achieved the seeds develop and the fruit swells—the seeds giving the fruit a superior nutty flavour. The Adriatic or common fig, on the other hand, develops its fruit without pollination of the female flowers but the seeds are only hollow shells without the inner kernel and embryo; in other words they are not viable. The White San Pedro develops fruit without pollination at the beginning of the season when it bears its first crop, but for its second crop the flowers must be pollinated. The first flowers are hermaphrodite. The Caprifig produces both male and female flowers but the males, located near the opening of the fruit, become dried up and make the fruit practically inedible.

In the first three kinds (Smyrna, White San Pedro, Adriatic) the styles of the flowers are long, but in the Caprifig they are short. The short styles permit *blastophaga* to lay its eggs but the long styles prevent it from doing so. Therefore *blastophaga* needs the Caprifig—it cannot breed otherwise—and as the fig grower needs *blastophaga* he also needs the Caprifig. From very early times 'caprification'—the hanging of branches of Caprifig amongst the trees of the edible figs—has been practised in fig cultivation. *Blastophaga* covered in pollen emerges from the Caprifig, enters the opening in the fruit of the other figs and then crawls over the long styles searching for a place to lay its eggs and at the same time pollinates the flowers.

Blastophaga cannot live in northern climates, therefore the Adriatic fig, which does not need the *blastophaga*, is the only one that can be used for producing fruit. It was introduced into England for this purpose a long time ago, though exactly when is not known. Cardinal Pole certainly introduced fig trees from Italy in the early part of the sixteenth century, and in the twelfth Thomas Becket is said to have planted the fig at Tarring Manor in Sussex, where indeed the remains of a fig garden still exist. But it is quite likely that it was the Romans who first brought it to England. They brought the grape, so why not the fig?

Although it is sub-tropical it is extensively cultivated in areas where fairly low winter temperatures are experienced, and today it is not uncommon for it to be grown in the open as a standard tree in the south of England. It has, in fact, even been grown in Cambridgeshire, which is noted for its cold winters. It can withstand temperatures as low as 10°F (−12°C) during its dormancy period, but in the spring when the trees are sprouting severe damage can be caused if the temperature goes below 30°F (1°C).

Where the dormancy period is short (ie in warm countries) it is not unusual to obtain three crops of fruit each year. In England, if a heated greenhouse is available, it is possible to obtain these three crops but the usual aim is for two only, and one crop only if it is grown outdoors or in an unheated greenhouse.

Whatever the aim—one, two or three crops—it is vital to understand the fruiting characteristics of the fig tree. It is tip bearing by habit, but both one- and two-year-old wood bears fruit. During the summer the new growth commences to bear small or embryo figs and these are produced singly or in pairs in the axils of the new leaves. In a warm temperature these develop into mature fruit but outdoors in cool temperate climates this will not happen and they will need a second season in which to mature. When there has been an early and warm summer some of these embryo figs will begin to develop before the onset of cold weather, but as they will not have time to mature and ripen they should be removed. Their removal will encourage further figs to be produced and these will mature during the following year. These further figs will form more at the base of the shoots than at the tips and therefore stand a better chance of surviving a severe winter.

Ripe or mature wood growth is required for fruit. In rich soil growth becomes lanky and does not have time to mature. In alkaline soil the tree remains smaller, the fruit develops well and has a higher sugar content, though high alkalinity may cause the leaves to fall. It will do quite well on a chalky soil especially where there is about 18in of loam over the chalk. Its requirements, then, in respect of soil are for a loam with a fairly good lime content which should be retentive of moisture yet well drained, but its roots should not be allowed to wallow in this unfettered. It is vital to restrict root growth in order to obtain fruitfulness. A special bed can be made for it by digging a hole 3ft deep and 3-5ft wide. If the soil is loamy put about 12in of brick rubble in the

H

bottom and ram this down hard. If the subsoil is clay put in 6in of brick or stones and cover this with concrete. The hole can then be filled with two parts of turf loam and one part of old mortar or chalk nodules. The use of pots is also a very effective way of restricting the roots. Whatever method is used rich soil must be avoided, but humus is required to retain moisture in summer.

The propagation of the fig can be by cuttings or layering. The cuttings should be short jointed shoots of the previous year's growth, about 8-12in long with an inch of older wood at the base. They should be cut in October or November and inserted 6in deep in a warm sheltered position. To protect them from frost they should be covered with peat or litter. Uncover them when all danger from frost has passed but leave them where they are until the following autumn when they can be lifted and planted where required. The layering of branches should be done in the summer. Bend a branch down to the soil, secure it firmly with a peg and then cover with a few inches of soil. By the autumn it should have rooted, when it should be detached from its parent and planted at once.

Trees bought from a nursery can be planted outdoors in March. If a tree is to be grown against a wall it should be a south- or south-west-facing wall and at least 10ft high. If more than one tree is to be grown they should be planted 15ft apart. When growing fig trees against a wall the fan system should be used. The main thing in pruning is to prevent overcrowding, so that the sun can get to each shoot and branch. The main pruning can be done in March when any damage that has been caused by frost will be seen, but after this any buds or young shoots likely to cause overcrowding should be removed. When these buds are removed early the process is no more than disbudding. Any lateral shoots that are growing too long can be nipped off at the sixth leaf.

In the beginning harder pruning is required to build up a tree with a good framework. Later pruning should be minimized to encourage fruiting. The fig tree extends its growth from the terminal buds and its old wood becomes naked—with neither fruit nor fig leaf. Therefore another aim must be to maintain as many one- and two-year-old shoots as possible by cutting back some of the branches to suitably placed joints—this should be done in the autumn as soon as the leaves have fallen. In the spring new shoots will grow from the stubs and some of these can be selected and tied in as required when they have made sufficient growth. By first building up a fan-shaped tree with five or six branches and then in succeeding years cutting back two or three of these each year new wood is maintained uniformly over the tree.

The standard tree should only be grown in warm temperate areas or a well-sheltered position. The same principles as described for the fan tree apply. If any of the shoots on the main leaders are growing more strongly than the others they can be pinched back. Lanky ones should be removed because fruit will only ripen on short, stocky shoots.

When grown in the greenhouse the tree can be kept either in a pot or against the wall of the house. Remember, though, that it does not require a rich soil. However, a mulch of well-rotted manure, if available, is very beneficial to help maintain the moisture it needs for its foliage. The leaves should be syringed daily and the soil thoroughly watered. This supply of adequate moisture should commence as soon as the tree begins to come into leaf and continue until autumn, apart from the time when the fruit is ripening—too much water at that stage may spoil it.

With heat in the greenhouse two crops of fruit should be obtained. Awaken the tree from its dormancy as early as possible so that the first crop is obtained in June or July and the second by the end of September. If growth stands still it can be encouraged with a light dressing of nitrogenous manure. If the tree starts its growth in February it should fruit in June. If it is started into growth in December in a temperature of 65°F (18°C) rising to 80°F (27°C) in later months a first crop is obtainable in March, a second in July and a third in October. However, care should be taken not to exhaust the tree or there will be poor fruiting in the following year; it should be fed twice weekly with liquid manure.

Pot cultivation can be practised either indoors or out, or a combination of both. The restricted roots will give only a small tree but a reasonable crop will be obtained. The pot can be 9, 10 or 12in. A recommended compost is seven parts good loam, three parts sharp sand and three parts peat, to which should be added 4½oz superphosphate, 4½oz hoof and horn manure, and 2½oz sulphate of potash per bushel.

The tree should be either a two-year-old or a maiden and potted up in the autumn. Every autumn it should be repotted, shaking off some of the old compost and giving it some new. In a pot it will need plenty of watering. Placed outdoors, on a patio or roof garden, it fulfils a decorative function. If greenhouse space is available it is ideal if it can take up its winter quarters there.

The principle of pruning, root restriction and fruiting as described for the other methods of cultivation apply equally to the tree grown in a pot. And the fruit will be the same.

When mature the fruit is soft to the touch and it can be harvested by twisting it at the neck or by cutting. Properly ripened fruits are nutritious. Eaten fresh they are rich in calcium, iron, and the vitamins A and C. Their sugar content is high and acid content low. They are more alkaline and contain more mineral matter than most other fruits or vegetables and their natural laxative effect has been valued for a long time. Also they are said to stimulate blood production and to be useful for curing anaemia. *The Complete Herbal* by Nicholas Culpeper published in 1653 says that a syrup made from the green fruit 'is excellently good for coughs, hoarseness, or shortness of breath, and all diseases of the breast and lung'. Such medicinal claims for the fig may or may not be true but ripe figs for dessert are extremely delicious, especially if they are cut in two and allowed to soak in an orange liqueur or sherry an hour or two before required and then served with sweetened whipped cream. They can also be sprinkled with caster sugar and baked in a hot oven until soft, and when cold served with whipped, slightly sweetened cream.

There are many varieties of fig and it is not possible to list them all; in any case the fact that the same fig sometimes has different names in different countries causes confusion. For example, the fig known as Negro Largo in Britain is San Piero in Italy, Aubique Noire in France, San Pedro Black or Brown Turkey in California. The varieties which follow are the usual varieties in Britain. Growers in USA will have a much greater variety to choose from, including Smyrna figs.

VARIETIES OF THE COMMON FIG

BROWN TURKEY—the hardiest variety for growing outdoors. It also forces well in pots. Fruit is large and brownish purple, with dark red flesh. Rich sweet flavour.

BRUNSWICK—another good outdoor variety, especially against a wall. Provided roots are restricted it is a good cropper. Fruit is large and green with a brown flush, and has orange-red flesh. Flavour is good.

BLACK ISCHIA—hardy. Fruit is small and purplish black, with red flesh. It is sweet and juicy and has a good flavour.

WHITE MARSEILLES—fairly hardy. It is good for cold greenhouses and also forces well in pots. Fruit is of a medium size and pale greenish white with white flesh. It is sweet and rich in flavour.

WHITE ISCHIA—a good early ripening variety for the greenhouse where three crops is the aim. Fruit is small to medium, green, with white flesh. Well flavoured.

NEGRO LARGO—good for the heated greenhouse and does well in pots. A good cropper. The fruit is large, the skins are black and tender, the flesh and juice red. Sweet and juicy.

Something may one day be done with Smyrna and White San Pedro in cool temperate climates. It has, for example, been found that by using hormone sprays on the Smyrna type the figs set and develop without the aid of *blastophaga*. Then, too, White San Pedro can develop its first crop of fruit without pollination so that, in theory, if one crop only is required and if the temperature and other conditions are right *blastophaga* is not required.

Fuchsia berry

Classification   : *Fuchsia* species.
Physiology   : Semi-hardy flowering shrubs.
Origin   : Peru, Mexico and New Zealand.
History   : Berries probably used by Incas and Aztecs long before arrival of the Spaniards. Introduced to Europe late eighteenth century. Today widely cultivated in USA and Europe, but purely as an ornamental.
Recommended site   : Greenhouse or conservatory—pot shrub. Outdoors (New Zealand species only).
Culinary uses   : Eaten from the hand.

There are about 100 species in the genus *Fuchsia* and it is not generally realized that a number of them offer edible berries. Some were undoubtedly known to the Incas and Aztecs and possibly cultivated by them. One species was, in fact, discovered growing in the ruins of an Inca city in the Andes. Similarly, a species native to New Zealand provided edible berries for the Maori. But the fruit-bearing species does not compare with the really lovely fuchsias known to most people —these beauties are hybrids and are the result of patient breeding over the past 100 years. Even so the fruit-bearers themselves do offer quite useful flowers.

In their natural habitat in South America they are most usually to be found growing either in forests or in moist places in the mountains. In cool temperate climates the South American species require to be cultivated in a greenhouse or conservatory.

They can be propagated either from seeds or from cuttings. Fuchsia seed does not maintain its viability for very long but it can be sown at any time of the year provided a temperature no lower than 55°F (13°C) is available. If no heat is available seed cannot be sown before April. The seed should be thinly sown in trays and lightly covered with a mixture of sand and compost. The trays should then be placed in the greenhouse or frame and covered with a sheet of glass and brown paper. Covering the tray prevents the compost from becoming dry; no watering is then necessary until germination has taken place. Germination is usually erratic and if possible each seedling should be pricked out as soon as it is large enough to move. When it has developed about four pairs of leaves it should be potted up into a 3in pot.

Propagating from cuttings of green wood or fully ripened wood is quite easy. Green-wood cuttings, taken as early in the season as possible, should be placed in a shady part of the greenhouse, and if bottom heat is given and ventilation excluded rooting should commence in about a week. Half-ripened or fully-ripened wood can be used from May to September, the cuttings being placed in a cold frame.

The fuchsia likes a rich, well-drained soil. A good compost for it when grown in a pot is three parts loam, one part peat, a half-part sand, to which should be added a liberal sprinkling of bonemeal. It does not need a great deal of attention but will require plenty of ventilation during the summer. Fresh air is required to ripen its wood and it is beneficial for it to stand outdoors during part of the summer. It should, however, be back in the house before frost is able to injure it. As long as a temperature of about 40°F (4°C) is maintained during the winter it will do quite well.

One of the species from Peru which provides edible berries is *Fuchsia corymbiflora*. This is a semi-climbing shrub, which does not have a great number of branches, and which grows to a height of 4-6ft. The flowers are scarlet, shading to deep red. Because of their length and colour they are quite showy. The berries are purple and are said to taste like ripe figs. Various other species from South America provide sub-acid to sweet berries.

If you have no greenhouse there is a species which is almost hardy. This is *Fuchsia exorticata* from New Zealand. In its natural habitat it grows to about 40ft and has a massive trunk. In the milder parts of Britain this grows to a tall shrub but elsewhere to a low bush only.

Fuchsia berry

It is remarkably different from the other fuchsia species and its flowers are produced on its trunk right down to the ground, as well as on the branches.

The flowers are 1in long, the calyx is yellow and the sepals violet-green. The pollen of the flowers is bright blue and this gives the tree a purple-blue sheen when it is in bloom. Maori girls used this blue pollen as a face powder to beautify themselves. The berries from *Fuchsia exorticata* are purple-black and sub-acid.

Goumi

Classification	:	*Elaeagnus multiflora* (*E. edulis*).
Physiology	:	Hardy, deciduous, low, bushy shrub 6-10ft tall.
Origin	:	China, Korea, Japan.
History	:	Cultivated in Japan for its fruit, but little done elsewhere to improve it.
Recommended site	:	Outdoors—sheltered position.
Culinary uses	:	Good for pies, tarts, jams and jellies.

There are about thirty species of *Elaeagnus*—some deciduous, some evergreen—and they are related to *Sheperdia* (buffalo berry) and *Hippophae* (sea berry). Of these species *Elaeagnus multiflora*, known in the USA as goumi, offers most scope for the pomologist.

It is a bushy shrub growing 6-10ft tall and eventually having as much spread to it as it has height. It is, therefore, quite tubby or rotund in build. In Britain it is usually deciduous, although in a very sheltered position it may be semi-evergreen. In China and Japan it grows wild but in the latter country it has for a long time been cultivated for its fruit. A little was done with it some years ago in the United States, and it was thought that by selection, breeding and improved cultivation a really first-class fruit could be obtained which would rival the gooseberry, currant and cranberry. Yet, like many a plan delayed in the corridors of public administration it still awaits development.

It is no more difficult to propagate and cultivate in the garden than the usual bush fruits. It can be propagated either from seed, cuttings or by layering. Seed should be sown in trays in light soil in spring and in a temperature of 55°F (13°C). Cuttings, 3-4in long, should be

121

Goumi

taken from the young side shoots with a thin heel of the old wood, and inserted in a cold frame in July or August. Layering can be commenced in spring. Transplanting should be done from October to December. The shrub will grow well in any ordinary but dry soil. An open sunny position is best, provided it is fairly sheltered. It can also be planted on a bank or against a wall facing south or west. The only pruning necessary is to keep the bush in a convenient shape, remembering that fruit will be borne on new growth.

During April and May silvery, yellow-coloured flowers resembling small fuchsias will appear. Usually they are borne solitarily in the leaf axils of the new shoots. The flowers are fragrant. Unlike its cousins *Sheperdia* and *Hippophae* the flowers are not one-sexed. Pollination offers no problems.

The fruit ripens in July and is borne in great profusion, hanging heavily along the underside of the branches. The bush is at this time very attractive. Unfortunately birds also find the fruit attractive and will, if given the chance, quickly strip a bush.

The fruits are about a half to three-quarters of an inch long, oblong or oval, and flat at the ends. They are orange or reddish orange with very small silvery white dots. At first they are very astringent but with maturity they are pleasantly acid and juicy, too acid to be eaten raw but good in pies, tarts, jellies etc.

OTHER FRUITING SPECIES OF INTEREST

SILVER BERRY (*Elaeagnus argentea*; syn *E. commutata*)

A native of North America. It grows 6-10ft tall. In habit it is slim and erect and has slender branches. It suckers freely and spreads by this means. A handsome shrub in that its leaves are a lustrous silvery white on both sides. In May fragrant yellow flowers are borne in great profusion, often as many as three in each leaf axil.

The roundish, egg-shaped fruit is about one-third of an inch long and has a silvery colour. The flesh of this fruit is dry and mealy.

RUSSIAN or WILD OLIVE, OLEASTER (*Elaeagnus angustifolia*)

From southern Europe and western Asia. This is a deciduous small tree or shrub which grows 15-20ft tall. The branches are spiny with silvery, willow-like leaves. The young shoots are covered with glistening silvery-coloured scales which become dark in the second year. Because of the whiteness of its twigs and its silvery leaves it is a striking tree, especially when grown in the proximity of dark evergreens.

The fragrant flowers appear in June, one to three in each leaf axil. The fruits are oval and about half an inch long, though larger on some varieties. In colour, the fruit is silvery amber; in taste and texture it is sweet, dry and mealy.

This species is very similar to that which follows and both have been cultivated in Turkey, Arabia and surrounding countries, the fruits being used for making sherbet.

TREBIZOND DATE (*Elaeagnus orientalis*)

Similar to the above but the fruit is better; it was once commonly sold in the markets of Turkey but the species is now rare. The flowers are also more fragrant and contain much nectar. Indeed, at one time in Persia the perfume from the blossom was said to have a very powerful influence on feminine emotions, so much so that the men would lock up their wives when the tree was in blossom.

Grape

Classification	:	*Vitis vinifera.*
Physiology	:	A deciduous climber or woody vine.
Origin	:	Probably Armenia and Caspian Sea area.
History	:	Cultivated from earliest times, and today throughout the world, wherever climate is suitable. Introduced into England probably by Romans, but outdoor cultivation declined and is only now being revived.
Recommended site	:	Outdoors—southerly aspect.
Culinary uses	:	Fresh for dessert. Wine making.

Vitis is a genus of about sixty species, most of which are deciduous climbers. They climb by means of tendrils which they coil around any suitable support. Some of the species are decorative and their climbing habit makes them useful for pergolas, trellis work or on walls.

But the principal species as far as the grape grower is concerned is *Vitis vinifera*, although there are some other useful species. Some of those native to North America, for example, produce useful grapes which have been crossed with *vinifera*.

Grape cultivation must be nearly as old as man. No one can say how long ago or where it began. Certainly viticulture was practised in Egypt in the 4th Dynasty (2400 BC) because details of grape and wine production are revealed in the hieroglyphics of that time. The 'fruitful vine' is associated with the Jewish people and was cultivated in Palestine in Old Testament times. It is, in fact, the first cultivated plant to be recorded in the Bible.

It is thought that *Vitis vinifera* originated somewhere in Asia Minor, the cradle of so much of the earth's life. From there it spread westwards throughout southern and central Europe as well as eastwards to India. Today it is cultivated throughout the world, wherever the climate is suited to it.

By the third century AD it had reached England, brought no doubt by the Romans, and its cultivation was later given impetus round about the time of the Norman conquest. Vineyards became fairly numerous and thirty-eight were recorded in the Domesday Book. Gloucestershire had most, closely followed by Kent. Some monasteries had their own vineyards. But by the twelfth century wine making in England began to decrease in favour of imports from the Continent. During the eighteenth and nineteenth centuries grape cultivation was confined to the production of fresh dessert grapes for the rich man's table. These grapes were grown at first on the walls of large gardens and then later in heated glasshouses or conservatories. Varieties were selected which produced the best dessert grapes under these new sheltered methods of cultivation. Attempts were made from time to time, by enterprising gardeners, to re-establish outdoor cultivation, but the indoor varieties available were only successful in the open garden in exceptionally good seasons.

Had these experimenters been able to use varieties which mature their fruit earlier their efforts would have met with more success. Today 'early' varieties are available which can be expected to crop reliably in the English climate. Amongst these varieties is Wrotham Pinot which was found growing near Wrotham in Kent, and it is thought that this was a variety at one time grown in local vineyards. There are also hybrid varieties which have been bred in Continental research stations, some of them East European and Russian, and bred for special climatic conditions which make them acceptable for outdoor growing in Britain.

Today an increasing number of gardeners are beginning to be interested in these outdoor varieties. What has been done with the tomato is being done with the grape. Yet, even so, most people in Britain think of grape growing in terms of a heated greenhouse or conservatory. Therefore, as the *outdoor* grape is still very much an unusual fruit it is outdoor cultivation which is here considered, together with cloche and pot cultivation.

Grape

The first consideration of course is climate, and at the outset it can be said that the earlier varieties are successful outdoors anywhere south of a line from the Wash across to Wales, and with some of the very earliest varieties we can push this line even farther north. Altitude must, however, be taken into account because it has been found that within the same region in southern England fruit ripens three days later for every extra 100ft above sea-level.

The grape vine is very hardy and it should not be treated as though it were a tender plant. It can withstand a temperature falling as low as $-4°F$ $(-20°C)$ but unusually severe winter conditions with persistent temperatures around $0°F$ $(-18°C)$ would destroy it. The most suitable climatic conditions are a dry, warm summer and a cool winter. Although the vine flowers late it is susceptible to spring frosts and if these occur after it has started new growth they can cause trouble with the young shoots. Its susceptibility to frost is about equal to that of the tomato plant and planting in a frost pocket should therefore be avoided. High winds in autumn can batter and bruise the ripening berries so that any position exposed to south-westerly gales should also be avoided, or else a wind-break provided. The site chosen should face south-east to south-west to ensure that the vine is exposed to the maximum sunlight available.

The fruit of thick-skinned eating varieties can be left unpicked until right into November. Indeed, even after several frosts which have cut off all the leaves the fruit is undamaged and tends to become sweeter. Because of this it may still be possible, by using a cloche, to pick fruit at Christmas. To be able to have freshly picked fruit at such a time is surely worth consideration.

The choice of soil is not greatly important as the vine seems to do just as well on anything from chalk to clay. Some varieties (eg Wrotham Pinot) possibly do better on chalk sub-soil. Waterlogged clay should be avoided as this may cause the roots to rot in winter.

The spacing of the vines will depend on the method of training desired or adopted, but the general practice in England is to space the plants 3ft apart and the rows also 3ft apart. There is no reason why, to save space, the rows cannot be planted much closer together, except that this tends to make cultivation more difficult and also prevents the sun from getting fully to some of the vines. Planting can be carried out from November to March. A deep hole should be dug so that its roots can be spread out. Although not essential it is a good plan to fill the hole with a good rich soil so that in its early stages the vine is well nourished. It will then be helped to grow quickly and its full fruit-bearing life hastened.

The usual method of propagation is to use cuttings 8-14in long and these should be from wood produced during the previous year (a supply can be obtained from wood removed in the course of pruning and training). There should be a bud within an inch of the top end and another within an inch of the other end. The cuttings should be tied together in a bundle and buried to within 2in of their tops in a damp border but out of the way of cold wind. In March they should be lifted and planted out individually 3-4in apart in a trench and with only their tops above the soil. During dry weather the soil should be kept moist. In November the young vines may be planted where required. If good soil is used to give them a start in life they may grow as much as 7ft in the second year and produce their first grapes in the third.

Propagation can also be by layering. If shoots are pegged down almost every bud that is in contact with the soil will form roots, and in the following autumn these can be severed and transplanted. It is, however, not always convenient to use layering as a means of propagation because it may interfere with the method of cultivation or training.

Although vines can be grown as cordons, espaliers, fans or bushes, for the worthwhile production of grapes in the open vineyard the cordon is invariably used. Various methods can be and have been devised to suit varying circumstances but these methods are based on the principles that (1) grapes are usually produced on the *current year's shoots* which grow from the *previous year's wood*, (2) a vine uncontrolled grows rampantly at the expense of ripening its fruit—in a cool climate this is a particularly important point to watch. It follows that wood which has finished fruiting is no longer useful (except to be used for propagation) but one-year-old wood is necessary to replace that which has been removed. A combined system of pruning and training is therefore required. In a nutshell the principle is the same as with the cultivated blackberry except that there the new wood grows up from the soil whereas that of the vine grows from a main stem.

Grape

The method usually employed nowadays in the open vineyard in England is one devised by Dr Guyot and known as the Guyot system. Briefly described it is as follows. After the first season's unrestricted growth the longest stem, or rod as it is often called, is selected and pruned down to about 3ft. Another stem is also selected but this is pruned down to form a short spur with three buds. All other growth is completely removed. The longer stem or rod is then pruned of all side growth and fastened along a horizontal wire about 1ft from the ground. As the fruiting laterals develop from this horizontal stem about 2ft 6in from the ground. To eliminate the need to tie the laterals to the top wire, two wires can be loosely run along the top and the laterals simply tucked between them. Meanwhile two new vertical stems are allowed to develop from the buds on the short spur and these are tied to a 6ft upright cane. At the end of the season the wood which has fruited (ie the horizontal stem with the vertical laterals) is cut right back whilst the stems which were tied to the upright cane are reduced to one long and one short spur as in the previous year. This process is repeated each year, a longer fruiting stem or bearer being allowed as the vine matures.

A specialized adaptation of the Guyot system is now known as the Double Dwarf Guyot system. In this system, instead of using one long horizontal stem or bearer, use is made of two which are kept to 2ft 6in long and bent either way; this requires that three stems instead of two should grow up in the middle as replacements in the following year. These replacements grow up the cane or stake in the same way as in the previous system but are topped when they reach the required height of 2ft 6in.

The advantage of either system is that the vine is kept low and can be adapted to cloche cultivation. The bottom wire along which the horizontal bearer is trained is, in England, usually kept at about 1ft from the ground so as to obtain as much warmth as possible from the soil, but in areas where there is a definite danger from spring frosts it should be kept higher.

The Double Dwarf Guyot system is particularly suited for use in conjunction with a low wall. Twin wires at the top are not necessary in this case. All that is needed is a single wire about 2in out from the wall. A wall system is particularly useful for cloche cultivation and ensures a satisfactory crop. The cloche consists of nothing more than

V Fig tree—pot-grown. Note that though root restriction gives a small tree
a reasonable crop is obtained

VI (left) *Harvesting grapes. Simple cloche protection ensures a satisfactory crop;* (below) *pruning for the Double Dwarf Guyot system of training. Note the two stems bent either way and the replacement stem in the middle*

a frame with very strong plastic fixed over it. At the beginning of the season when the weather is still cold the cloche can be closed right down simply by hooking the frames tight against the wall. As the season develops and ventilation is required, and as the fruiting laterals begin to grow up between the wire and the top of the wall, the frame is moved out slightly and fixed to the wire. Each end of the wall cloche must of course be closed, otherwise there will be a dangerous through-draught.

One other little-practised method of cultivation—pot cultivation—can be mentioned. In days gone by this was often used in large houses because it was considered quite ornamental, and so it is. The two best methods of training pot vines are essentially Guyot methods. In the first, a single long bearer is trained in a large loop or circle over the pot, and the two short replacement stems grow up a cane in the centre. In the second, the double bearers are grown on an inverted T-shaped structure.

It is as well to be on your guard against the pests and diseases which afflict the grape vine. Wasps can be troublesome. They usually disappear before the end of September but early varieties ripening before that time are liable to attack. If the grapes are left unprotected birds will also make a feast of them. Much more serious is a nasty aphis-type of infection known as phylloxera. This has been a scourge on the Continent, where it has been necessary to use rootstock from American species that are resistant to it. Up to the present, however, phylloxera has never caused trouble in England.

There are three fungus diseases which can and do occur in England. Powdery mildew occurs early in the season and can be controlled by sulphur (or alternatively the proprietary Karathane can be used). The easiest method is to blow powdered sulphur on to the vines in spring when they are about 6in long, and then again in early summer when the flowers are in blossom. Downy mildew does not usually occur until after the flowers have blossomed in June. Copper sprays are quite effective against this but it is better not to use them until after the fruits have set as they tend to damage the flower trusses. Another fungus trouble is botrytis which can cause fruit to rot when it is almost ripe. It is especially troublesome in a wet autumn. The sulphur used to prevent powdery mildew will, if it has been blown into the trusses of flowers and remains there, help to prevent this trouble also.

Grape

The flower clusters from which the grapes will come begin to form during the year preceding their bloom, though they may not become apparent until in bloom. At this time any laterals which are sterile (ie those not carrying flowers) should be removed so that more sap goes to those which bear the grapes. Also, those shoots bearing the flowers should be stopped at a point one or two leaves above the grapes.

Outdoor grapes are small but if they are to be used for wine making this does not matter. Whether they are thinned or not the actual weight of the bunch will remain much the same. In England an individual vine should be allowed to give up to 3 or 4lb of grapes each season. If all the grapes in the bunch are left to develop and ripen they will be small, but if, say, half of them are removed the remainder will grow much larger. For table use they should, then, be thinned. This should be done when they are about the size of small peas. A pair of long nail scissors is the ideal tool. The aim should be to remove grapes inside the bunch and any on the outside that may spoil the shape of the bunch. When you are thinning try to imagine the bunch on the table before a favoured guest.

It is not necessary to describe the grape as a fruit, but remember that they can be black, blue, red, amber (gold), or green (white) in colour. In many varieties they are covered with a white bloom. Grapes contain grape sugar (glucose or dextrose) the quantities of which differ according to the variety. All grapes will produce wine but those with the most glucose ferment most readily.

VARIETIES SUITABLE FOR OUTDOOR OR CLOCHE CULTIVATION

There are today throughout the world nearly 10,000 varieties of grape. Below are listed a few that are considered suitable for outdoor or cloche cultivation under the climatic conditions of Britain. The early ones, listed first, begin to ripen from the middle of August.

PIROVANO 14—a very early red to black grape of medium size. Good flavour. In good conditions it will give good crops and in the worst years will ripen. The flowers, however, can be damaged by continual bad weather. A table grape.

PRECOCE DE MALINGRE—a very early white grape. It is a very old grape in France but seems to do better in England, and has been found growing quite well in Upsala, Sweden. A good dual-purpose grape for table or white wine.

SIEGERREBE—very early. One of the best German hybrids. Large golden sweet-flavoured grapes with fine muscat flavour. Very good for table or wine.

MARSHAL JOFFRE—early, and a French hybrid. It has been found to be a good cropper but is rampant in growth and double spacing is recommended. For table or wine.

MUSCAT DE SAUMUR—very early. A medium-sized golden, muscat-flavoured grape for the table.

NOIR HATIF DE MARSEILLE—a very early black, muscat-flavoured grape. It does well in the open but prefers a fairly rich soil. Under cloches it is very prolific. The grapes are small but of very good flavour. Good for table and wine.

MADELEINE X SYLVANER 28/51—an early fruiting German hybrid yielding regular crops of good flavoured white grapes which make excellent wine.

MADELEINE DE ANGEVINE 7672—early mid-season. A new German hybrid. This is proving to be an exceptional cropper giving plenty of white grapes of medium size. Good for white wine.

GAGARIN BLUE—very early. This is a Russian hybrid, the result of a cross between *Vitis vinifera* and *Vitis amurensis*. It produces medium-sized, slightly oval blue-black grapes which have a wonderful bloom to them. The flavour is excellent. This is a very special grape and good for table or wine. In Russia it is used for red wine.

TERESHKOVA—very early. Another new Russian hybrid. The oval-shaped grapes are of medium size, are a beautiful purple-red colour and have a delicate muscat flavour. Ideal for the table.

Grape

REISLING SYLVANER—mid-season, and an excellent white grape. It is a noted hock grape, but as it is large and has a good flavour it is equally suitable for the table.

SEYVE-VILLARD 5/276—mid-season, and another standard white wine grape. It is suitable for a poor but well-drained soil, gives large crops and ripens in the open almost every year. It makes an excellent white wine.

SCHUYLER—mid-season; an American hybrid. This gives large crops of medium-sized black grapes of good flavour. An excellent grape for eating.

OLIVER IRSAY—mid-season; a white grape with muscat flavour and of medium size. Prefers a good soil. Ripens well against a wall or under a cloche. For the table.

LEON MILLOT—mid-season; a good French hybrid. Medium-sized black grapes with good flavour. Like the variety Marshal Joffre it is a rampant grower and needs double spacing. It is good for covering walls and gives heavy crops. For the table.

EXCELSIOR—mid-season, normally ripening well in the open and giving masses of medium-sized white grapes with a non-muscat flavour. For the table.

SIEBEL 13053—mid-season, and considered to be, at the present time, the best black grape for wine making. It produces an excellent red wine. Grapes are produced abundantly and they ripen in all but the worst years.

MUSCAT HAMBURGH—a late and superb black grape with a good muscat flavour. This is a regular and reliable cropper under a cloche and is considered to be superior to the old variety Black Hamburgh which is the usual greenhouse grape. Excellent for the table.

WHITE FRONTIGNAN—a late medium-sized white grape with a

very high muscat flavour, one of the best. It is, however, only suitable for a cloche or cold greenhouse. For the table.

GOLDEN CHASSELAS (*Chasselas d'Or*)—the standard French dessert grape but also grown extensively in France for wine making. The slightly golden grapes are round, of medium size, and have a non-muscat flavour. They can be left to hang until Christmas.

CHASSELAS ROSE ROYALE—late; very similar to the previous variety but the grapes when ripe have an attractive reddish hue. For table or wine.

CHASSELAS 1921—late; again similar to the preceding two but the grapes, which are a pale golden colour, are slightly larger. The flavour is good. This is a Swiss grape and is used for Swiss Fendant wine. For table or wine.

MUSCAT QUEEN—late; a large white grape with a muscat flavour. This is a fine Hungarian grape but it normally requires a cloche for ripening. For the table.

BRANT—late; a well-known Canadian hybrid. It has a fair flavour and is very prolific and reliable. The black grapes are small but they always ripen. For eating, and it also makes an excellent wine.

STRAWBERRY GRAPE—an American grape, sometimes called Concorde. The black grapes are carried in large bunches and have a flavour which is sometimes considered to be like strawberries. For eating.

WROTHAM PINOT—a late variety, related to the Pinots of Champagne and Burgundy. It was found growing near Wrotham in Kent and is thought to be a descendant of the variety grown in English vineyards long ago. The grapes are black and small and the leaves have a dusty look—similar to the Pinot Meunier of France. In reasonable conditions it is extremely prolific and a consistent bearer. It seems to do best in the Thames area. Suitable for wine.

Grape

HIMROD—late; an American hybrid. It is a seedless grape and therefore of some interest. The grapes are white and have a good flavour. It ripens quite well under cloches.

Quite apart from its fruit it should not be forgotten that the grape vine has outstanding ornamental worth. Its climbing habit, beauty of leaf and the fact that it can be easily trained make it invaluable in the modern home and garden. If you tire of growing it for its fruit it will always give joy when clematis or roses are allowed to scramble about with it. It can in fact be used to provide both ornament and fruit if it is planted outdoors and then permitted to come indoors by passing the stem through a small opening. By doing this it is possible to achieve a wonderful effect in a modern furnished sun-lounge and to have the grapes to hand for eating.

Guava

Classification	:	*Psidium guajava.*
Physiology	:	Small, evergreen tree or shrub growing 6-30ft tall.
Origin	:	Tropical America—Colombia, Peru.
History	:	Introduced to many tropical countries by the Spaniards. Today it is occasionally cultivated in the Mediterranean area.
Recommended site	:	Heated greenhouse, in large pot or tub.
Culinary uses	:	Eaten from the hand; eaten fresh with cream; cooked for pie filling; for jellies and preserves.

Psidium is a genus consisting of about 140 species of shrubs or small trees, all originating in tropical America, the West Indies and Mexico. Of these 140 species only two or three and principally *Psidium guajava,* are of interest for their fruit.

Psidium guajava is a small long-lived evergreen tree or shrub which, if allowed to grow naturally will develop into a large and many-branched bush. Its bark tends to be bright and smooth and something like the bark of the eucalyptus tree. Its leaves are light green with conspicuous veins, usually reddish in colour. In a climate suited to it the tree will grow nearly as fast as a peach tree and may need nearly as much space.

The Spanish conquistadores found the tree growing extensively from Colombia to Peru. The fruit was well known to the Aztecs, who called it the sand plum; the name guava is thought to be of Haitian

135

origin. The Spaniards seem to have introduced it to other countries. Today it is cultivated throughout the tropical world as well as in many sub-tropical climates. Occasionally it is grown in the Mediterranean area.

Propagation of the guava can be from seed; it is said to be viable for a year after its extraction from the fruit but if you take it direct from the fruit it is as well to sow it as soon as you can. Any normal seed compost is suitable. It should be sown a quarter of an inch deep and then kept in a fairly warm place. Germination normally takes 2-3 weeks. The compost should be kept moist but once the seedlings appear they should not be watered too liberally. There is considerable variation in the seedlings so that, by selection, there is scope for improvement.

Layering is the easiest method of propagating vegetatively. When laterals are taken for layering it will be found, however, that these tend to remain dwarf and that their main branches try to grow horizontal and take on a drooping manner. They produce fruit-bearing shoots all along their length.

The guava is fairly hardy in respect of transplanting and will withstand considerable pruning of its roots at this time. This should be of great help if it is to be grown in a pot. Under suitable conditions plants come into bearing when about 4 years old.

In Britain it requires a hot-house if it is to flower and fruit satisfactorily. It may be grown in a large pot or tub, or in the greenhouse border against the wall. It should be provided with a good sandy loam (the ideal soil is four parts sandy loam, one part cow manure, one part silver sand). Planting should be done in early spring. During its growing period it should be watered freely but given little at times when it is resting. During the winter it should be given a temperature of not less than 50°F (10°C) and then, when temperatures rise, watering should be increased.

It does in fact grow and fruit well in places of extreme climate. For example, in Sind in India, where maximum temperatures may rise to as high as 114°F (46°C) in summer and fall as low as 40°F (4°C) in winter but where annual rainfall is seldom above 7in, the tree is very successful. In another part of India where the temperature range is 112-50°F (45-10°C) and the average annual rainfall is 29in very high quality fruit is produced. But the trees are, in fact, sensitive to very low temperatures. At 26°F (−3C°) they may be damaged badly. In the USA it has been found that in a cool summer when the average temperature is below 60°F (15°C)—even if this follows a mild winter—the trees tend to stop growing and eventually die from lack of heat. It may, therefore, be deduced that for successful cultivation in Britain and similar latitudes temperature should be as high as can be managed but with low humidity, and in the winter not less than 45°F (7°C).

It is by nature a bush-like tree and tends to produce suckers near the base of its trunk. These should be removed as soon as they appear. Any water shoots should also be removed. Pruning should be done in February. If it is to be grown as a pot tree it should be trained to a goblet shape, using three or four good branches and removing the others. When it has reached the age of 4 years and its framework has taken on a nice shape there should not be much further trouble from water shoots and suckers. Any shoots which subsequently grow into the centre of the crown should be removed, as also should any dead wood.

A seedling assumes an upright form and its main branches always tend to grow in a vertical manner, producing fruit mainly at their tips and not much lower down. However, the tree lends itself to easy training and when it is to be grown in the greenhouse border against the wall it is not difficult to obtain a good espalier, by growing only three lateral branches and nipping out other side shoots. The three branches should be allowed at convenient height but there should be about 1½ft between them. The young branches bend well and can be conveniently tied to wire or posts so that they are horizontal at the required height. As they mature they will keep their horizontal position and will require no further support or training. From those horizontal laterals verticals are induced to grow until they meet the horizontal lateral at the next level, so that the finished product takes on a net-like pattern. Fruiting spurs are encouraged to grow on all the verticals by keeping any further shoots in check. By this method stems are exposed to light and air, which induces more flowers.

Flowers appear from spring to midsummer, depending on temperature, but usually when the tree is making new growth at the beginning of the new season. They are white and about 1½in in diameter. They are borne singly, or two or three together in the axils of leaves, intermittently, on young shoots. Little is known about pollination but the flowers are hermaphrodites and there seems to be little trouble. Pollination is usually satisfactory.

If adequate temperatures can be maintained (ie a good dry summer temperature) and if there is plenty of light the fruit of some forms may be ripe 3-4 months after the opening of the flowers. The tree not only thrives better but it also produces fruit of better quality in places of extreme climate. In a humid climate the fruit develops an insipid taste.

Guava fruit varies considerably in its form. Some trees produce fruits which are nearly round, some more oblong fruits and some pyriform. They vary in size from little more than 1in long to as much as 4in or more. The skin surface also varies from smooth and waxy to ridged and waxy, and the colour of the flesh from white to yellow and pink to red. The texture and flavour also vary. The best have a slightly sweet flavour blended with muskiness and mild acidity but some may be too tart or too musky.

The fruit is best when fully ripe, yellow and soft to the touch, and plucked fresh from the tree. It is damaged by rough handling or if it is allowed to fall to the ground. The guava emits a sweet aroma, and is both pleasantly sweet and acid. It is wholly edible—the skin being papery and almost a part of the pulp. Except for its penetrating strong aroma in the advanced stage of ripening and the hard seeds in the inner part of the pulp the guava is considered to be among the most delicious and luscious of fruits. It is an excellent source of vitamin C and also of minerals such as calcium and phosphorus. Immature or unripened fruits, however, are highly astringent and not edible.

Guava can be eaten in many ways: out of the hand; sliced and served with cream; made into drinks; stewed; used in pies; preserved. One of its best-known uses is in the making of a pleasant, musky jelly.

VARIETIES AND SPECIES

The main varieties of guava are ordinarily considered to be two—the white guava (with white flesh) and the pink guava (with pink flesh) but the following species are also of interest.

STRAWBERRY or CATTLEY GUAVA (*Psidium cattleianum*)

This is a bushy shrub, a native of Brazil and hardier than *P. guajava*. It is more tolerant of cool summers and more resistant to frost. Taken to south China at an early period by the Portuguese, it then came to Europe and was incorrectly named Chinese guava.

The fruit is roundish and of 1-1½in diameter—much smaller, therefore, than the ordinary guava. Some forms bear coppery red fruit, some purplish red and some sulphur-yellow (*Psidium cattleianum lucidum*). It is said to be sweet and aromatic, suggestive of strawberry. Because it has not the muskiness of ordinary guava it is preferred by some people.

CAS (*Psidium friedrichsthalianum*)

Native of Costa Rica. This has sulphur-yellow fruit with white flesh, is more acid and is only suitable for jelly or preserves.

Guelderberry

(HIGH BUSH CRANBERRY)

Classification : *Viburnum opulus. Viburnum trilobum (V. opulus americanum).*

Physiology : Deciduous ornamental shrub growing 6-10ft tall.

Origin : Europe, including Britain. North America.

History : The *Viburnum* species have been cultivated purely for ornamental purposes. No serious attempt appears to have been made to grow any of them for their fruit.

Recommended site : Outdoors—fairly moist location.

Culinary uses : Mainly used as a substitute for cranberries but can also be used for wine making.

The *Viburnum* species number about 100 and several of them warrant consideration for their fruit. In Britain the best known of the species is *Viburnum opulus* or, as it is commonly known, guelder rose. It is, in fact, a native of the temperate regions of Europe—woodlands and thickets in damp places being its natural habitat.

It grows in the form of a clump of erect, greyish branches. In the autumn its leaves colour beautifully, especially when grown on chalk, and red translucent berries hang long after the leaves have gone. It is a handsome shrub and also hardy, requires little cultivation, and will thrive in any good loamy moist soil. Little pruning is necessary.

Propagation can be from seed, and to the pioneer fruit grower this method offers good opportunity for obtaining better fruit-producing forms. Cuttings offer an easy method of propagation because these root easily if they are from nearly ripe wood, taken in late July or August.

White flowers are produced in late May and early June in an inflorescence about 3in across. This and some others of the *Viburnum* species have a very unusual side to their character. In the inflorescence there are two distinct kinds of flower. One kind is more showy than the other—it is larger and is on the outside of the inflorescence. The other is smaller and on the inside. You may think that the larger flowers are the males but they are not. They are completely sterile and their function is to attract insects which will pollinate the fertile flowers. It can almost be said that they are soliciting for the others. The fruit which is in due course produced is a bright red drupe or berry, nearly round or oval and about one-third of an inch in diameter. The seed is large and hard and the fruit too sour and astringent to eat uncooked, though there is a great deal of variety to be found in different forms. Some forms bear berries which have a pleasant acid taste and are a good substitute for the cranberry in making jelly, preserves or sauce. They can also be used for wine making. If the fruit is to be used solely for wine making a yellow-berried variety (*Viburnum opulus luteum*) might be considered; otherwise, as a cranberry substitute, the normal red-berried kind should of course be grown.

The late season of ripening and the easier cultural requirements as compared to the cranberry (especially in those areas where a lime or chalk soil prevents successful cranberry cultivation) commend it for some attempt at improvement. Its variety of form offers scope for the plant breeder.

A species or form which is said to be superior for its fruit is *Viburnum trilobum* or *Viburnum opulus americanum*. Some consider it a native of North America, others a variety of the European species. In its general characteristics it differs little from the European except that the lobes of its leaves are longer. It may well be that the early settlers took a better fruiting form of the European species with them to America, but there is no proof of this.

Viburnum opulus and *opulus americanum* are the best for setting fruit in Britain.

OTHER USEFUL SPECIES

WILD RAISIN or SHEEPBERRY (*Viburnum lentago*)

A native of Canada and north United States. This is a shrub or small tree but sometimes grows to 25ft with numerous spreading branches. It prefers a rich, moist soil.

The flowers are fragrant, creamy white and appear in May and June. When in bloom it is attractive because the flowers, although small, are very numerous. They are ovoid, bluish black and have a bloom. They vary greatly in size and quality. Like guelderberry they possess flat, hard seeds. The best forms produce fruits that are half an inch long, pulpy, sweet, juicy and pleasant to eat.

STAGBERRY (*Viburnum prunifolium*)

Another native of North America and closely related to the wild raisin. Its leaves, however, are smaller and in some respects resemble those of the plum tree. It is a handsome tallish shrub or small tree, growing up to 25ft. When young its branches are a reddish colour. In its natural habitat it tends to grow on hillsides in drier soils than those preferred by most of the other species.

Flowers are uniform and perfect (ie none are sterile); they are produced during June. Fruits are dark blue when ripe, ovoid, half to two-thirds of an inch long and sweet.

HOBBLEBERRY (*Viburnum alnifolium*)

Native of the more mountainous regions of North America. It will only do well in an acid soil and seems to do better in more exposed positions.

It is a strong growing shrub, 3-10ft tall. Its central stems grow erect, but the others are spreading and often prostrate. Where these lower branches come in contact with the ground they will often take root at their nodes, and it is because of this characteristic that it acquired the name of Hobblebush. The unsuspecting person walking near these shrubs was presumably tripped or hobbled by the rooting branches lying flat on the ground.

It is another handsome shrub. Its branches are greyish purple and in the autumn the leaves are at first bronze and then change to a beautiful red. The flower clusters are from 3-5in across; the sterile flowers are nearly 1in in diameter and are carried on long stems, whilst the female flowers are on short stems. The slightly oblong fruits are at first red but later turn to dark purple. When ripe they are sweet and the birds are fond of them.

VIBURNUM CASSINOIDES

Native of North America. This is a shapely bush with a well rounded figure or form, growing 6-8ft tall. It does not like chalk soil. Its leaves colour very well in the autumn.

Flowers are uniform and perfect, yellowish white and appear in June. Fruits are one-third of an inch long, bluish black and sweet.

VIBURNUM NUDUM

Native of eastern North America. Very similar to *cassinoides* except that its leaves are glossy. Flowers are uniform and perfect, yellowish white and appear in June. Fruits are one-third of an inch long, bluish black and sweet.

Holboella

Classification	:	*Holboella latifolia; Holboella coriacea.*
Physiology	:	Handsome, evergreen, twining climbers. Can climb to 20ft.
Origin	:	Himalayas, China.
History	:	In their native habitat their fruit is eaten by the local people but there is no record of cultivation for fruit.
Recommended site	:	Outdoors—very sheltered position. Indoors—cool greenhouse; conservatory; sun lounge.
Culinary uses	:	Eaten from the hand.

Holboella belongs to the Lardzibalaceae family and is, consequently, related to the akebias. It is a very small genus of which only two species are here dealt with. Both are luxurant evergreen climbers but *Holboella latifolia*, a native of the Himalayas, is rather tender. Although it will thrive in the milder counties of south-west England it usually needs cool greenhouse protection, or at least a wall. It is, in fact, normally cultivated as an indoor climber.

In a greenhouse, conservatory or sun lounge it can be grown in a large pot and trained up suitable supports. A recommended compost in which it can be grown is four parts loam, one part sand, one part leaf mould. During the winter minimum temperatures should be not less than 40°F (4°C); in the summer it should be watered freely and the foliage sprayed except when it is in bloom. Its propagation is from cuttings taken in the spring from new growth and inserted in sandy soil in a warm temperature. It can also be propagated by layering.

VII Grapes in an open vineyard in Sussex. Riesling Sylvaner produces a good crop for wine

VIII (above) *Ripe guava fruit is soft to the touch. It should be handled gently to avoid damage; (below) harvested litchees. When fruits are taken individually they should preferably be snipped off with a portion of stem*

Fragrant female and male flowers are borne on the same plant but pollination by hand is necessary. They appear in March, the females are purple and the males white. The fruit is an oblong or sausage shape, 2-3in long and about 1in wide, purplish in colour. Many black seeds are contained in the white pulp which in taste is rather insipid. However in the Himalayas the local people eat the fruit and it is considered to be very palatable. It is generally eaten from the hand but with experimentation other good ways of using it may be found.

The other species, *Holboella coriacea*, comes from Hupeh, China and is a more vigorous and hardy species. Outdoors in a suitable sheltered position it will grow to a good height, perhaps up to 20ft. A sandy loam suits it fairly well and its propagation is the same as for the other species.

Flowers are produced in April and May. The females are purple and the males greenish white. Females are slightly larger than the males and appear on the main stems, whilst the males appear in groups of corymbs at the ends of the previous year's growth or in the leaf axils.

The fruit is oblong shaped, purple, about 2in long and 1in wide. The seeds in the white pulp are jet black and the taste of the fruit is generally considered to be insipid.

K

Hottentot fig

Classification	:	*Carpobrotus edulis.*
Physiology	:	A half-hardy, woody succulent, which trails and spreads up to 6ft.
Origin	:	South Africa.
History	:	Fruit eaten by native people of South Africa. Medicinal properties recognized in Cape pioneering days. Now naturalized in milder parts of Europe. Not cultivated for its fruit.
Recommended site	:	Sunny greenhouse or sun lounge—pot plant.
Culinary uses	:	Eaten raw, preserved or used for jam or syrup.

The genus *Carpobrotus* belongs to the *mesembryanthemum* group by which name the various species are often called. As is implied by the name, *Carpobrotus* provides edible fruit (*karpos*, fruit; *brotus*, edible). The principal species is *Carpobrotus edulis* or Hottentot fig.

The Hottentot fig is a native of southern Africa where its habitat is in harsh arid conditions. It is now very common in Mediterranean countries and is also naturalized in the milder parts of Britain. Very often it is planted at seaside resorts where it acts as a bond in sand dunes. It is a half-hardy, prostrate or trailing succulent, perhaps spreading as much as 6ft on the ground and forming a flower-spangled mat. The stems are woody and the leaves fleshy. The leaves are numerous and triangular shaped, about 3in long and tapering to a point.

The leaf juice, which is astringent, contains malic and citric acid

146

and their calcium salts. Ever since Cape pioneering days the juice has been used in cases of dysentry and, because of its mild antiseptic properties, for malignant sore throat—the juice mixed with vinegar and honey is said to make a good gargle.

The Hottentot fig is quite easy to grow but it requires a well-drained, preferably sandy soil. If grown outdoors it needs to be in a well-drained sunny rock garden or border. But to ripen the fruit it is best to have it in a greenhouse or sun lounge and on a sunny shelf.

Propagation is fairly easy from seed sown in March. The seeds should be sprinkled on top of the seed compost and not covered. They should then be placed in a temperature of 65-70°F (18-21°C), but kept moist and shaded until the seedlings are large enough to be pricked out. Cuttings will also readily root during warm weather in summer. These should be inserted in a compost of equal parts of sand and peat and subsequently sprayed from time to time to keep them moist until roots are formed. As soon as they are big enough they should be planted in individual pots. Compared to other succulents grown as indoor plants, and with which you may be familiar, the Hottentot fig grows into a large plant and therefore requires a good-sized pot. Placed in a sunny greenhouse on a bench it can be allowed to trail.

It is not a desert plant but belongs to arid or steppe-like country, and like the camel of the desert it can store up water for a waterless or rainless day. It can, in fact, survive long periods without water. Because of this, although it should be well watered during the summer such watering should only be given when the soil has dried out. During winter, especially if the weather is cold, water should be withheld.

The flowers have lustrous pale lilac, yellow or orange petals and the yellow stamens are numerous. Normally it will fruit in its second year but to ripen this fruit as much warmth and sunshine as possible is needed. It is at first green and fleshy, and is not ready for eating until all green has gone from it and it has turned completely brown and shows signs of shrivelling. In appearance it is then fig-like and has a sweetly acid taste. It can be eaten raw, preserved, dried or used for jam. It also makes a very good syrup which is said to be laxative.

In South Africa Hottentot women have used an infusion of the fruit during pregnancy to ensure an easy birth. Then, afterwards, the newly-born babe is smeared all over with juice from the leaves and fruit. This is said to make it grow up nimble and strong!

Huckleberry

(BLACK HUCKLEBERRY)

Classification	:	*Gaylussacia baccata (syn. G. resinosa).*
Physiology	:	Deciduous, acid-loving shrub, growing 1-3ft tall.
Origin	:	North America.
History	:	Although the Americans from days of the early settlers have always used the fruit it has never been cultivated nor received the same attention as some of their other berried fruits. Little known in Europe.
Recommended site	:	Outdoors in lime or chalk-free soil.
Culinary uses	:	Good for tarts, pies, sauce. Same uses as cranberry.

The genus *Gaylussacia* belongs to the Ericaceae family and is, therefore, related to *Vaccinium*. The huckleberry does, in fact, closely resemble the bilberry and it could have been included under the heading for bilberry or blueberry (please see), but because it is recognized as a separate genus it would be bad form not to give it its own heading.

Huckleberries are well known for their fruit in their native land—North America. The berries growing wild were soon utilized by the early settlers. Yet, although their relations, the blueberries, have been cultivated, selected and consequently improved, very little has been done with the huckleberries. As far as Europe is concerned they are hardly known.

148

Most common is the black huckleberry (*Gaylussacia baccata*), a deciduous shrub growing up to 3ft tall and carrying numerous grey brown rigid branches. Generally the huckleberries require a moist soil but black huckleberry in its native habitat is found in dry, sandy or rocky soil. It is, therefore, considered that it will put up with drier conditions elsewhere than most of the other species. It is not difficult to grow provided the soil is not chalky and has not a high lime content. No special pruning is necessary. Best propagation results are from cuttings taken from the tips of the current year's growth in August and inserted in sandy peat in a cold frame. Seed should be sown in sandy peat in the spring. They should be planted out from October to April and spaced 3 x 3ft apart.

Pink or pale red flowers appear in June and are arranged in short, one-sided racemes. The berries are shiny black, round and about a quarter of an inch in diameter. They are sweet and very pleasantly flavoured. They are, however, more 'seedy' than blueberries: each contains ten seed-like nutlets. This may be the reason why the huckleberry has been less favoured than the blueberry, but it does have a good taste and ought not to be neglected.

OTHER HUCKLEBERRY SPECIES

DANGLEBERRY or TANGLEBERRY (*Gaylussacia frondosa*)
    This grows 3-6ft tall in moist woods and thickets. Woodland conditions and a peaty soil, therefore, suit it best—ie peat soil with an abundant addition of leaf mould or other humus. The best position is in partial shade, the soil kept moist but not allowed to become waterlogged.

Greenish purple flowers appear in June. It produces fewer flowers than black huckleberry but the berries are larger. They are borne on drooping stems, are dark blue with a whitish bloom and sweet and pleasing to the taste.

BOX HUCKLEBERRY (*Gaylussacia brachycera*)
    A deciduous shrub with box-like leaves; growing up to 1ft. It is fond of a moist peat soil. Pinkish white flowers appear in May and June. Berries are blue.

Huckleberry

BEAR HUCKLEBERRY (*Gaylussacia ursina*)
Deciduous shrub 2-6ft tall. Flowers are white or red and appear in May or June. Berries are black.

DWARF HUCKLEBERRY (*Gaylussacia dumosa*)
Deciduous spreading shrub. Grows to 1ft tall. It spreads by means of underground stems or rhizomes. Flowers are white and appear in May or June. Berries are black.

Japanese quince

(JAPONICA)

Classification	:	*Chaenomeles* species.
Physiology	:	Hardy, deciduous shrub of spreading habit and with spiny branches.
Origin	:	China; Japan.
History	:	Has been cultivated in England since the eighteenth century, since when there has been some confusion about classification.
Recommended site	:	Outdoors—preferably against a sunny wall.
Culinary uses	:	Used for jellies, conserves or for flavouring apple or other pie fruit.

There are only three true species of this genus but there has always been some confusion about their classification. The first of the species was found in the Hakone mountains in Japan in 1784 and was introduced into Britain under the name of *Pyrus japonica*; later botanists decided that it was not a pear (*Pyrus*) but a quince (*Cydonia*). Meanwhile, however, another species had been introduced into the country, and although a native of China it was erroneously given the name of *Cydonia japonica*. The botanists then had further thoughts and came finally to decide that the species not only did not belong to the genus *Pyrus* but that they did not belong to the genus *Cydonia* either. Now they have their own genus—*Chaenomeles*—and the erroneously named *Cydonia japonica* becomes *Chaenomeles speciosa*. It is often, however, still referred to by its old and incorrect name.

Japanese quince

There is yet another cause of confusion. This is a species known often as *Cydonia sinsensis* and classed with the Japanese quince or japonica; it does not, however, belong to the same genus. It is closer to the true quince (*Cydonia*) but even so it is now considered that it has its own genus—*Pseudocydonia*.

Then, also there has been considerable hybridization between the *Chaenomeles* species, and nurserymen often offer numerous cultivars. These cultivars have been bred in the main for the ornamental value of their flowers rather than for their fruit. However, to avoid further difficulties only the three true species of the genus will be here described. Their cultivation, both simple and similar is dealt with first.

Chaenomeles will grow in any soil and in any location, but where fruit is the main consideration a sunny position should be chosen. A sunny wall is ideal. When choosing a site do not forget their considerable ornamental value, especially as they flower in early spring when there is not much other colour around.

They can be propagated from seed sown in the autumn in well-drained pots and then left outside in a cold position all winter and, preferably, moved into a cold frame in early spring. Or they can be propagated from cuttings taken from the ends of half-ripened wood in July. Or branches can be layered in the autumn, or suckers taken up in November or March.

Any planting should be carried out between November and March. Once established, pruning consists of removing surplus wood after the flowering has finished. Old wood and thin branches should be cut out and side shoots should be shortened. Those grown against a wall and, as mentioned, this is the ideal way of growing them, benefit from regular pruning once a good framework of branches over the wall has been established. Shorten the branches after flowering, and then again in late summer, after the season's growth, cut back any outward-growing shoots.

The ripening fruits become quite ornamental and can be allowed to remain until they fall. They are too sour and astringent to eat raw. They are very hard but contain a rich, aromatic lemon-like juice which imparts a distinctive and pleasant odour to other fruit cooked with them. They are, therefore, esteemed for jellies, conserves, and the flavour they give to apple and other pie fruit. Japonica jelly makes an excellent condiment with meat.

JAPANESE QUINCE (*Chaenomeles speciosa*, syn. *lagenaria*)
(*Cydonia japonica*)

This, as previously explained, is a native of China but has been wrongly named Japanese. It is a deciduous shrub with a wide, spreading habit. It may eventually grow 10ft tall and 20ft wide, but usually it is seen much smaller than this. Its spiny branches tend to become dense and interlacing if some of them are not judiciously removed.

It will usually commence flowering from February onwards until June, sometimes even earlier. The flowers are red or reddish orange and are produced on the old wood in clusters of two to four. The fruit, which remains a long time on the tree, is stalkless, globular or ovoid, roughly 1½in in diameter, greeny yellow and minutely speckled with brown spots. It is five-celled and each cell has numerous seeds, as in the other two species.

DWARF QUINCE or MAULES QUINCE
(*Chaenomeles japonica*; syn *maulei*)

A true native of Japan. This was the original species discovered in the Hakone mountains in 1784 and first named *Pyrus japonica*. It is a small, low-spreading, deciduous spiny shrub. Normally it will grow to about 3ft and somewhat wider. Its flowers—flame-coloured to blood red—appear from April to June and are very abundant, occurring in clusters in the joints of one-year-old wood. A very attractive shrub.

Apart from its smaller size at maturity it can be distinguished from the previous species by its minutely warted twigs and its leaves, which are more rounded and more coarsely toothed.

The fruit is freely borne. They are apple-shaped, 1½in in diameter, yellow and flushed with red where the sun touches them; very aromatic and make excellent jelly.

CHINESE QUINCE (*Chaenomeles cathayensis*)

This is most probably a native of China but its true habitat is not known. It was first collected in Hupeh, China, but it was already a cultivated plant and not a wild specimen. It is a deciduous shrub with an open spreading habit and growing 8-10ft tall. Its branches are armed with tiny spurs. Flowers are in clusters of two or three, appearing in April, and are white suffused with pink.

This species provides the largest fruit of the three, egg-shaped but contracted at the base, 4-6in long and 2½-3½in wide.

Jujube

(CHINESE JUJUBE; CHINESE DATE)

Classification	:	*Zizyphus jujube* (*Z. sativa*).
Physiology	:	Deciduous, sub-tropical, thorny tree, growing to 40ft.
Origin	:	China.
History	:	Cultivated in China for perhaps 4,000 years. Now grown in many sub-tropical countries. Known in England as far back as 1640 but its tenderness has kept it a rare tree in this country.
Recommended site	:	Outdoors—exceptionally mild sunny position. Indoors—warm glasshouse.
Culinary uses	:	Eaten fresh; or dried; or preserved.

There are a hundred or so species of *Zizyphus*; its representatives grow in all the world's continents but only a few species provide fruit. It has been cultivated in China for hundreds, even thousands, of years. It is one of the principal fruits of that country and hundreds of varieties have been bred.

The most noted characteristic of the tree is its thorns: there is a species which is very common around Jerusalem and it has been suggested that it was from this tree that the crown of thorns was made.

The jujube is a deciduous tree growing up to 40ft. It has a spreading habit and carries spiny branches. The spines are in pairs—one straight and up to a quarter of an inch long, the other curved and shorter. There are, however, varieties which are spineless.

It is a tree which will stand all kinds of soil, growing even in badly drained and poor soil; deep sandy loams are, however, said to be best for good growth and fruiting. It is able to adapt to a wide range of soils and to withstand both drought and waterlogging because it quickly develops a deep tap-root system. This tap-root growth may limit its suitability as a subject for pot cultivation, but on the other hand, given the right soil and moistures, it may not need to push its roots downwards. It grows best in a hot dry climate and excessive humidity is a limiting factor to satisfactory fruiting. During the winter, while it remains dormant, it can withstand frost.

Propagation can be from seeds. As the seeds are contained in a very strong outershell (endocarp) it is necessary to break or crack this or germination will be a very lengthy process. Care must, however, be taken not to injure the living seeds or embryos. They should then be sown several to a pot and kept in a warm place. The soil must be kept moist and they should germinate in about two weeks.

To propagate the varieties which are grown commercially it is necessary, of course, to propagate by vegetative means. In China it is common practice to take cuttings from the roots. These root cuttings are from 4-6in long and have a diameter of not less than three-sixteenths of an inch.

When seeds have germinated and formed four leaves they may be transplanted into their own individual pots. If outdoor growing is intended a warm sheltered position should be selected. Under suitable conditions seedlings usually begin to bear fruit from their third to fourth year.

During its young life, until it begins to bear fruit, the tree should be pruned with the aim of building a good frame. No hard-and-fast rules can be given as much will depend on the circumstances of its location. When it begins to bear fruit, pruning of the branches may be practised annually. Fruit is borne in the axils of the leaves on the young growing shoots of the current year so that it is necessary to encourage each year a good healthy growth which will provide the largest fruiting area. This pruning should be carried out whilst it is sleeping during the wintertime. The smaller shoots are pruned back leaving a short stump from which new growth will commence in the spring. If there is any overcrowding the old and thin branches should be cut right out.

Jujube flowers are small, less than a quarter of an inch across, greenish yellow and borne in clusters of two or three together on short stalks in the leaf axils. Excessive humidity limits its fruiting capacity but during the fruiting season it does require adequate watering.

The fruits that develop become mahogany brown as they ripen. They are round to egg-shaped, about the size of a small plum, half to one inch long, and contain white crisp flesh with a single large pointed stone. They have a pleasant acid taste when eaten fresh but are much better when dried. They can be picked when they are still firm but have developed a light yellowish scarlet colour with a brownish hue. Generally they are only fit to eat when the skin has attained its full colour although there are some varieties which may be eaten when still green.

They are a rich source of vitamin C as well as containing vitamins A and B. They can be eaten fresh or semi-dried. They can be candied or crystallized and this is done by puncturing the thick skin thoroughly all over to permit full penetration of the syrup. This makes an excellent confection and they are then usually called Chinese dates.

OTHER SPECIES OF INTEREST

INDIAN JUJUBE (*Zizyphus mauritania*)

This is a native of India and is sub-tropical. It is an evergreen shrub, not so spreading as the Chinese jujube but reaching about the same height (40ft). It thrives in a hot dry climate where winter temperatures do not go below 15°F (-9°C). The fruit is smaller than in the Chinese species.

ARABIAN JUJUBE (*Zizyphus spina-christi*)

This is a native of Arabia but grows wild from Algeria to the eastern Mediterranean area. It is a shrub or small tree growing up to 30ft. Its branches bear pairs of stout spines at the base of each leaf. This is the species which grows around Jerusalem. The fruits are berry-like, about the size of a hazelnut, globular and about a third of an inch in diameter.

ZIZYPHUS ROTUNDIFOLIA

This is a species often used as a rootstock and cultivated varieties budded on to it do not grow so large. It also provides good-quality fruit.

Juneberry

Classification : *Amelanchier* species.
Physiology : Deciduous, hardy, small trees or large shrubs.
Origin : Principally North America.
History : Wild berries used, especially in North America, but very little has been done to improve them. Cultivated as an ornamental in Britain.
Recommended site : Outdoors.
Culinary uses : Best forms of the berries used fresh for dessert; pies, jams etc.

There are some twenty-five or so species of *Amelanchier* and many of them are used for food in many parts of the north temperate zone. They are closely related to the apples and pears but differ from them in that their fruits are juicy and berry-like. Because of natural hybridization which has taken place among the species, especially in North America, it is exceptionally difficult to distinguish between them. The following notes are therefore general.

Some of the *Amelanchier* species are dwarf shrubs 2-3ft tall, with many stems; others are small trees with slender, straight stems which may reach a height of 40ft and have a diameter of 8-10in. They are unarmed, that is to say they have no thorns, spines or prickles. The flowers are mostly white but some are pink, and they appear in early spring. The leaves, when young, are usually copper coloured and turn red or gold in the autumn.

They are, in fact, grown in Britain for their ornamental value but in some countries, especially in North America, they are valued for their fruits. The North American Indians, for instance, crushed the berries and dried them to form a kind of cake. This 'fruit cake' they would take on their long journeys to provide them with sustenance.

The various species will grow on all soils, including chalk, and they thrive under conditions that are suitable for apples and pears. They are also tolerant of varying moisture conditions. All of them are very hardy and they can, therefore, be considered for those parts of the country where there is a limitation on the kinds of fruit that can be grown. They are readily propagated from seed sown in spring. The bushy kinds can be divided in the autumn. Grafting and budding can be practised. The means of improvement are therefore simple.

As the name implies, the fruits are normally ripe during June. They are berry-like pomes with a cavity at the top; in some species no bigger than a pea or currant, but in others they may be the size of a small crab apple. They are sweet and juicy. In colour they vary from a dark red to purplish blue and black. All, in varying degrees, are covered with a bloom. Because the various kinds of Juneberries are very variable in their fruits there should be scope for improvement through selection and breeding.

The berries may be served uncooked for dessert; they are excellent for pies, or for preserving for winter use.

INDIVIDUAL SPECIES

Due to the fact that the North American species are so closely related it is difficult to give a really worthwhile description of individual species. Botanists have not agreed on the naming of some of them. The following descriptions and names must only be taken as a rough guide.

JUNEBERRY or SHAD BERRY (*Amelanchier canadensis*)

From eastern and central North America. Growing 20-30ft tall. In April when heavily laden with small white flowers in nodding racemes it is very eye-catching.

The berries ripen in June and are round, about a quarter of an inch in diameter, dark red or purplish maroon. They are of a sweet and pleasant odour but vary in flavour.

MOUNTAIN JUNEBERRY (*Amelanchier alnifolia*)
From western North America. A shrub 6-8ft tall. White flowers in erect racemes appear in April, followed by purplish or blue-black berries. Sweet and juicy.

SWAMP SUGAR PEAR (*Amelanchier oblongifolia*)
From eastern North America. A large shrub 10-15ft tall, spreading by means of suckers. White flowers in April. Its berries were used, fresh or dried, by Canadian Indians, and according to one early traveller from the Old World they were said to make an 'excellent plum pudding'.

QUEBEC BERRY (*Amelanchier stolonifera*)
From eastern North America. A low spreading shrub 3-5ft high. Forms a small thicket of stiff erect stems and spreads by means of underground suckers. White flowers bloom in April. Berries ripen in July, they are purplish black, glaucous, sweet and juicy.

FLORIDA JUNEBERRY (*Amelanchier florida*)
From western North America (south-east Alaska to north-west California). Closely related to *Amelanchier alnifolia*. A shrub or thicket of stems 10ft high. Flowers are white, borne five to fifteen together in erect racemes. Berries are purple-black and juicy.

AMELANCHIER X SPICATA
This is a hybrid which is thought to be a cross between *oblongifolia* and *stolonifera*. It has been grown for over 100 years. It forms a dense thicket of stems 6-12ft high. Flowers appear in late April and May. The berries are blue-black.

EUROPEAN JUNEBERRY or SNOWY MESPILUS
(*Amelanchier ovalis*)
From the mountains of central and southern Europe. A large tree or small shrub growing up to 10ft tall. Flowers are fewer than on the other species but are much larger, often being 1½in in diameter. Berries are first red, then black, are covered with purplish bloom and are about the size of a blackcurrant. Not particularly palatable but can be used for jam or wine making.

159

Juneberry

KOREAN JUNEBERRY (*Amelanchier asiatica*)

From Korea and Japan. This is a beautiful flowering tree which may grow to a height of 40ft. Its berries are bluish black and, like the North American species, are far superior to the European.

It is necessary to mention that the birds relish Juneberries. However, even as God created man so did He create the birds and by Him the birds are fed.

Killarney strawberry

(TREE STRAWBERRY)

Classification	:	*Arbutus unedo.*
Physiology	:	A small, evergreen, ornamental tree growing to about 20ft tall.
Origin	:	Eastern Mediterranean; Ireland.
History	:	How it came to be a native of Killarney is a mystery. Cultivated in warm temperate areas as an ornamental.
Recommended site	:	Outdoors as ornamental.
Culinary uses	:	For jam or wine.

Arbutus is a genus of evergreen trees noted for their attractive foliage, lily-of-the-valley-like flowers, and strawberry-like fruit.

The best known species in this country is *Arbutus unedo*. Although it originated in the Mediterranean, and probably the eastern Mediterranean area, it is also found growing wild in Killarney in Ireland where it forms thickets along the shores and islets of the lake of that name. How it came to be a native of these parts is not known. Legend has it that the tree appeared as a miracle to give comfort to a Spanish monk pining for his monastery in Spain. More scientifically, it has been suggested that the tree spread from Brittany during the early post-glacial period when the climate was warmer than it is now and that it then managed to survive in a few favourable places and eventually became acclimatized. It could, of course, have been introduced by the Romans or even the Phoenicians.

It is a small, beautiful tree or shrub, depending on the conditions in which it is grown. In England, for example, it often takes the form of a shrub growing to about 20ft. It is evergreen, the glossy leaves are

161

L

Killarney strawberry

laurel-like with a leathery texture, dark green above and pale green below. The young branches are reddish in colour but the older bark is brown and rough. The flowers appear in autumn in drooping panicles at the ends of the stems. They are urn-shaped and like small white waxy bells; they have been likened to lily of the valley.

Propagation is best done from seed and this should be sown under glass. It germinates readily but the seedlings have a tendency to damp off. The young seedling should be potted up as soon as possible and, when hardened off, transferred direct to its location as it is not able to withstand much transplanting. It will tolerate most soils. Although the genus *Arbutus* belongs to the Ericaceae family it thrives on a chalky soil. Also it is hardy and is known to have withstood a temperature of -22°F (-30°C). It does, however, fruit better in a mild district. Although there is self-pollination, cross-pollination is effected by bees. Because it flowers in the autumn it is only in the milder climates that self-pollination will be supplemented by insects.

The flowers take a whole year to develop into juicy berries and this means that flowers and fruit are on the tree at the same time, which is October or later. The tree is particularly attractive at this time of the year.

The berries are globose, measuring half an inch to three-quarters of an inch in diameter and have a rough surface. They are at first white, then yellow and finally rosy red in colour. It is from the colour and size of the fruit that it gets the name of Killarney strawberry or tree strawberry. Although juicy the berries are insipid and contain numerous seeds. They can, however, be made into jam or wine. In Corsica the berries are used to make a distilled liquor.

Kumquat

Classification : *Fortunella japonica. Fortunella margarita.*

Physiology : Small, evergreen, sub-tropical trees, 6-8ft tall.

Origin : China.

History : Cultivated in China and Japan for a very long time. Introduced into England in 1846 and to USA about 1850. Now grown commercially in California and Florida.

Recommended site : Indoors—warm greenhouse or conservatory—as pot plant.

Culinary uses : Eaten raw or as a preserve.

Fortunella is a genus of about six evergreen shrubs or small trees and is very closely related to *Citrus* in which genus it was originally included. However, it differs from *Citrus* in having small fruits with acid pulp and sweet edible skins or rinds. It was first introduced into Europe in 1846 by Robert Fortune, a British plant hunter collecting for the London Horticultural Society. But despite the fact that it makes a pleasing pot plant it has remained little known.

All parts of the tree are sweetly scented and their dark green, glossy leaves and small white flowers make them miniature orange trees. Although they may grow 6-8ft tall they can be kept much smaller.

In China and Japan the kumquat is widely cultivated for its fruit and there are many varieties in those countries. Elsewhere there are a number of hybrids not only within the genus but also inter-generic (eg between *Fortunella, Citrus* and *Poncirus*), but only the Marumi

Kumquat

kumquat (*Fortunella japonica*) and the Nagami kumquat (*Fortunella margarita*) will be dealt with here.

Both are more resistant to cold than orange or mandarin trees and can withstand quite lengthy cold periods. They quickly cease growth during cool weather (55°F, 13°C) and because of this are already inactive if cold weather follows. But, even so, in order to get results a well-lighted greenhouse with a winter temperature of not less than 40-50°F (4-10°C) is required. They should be planted either in pots or in the greenhouse border early in summer, after the new growth has been made. A good compost for them is equal parts of turf loam and leaf mould.

In propagating them from seed best results are obtained when the seeds are sown soon after being taken from the fruit, as they do not withstand much drying. They can be sown in any ordinary seed compost and germinated in a warm but airy situation. As soon as they are large enough the young seedlings can be planted into their own pots and allowed to grow on. They require little pruning except to keep them to a good and convenient shape. From the time the new growth commences they should be kept well watered and syringed during hot weather.

The flowers of both species are pure white, similar to those of the orange, and are single or clustered in the leaf axils. The fruits are slow to colour and ripen but with blossoming in the summer it should be possible to have fruit by Christmas.

The difference between Marumi and Nagami kumquat is in the fruit. Marumi, or round kumquat as it is sometimes called, is a bright orange-yellow, waxy, round, and about 1in in diameter. The pulp is juicy and acid-sweet. The rind is comparatively thick for the size of the fruit but is sweet and spicy. Provided the fruit is ripe and the pulp not too acid the taste of the rind blends with the pulp. The flavour is sweeter when the fruit has ripened in a warm rather than in a cool temperature.

The Nagami, or oval kumquat, is about 1½in long and three-quarters of an inch in diameter; in other respects it is similar to Marumi except that it is a little redder when fully ripe.

The fruit of both can be eaten fresh, or it can be preserved either in syrup or by being candied.

Lemon

Classification	:	*Citrus limonia.*
Physiology	:	An evergreen, sub-tropical, small tree or shrub growing 8-12ft tall.
Origin	:	Possibly central Asia.
History	:	When first cultivated is not known. It did not reach North Africa and Spain until AD 1000-1200 or thereabouts. Columbus is said to have taken it to America.
Recommended site	:	Greenhouse or conservatory — pot plant.
Culinary uses	:	For drinks, syrups, flavouring etc.

Citrus consists of only a few species but the fruits they bear are so well known and of such economic importance that they must be dealt with under separate headings (ie lemon, lime, mandarin, orange, pummelo and grapefruit) even though their cultivation is broadly similar.

The exact place from which *Citrus* originated is not known but it was possibly somewhere in the region of eastern India, Burma and southern China, though not in the tropical rain forests of that broad area. There is evidence to show that the fruit was known there in the days of early man.

But *Citrus limonia* or lemon was not known in the most advanced areas of civilization in China until a century or two before the Arabs brought it to North Africa and Spain. Its progress into Europe was helped by the returning Crusaders who had found it in Palestine. It was introduced to the New World in 1493 when Columbus took it to Haiti.

Lemon

Today it is widely cultivated in the Mediterranean area as well as in America, the largest production at present being in Sicily and southern California. In Sicily definite clones or varieties are not maintained, only types (eg oval, long, early-ripening). In California where varieties are maintained and each variety applies to one clone only, there is a variety called Eureka. This originated from a seed planted in Los Angeles in 1858 and was from a box of lemons from Sicily. Who can say what kind of fruit may come from a seed!

In 1577 the Dean of Windsor wrote that among the strange plants he had recently seen cultivated in England were lemons. He mentioned that they were grown in tubs which were taken indoors during winter and put outdoors during summer. This is still a good way of growing the lemon tree in these latitudes.

The lemon tree is considered to be closely related to the citron, if not an actual hybrid from it. Yet the appearance of the tree is different. In fact the branches of the lemon tree spread and droop more than the branches of any other *Citrus* species. It is a small tree or spreading bush, usually 8-12ft tall and carrying spines. The young evergreen foliage and flower buds are at first reddish but assume a pleasing waxy green as they develop.

Its propagation can be from seed and there is a very vital biological process which needs to be understood. Seed from most of the *Citrus* species (but not pummelo) is, in varying degrees, what is known as apomictical. Some of the *Citrus* species produce polyembryonic seeds —more than one plant being produced from one seed. One embryo may be from the fertilized egg and this may grow into a plant as variable as most plants normally are from seed. The other embryos —one or several—are formed adventitiously in the nucellus; these develop very much like the tree from which the fruit came and are little different to scions taken from that tree.

The lemon does not produce polyembryonic seeds to the same extent as the lime or orange, but even so apomictical or nucellar embryos do occur. The seedling which has been produced from the fertilized egg can sometimes be recognized by the fact that it is inclined to be stunted and is less vigorous than the nucellar seedlings. When so recognized the nucellar seedlings can be separated and grown on in the knowledge that they will all develop in a uniform manner and follow the characteristics of the parent tree. (Propagation from polyembryonic seed is dealt with more fully under Lime.)

Lemon seed should be sown half an inch deep in light soil in a temperature of 55°F (13°C) during March. Germination usually takes 20-30 days. Young seedlings are liable to damp off but otherwise they are vigorous. They withstand climatic rigours better than budded trees and will bear quite well. When about 3-4in high the seedlings can be transplanted into individual pots.

But it is by budding that better varieties can be perpetuated. There is a wide grafting compatability not only between the *Citrus* species but also between the closely related genera (*Poncirus, Agele, Fortunella*). Because of this some rootstock species may give a hardiness which will extend the climatic frontiers of the lemon tree. Budding onto seedling roots is the usual practice because of the predominance of nucellar embryo seedlings which provide uniformity. The seedling stems should be a quarter to three-eighths of an inch in diameter. Shield buds are inserted under the bark which has had a T or inverted T cut in it. The bud must not be completely covered by the flaps of the bark, but it must be bandaged so that the bud and the wound have an air-tight cover. August is the best time for budding.

A bud which has been set in cool weather does not start growth until warm weather comes. About 2 weeks after the bud has been set (the lower the temperature the longer the time) the bandage can be lifted sufficiently to see if the bud is either well calloused or dead. If it is still alive but not very well calloused it must be rebandaged and left for another 2 weeks, otherwise the bandage can be removed. The seedling top is usually cut back to the bud when it is ready to grow. Left to itself the budling will develop into a whip-like growth similar to that made by deciduous trees. It should, therefore, be pruned soon after the bud has started to grow. It will then branch readily and these branches sometimes start within a few inches of the union.

Propagation may also be from cuttings inserted in small pots of sandy soil in July. Leafy stem cuttings will root well when there is good light and atmospheric humidity; semi-hard cuttings will root more readily than cuttings of completely hard wood. Shoots may also be layered in October.

The lemon tree does not require the same depth of soil as do some deciduous fruit trees such as the peach—a tree which is often a subject for pot cultivation. It will thrive well in any well-drained loamy soil

Lemon

but it cannot stand waterlogged conditions. If you have a greenhouse suitable for indoor peach cultivation then growing the lemon, or for that matter any of the *Citrus* fruits, should give no problems. It can be grown in the greenhouse border or in a 12in pot and should be provided with a good fibrous loam. If grown in the border it should be top-dressed annually with well-rotted stable manure or compost. If grown in a pot, feeding will be necessary because of the restriction of the roots: this can be with a liquid fertilizer in which the nitrogen content is not high. It should be repotted annually or bi-annully, depending on the vigour of the tree, and this should be done early in the year after the main growth has finished.

The total heat requirement of the lemon is less than for the orange but it withstands cold less well than the orange. A temperature near 20-22°F (−7 to −6°C) is likely to injure lemon wood badly unless a night with a temperature as low as this has been preceded by two or three weeks of weather near freezing point at night and too cold during the day to permit any growth. A period with temperatures two or three degrees above freezing appears to increase the frost resistance of the lemon, but if damaged by frost it does not have the same ability to recover as does the orange tree. Flowers and very young fruit may be killed at a temperature of 29°F (−2°C); shoot tips may be killed at a temperature of 26°F (−3°C). The aim should be not to let the temperature in the greenhouse fall below 40°F (4°C) at night and by 45°F (7°C) by day during the winter. Spring temperatures should be not less than 50°F (10°C), rising to 70°F (21°C) by May. When the temperature falls to 50°F (10°C) the rate of growth is greatly reduced. Midsummer temperatures should not rise above 85°F (29°C).

The lemon tree needs plenty of light as well as ventilation and it should be placed outdoors whenever the weather is warm. It benefits by regular syringeing (during the summer this should be done daily) and the roots must never be allowed to dry out.

Citrus trees in general do not require the same amount of pruning as deciduous fruit trees. They do not respond in the same way and because of this it is not so easy to train young trees to the form required. Because the lemon tends to spread its branches it can more easily be pruned to shape than other young *Citrus* trees although it is not possible to train a fixed number of main branches. Branches that are clearly touching and crossing others, and shoots which will

168

obviously do so, are removed, as are also injured and dead branches. Shoots can be removed at any time during the summer, but the dead and larger branches should be removed and thinned, if necessary, during the winter.

When mature, the lemon is pruned more than other *Citrus*. A characteristic of *Citrus* trees is the production of what are known as water sprouts. These are long vigorous growths which occur on the upper side of spreading branchlets only a year or two old. These water sprouts grow much larger than the branches from which they spring and are out of proportion to the tree's symmetry. When these upright-growing water sprouts make the tree too tall or tangle with other branches they should be cut back to their point of origin. Except for those necessary to form the framework of the tree, any water sprouts starting from the centre of the tree should be cut out, but those starting well out on the branches will develop fruiting wood and these need not be cut out until they begin to be too tall.

The lemon tree under natural conditions tends to blossom almost continuously—the tree bearing fruit and flowers at one and the same time—but with the heaviest blossom in the spring. Spring blossom will certainly be heaviest when the winter has been too cold for much growth. Branches that are not bearing many flowers may sometimes be encouraged to blossom by ringing the branch.

The white, star-shaped flowers are large, and either solitary or in small clusters occurring in the axils of the leaves. Pollination does not normally cause a problem because if fertilization does not occur the fruit develops parthenocarpically. Normally the number of flowers borne annually is too many for all to set fruit. Temperature is the most important influence in determining the time when the fruit will be mature, but it may be from 7 to 14 months. Any water deficiency will affect the rate of growth. If the water deficiency continues for any length of time the fruits may be permanently reduced in size.

Fruit may not ripen until late in the year and it must be remembered that such fruit will be damaged when the temperature is at freezing point. But cool weather will not affect lemon fruits; they in fact develop the acid flavour which is expected of them in temperatures that are too cool for oranges to develop their best flavour.

When picking the fruit care should be taken so that it is not bruised or the peel broken with finger nail or punctured by any of the tree's spines, otherwise a mould will form when the fruit is stored. The best-keeping and best-quality fruit is that which reaches a good size while still green. It can be stored at 60°F (16°C) until the skin turns yellow.

If you intend to grow the tree from a seed it will usually commence maiden bearing in the eighth year and normal bearing in the tenth. From this tree you can then propagate budlings which will commence maiden bearing in their fourth year and normal bearing in their seventh.

Lime

Classification	:	*Citrus aurantifolia.*
Physiology	:	Evergreen, tropical, small tree or shrub growing 8-14ft tall. Usually carries spines.
Origin	:	Possibly East Indies or the nearby Asian mainland.
History	:	Believed to have been brought to Palestine and North Africa by the Arabs about AD 1000. Introduced further into Europe by Crusaders. Now grown in most citrus-growing areas.
Recommended site	:	Greenhouse or conservatory—pot plant.
Culinary uses	:	Used for drinks, syrups, flavouring etc.

The lime is another of those very important members of the genus *Citrus*. In some ways—in the use of its fruits, its physiology, its cultivation and its history—it is very similar to the lemon. It appears to have originated somewhere in south-east Asia and to have been brought to Europe through India and Persia by the Arabs, at about the same time as the lemon. But unlike the lemon, which may be a natural hybrid, there is little doubt that the lime evolved as a distinct species.

Returning Crusaders in the twelfth and thirteenth centuries introduced the lime into Europe, as they did the lemon. Columbus is said to have taken it to the New World and in the West Indies it can now be found growing wild. Mexico and Egypt are the two countries with the largest production today.

Lime

Allowed to grow naturally it tends to be a small shrubby tree, 8-14ft tall. Its spreading branches grow in an irregular manner and have short stiff twigs as well as small sharp thorns or spines. It is more tender than the lemon and far less resistant to the cold. Young growth, particularly, is not very resistant to frost.

Apart from the fact that one has to wait a few years for the fruit, it is quite feasible to propagate the lime from seed. Many varieties of the *Citrus* species produce what are known as polyembryonic seeds. From these seeds two or three seedlings may emerge. One of the seedlings may be the actual sexual offspring (ie the result of pollination and successful fertilization of the egg) and this sexual seedling will grow up and prove to be as variable as any such seedlings may be, different in many ways to its parents, bearing fruit inferior or superior to that of its parents. But the other seedlings which emerge from the polyembryonic seed are produced vegetatively, growing out of the cells of the nucellus of the seed. These vegetatively produced seedlings are called apogamic seedlings and they grow up identical to the parent (that is the mother tree from which the fruit and seed came). In a sense such seedlings can be compared with vegetatively produced suckers.

In some *Citrus* species nucellar embryos are always dominant in the seeds but the development of these nucellar embryos seems to be dependent on the prior pollination of the flower if not also the fertilization of the egg. (Citrus fruit can occur parthenocarpically without pollination.) Also, although a particular species produces mainly polyembryonic seed some varieties or clones may produce only monoembryonic seed. The lime is one of the species which produces mainly polyembryonic seed. Because of this it is possible to propagate lime trees with good-quality fruit from seed as well as by budding. The one disadvantage is that nucellar or apogamic trees have a thorny juvenile period and are slow to commence bearing. They may grow vigorously for 6 to 8 years before their first flowers appear. Compared with this a budling may commence bearing in its fourth year and this is of considerable economic importance to commercial growers. But if you can afford to wait, the apogamic tree will grow out of its thorny adolescence, will be hardier than the budling tree and will bear fruit and be as attractive as its mother.

The cultivation of the lime in most respects, is similar to that of the lemon and the reader should refer to the notes under that heading. Care should, however, be taken to see that temperatures in the greenhouse or conservatory do not fall lower than 40-35°F (2°C). Remember that it is more tender than the lemon. Also a little less pruning will be necessary. The lime tree tends to send up fewer water sprouts than the lemon. It makes a thicker, bushier and more spreading growth. Therefore pruning of the mature tree will consist of thinning out and shortening normal branches.

The flowers of the lime are also white but smaller than those of the lemon. They usually occur in clusters of a few together and, like the lemon, under natural conditions of light and warmth it may be blossoming for a large part of the year. The fruit rarely exceeds 2in in length and has greenish, very acid pulp and a thin rind which when the fruit is ripe is greenish yellow. Its flavour is distinctive. Like the lemon its juice is used for flavouring preserves, drinks etc.

When the juice is taken internally in quantity or applied externally it has the effect of sensitizing the skin to strong sunlight with the result that areas exposed to the sun are nicely tanned. If you are considering joining a nudist club a lime tree might help to provide a useful covering!

Litchee

(LYCHEE; LY CHEE; ETC)

Classification : *Litchi chinensis.*
Physiology : A round-topped, evergreen tree, reaching 35-40ft under natural conditions.
Origin : Southern China.
History : Cultivated in China for more than 2,000 years. It has the distinction of being the first fruit to be the subject for a work on fruit culture (Ts'ai Hsiang, AD 1059). Now grown commercially in a number of countries, including Australia, New Zealand and USA (Florida).
Recommended site : Cool or warm greenhouse.
Culinary uses : Eaten fresh; dried or preserved in syrup.

In the genus *Litchi* only two species are recognized and only one, *Litchi chinensis*, is cultivated for its fruit. This species appears to have been cultivated by people of Malaysian descent in southern China before the Chinese moved south. For more than 2,000 years it has been cultivated in China and there is now no known wild form of the species—apart from those which have escaped from cultivation. What is considered to be the first published work on fruit was written by a Chinese scholar Ts'ai Hsiang, in AD 1059 and dealt with litchee varieties.

Today in China neither the orange nor peach equal it in esteem.

174

Yet the spread of litchee to other parts of the world has been slow and has taken place only in comparatively recent times, despjite the fact that it is always a popular fruit. But it is grown extensively in parts of India and latterly in South Africa, and also commercially in Japan, Australia, New Zealand, and USA (Florida).

It is an evergreen tree tending to have a round-topped shape and, under natural conditions, grows to a height of 35-40ft. It is rather slow to reach maturity and tends to live to a good sturdy old age. Litchee is at all times a beautiful tree. The leaves are pinnate, leathery and shining, consisting of three to nine leaflets. When these leaves are young they have an orange or coppery red colour. Not only is the tree attractive when wearing new young leaves but also later in the year when bejewelled with clusters of rosy red fruit; being an evergreen it does not shed its leaves.

In climatic requirements litchee is tropical, but it can be, and is, grown successfully in sub-tropical areas. The climatic conditions in its native southern China are ideal for it: a large part of the year is moderately hot and humid and there is a period in winter which is foggy, continually cool but free from any frost. Seasonal variations in temperature are, in fact, considered necessary for proper fruiting. In winter a dry atmosphere with cold snaps between 35°F and 40°F (2-4°C) are considered beneficial for flowering and fruiting. However, old trees may be injured by brief periods of temperature as low as 25°F (-4°C) and young trees will not withstand temperatures below freezing.

The litchee can, therefore, be grown in Britain in a large greenhouse. It will tolerate a variety of soils provided they are well drained, but it does best in a deep, well-drained loam which is rich in organic matter. It is rather tolerant of wet soil and its roots will withstand immersion in water for some considerable time provided the water is moving—stagnant water causes the roots to decay. The tree benefits from the mycorrhiza fungi which grows on its roots (the benefit is mutual), and soils with a high organic content, which are well aerated and yet do not dry up (ie moist and acid soils) are the most suitable for the fungi.

Litchee can be raised from seed but such seedlings take from seven to twelve years before they bear any fruit. The seedlings are also very variable and most of them bear fruit inferior to that of their parents.

Litchee

The breeding of new varieties is, therefore, a very slow process. The seed also loses its viability within four or five days after being taken from its fruit. When left in the fruit it remains viable for two or three weeks. It must, therefore, be sown as quickly as possible, half an inch deep in a partially shaded place, and the soil kept moist. Germination takes about two weeks. Young litchees are very delicate and have a high mortality rate; it is desirable to give them an acid soil enriched with much humus.

The litchee can be propagated fairly successfully from cuttings which should be of two-year-old wood, but the most successful vegetative method is by air layering.

The tree grows slowly so that little annual pruning is required once the initial training and building up of a good frame has been achieved. Flowers are borne mainly on new shoots, and as the old branches very seldom bear flowers, removal of old growth to promote new is desirable; but because the fruit is harvested in branches along with shoots this serves the same purpose. If the tree happens to be making too much vegetative growth both root and shoot pruning may be carried out. Should the crown of the tree become too thick branches may be cut out, but it must be remembered that too heavy pruning causes a large amount of growth at the expense of flowering.

The flowers are small and whitish and without petals. They are borne in leafless terminal panicles sometimes as much as 1in long, and are either unisexual or bisexual. An inflorescence with several hundred flowers may set up to twenty or so fruits. The bee and the fly are the natural means of pollination. Flowering is in the spring and, as noted earlier, a chilling period during the winter is considered desirable to induce this. In most areas where litchee fruits satisfactorily there is a period of several weeks of chilling weather. A method sometimes practised is the scoring of a ring around a branch with a knife in the autumn to induce flowering on that branch in the following spring.

Under ideal conditions the crop will be on the tree about four months. Alternate spells of excessive watering and dry heat cause the fruit to split and fall to the ground. Splitting also occurs if the fruiting season is generally too dry. If the rind or shell of the fruit splits, the inner part, which is the edible part, will rot.

The fruit is ovate in shape and is covered with small rough tubercles. When mature the best varieties can be about 1in in diameter

IX *Medlar fruit, produced on short stems. The fruit is not ready for eating until November, or until it has been touched by frost*

X Mulberry tree and berries. The berries of a standard-type tree can be harvested by gently shaking them on to a sheet spread on the ground

and 1¼-1½in long. The colour of the skin or rind of most varieties is a rosy red when ripe, although some varieties remain green and some yellow. The rind is brittle and easily broken. If a piece of the rind is broken away at one end, then by pressing with the fingers the aril, or edible part, can be forced out into the mouth. The seed easily separates from the pearly white, translucent, fleshy and succulent aril surrounding it. The texture is pleasant. The fruit is sub-acid and has something of the flavour of the muscat grape together with its own distinctive and pleasant fragrance. It contains 10-15 per cent of soluble sugars and is a rich source of vitamin C.

The litchee quickly changes as it ripens and when ready for harvesting the coloured varieties become a bright rosy red. The maturity of the fruit can be judged by the flattening of the tubercles on the rind, giving a smoother appearance to the whole surface of the fruit. At maturity the fruits are harvested in their complete clusters or bunches, along with a portion of the branch and a few leaves. If harvested individually there is a risk that the rind may be broken where it is attached to the stem, and this quickly causes the aril inside to rot. If the fruits do have to be separated from the clusters they should be snipped off with a portion of the stem left on them. It is of no use picking the fruit while it is still green in anticipation that it will improve if kept a little; litchees harvested while still unripened remain insipid. Although fully ripe fruit may be kept up to three months at 30-45°F (1-7°C) in a refrigerator they will not keep longer than three days as a normal room temperature. They can be shelled and eaten days at normal room temperature. They can be shelled and eaten fresh, they may be dried like raisins, or preserved in syrup.

LONGAN (*Euphoria longana*)

Although only one species of the genus *Litchi* is cultivated for its fruit, there is a species of another genus which is very similar to it. This is the longan (*Euphoria longana*). It is, in fact, closely related to the litchee and at one time they were both classified together in the genus *Nephelium*. Pomologically the two fruits must be classed together and it is, therefore, dealt with here.

Longan is thought to be a native of Ceylon, southern India, Burma or China. It is found growing in areas, especially in China, where litchee is extensively cultivated or, more significantly, in adjacent

177

M

areas which are less favourable to litchee. It may, therefore, be considered to be a little hardier.

Longan is, in fact, a little more resistant to a cold, dry atmosphere and an alkaline soil than litchee. But it appears to require the same sort of check in a cool winter to induce it to flower well. As a tree it is generally stronger growing and carries larger leaves than litchee. The small flowers are borne on large upright and branched panicles. The fruits ripen later than litchee and are smaller, being less than 1in in diameter. The edible part, the aril, is similar except that it is not usually so sweet or sprightly.

Loquat

(JAPANESE MEDLAR; JAPANESE PLUM)

Classification	:	*Eriobotrya japonica.*
Physiology	:	Slightly tender evergreen shrub or small tree, growing 10-25ft tall.
Origin	:	Central China.
History	:	Cultivated for its fruit in China and Japan from antiquity. Now widely grown in sub-tropical areas. Introduced to Britain in 1787.
Recommended site	:	Indoors—pot plant. Glass lean-to—against the wall. Outdoors—only in well-sheltered sunny position.
Culinary uses	:	Eaten fresh for dessert. Used for jelly, jam and preserves. Stewed for pies.

The genus *Eriobotrya* consists of only a few species, all natives of eastern Asia. One species only is cultivated for its fruit. This is the loquat or *Eriobotrya japonica*. It is a native of central China but at some time was taken to Japan and in both countries it has, since antiquity, been cultivated for its fruit. Its cultivation in both countries has reached a very high development and several varieties of exceptional merit have originated there. Today it is commercially cultivated throughout the sub-tropical regions of the world. It arrived in the Mediterranean area in the nineteenth century, under the name of Japanese medlar, and is now widely grown in that area. It was introduced into Britain in 1787 but is still confined mostly to the gardens of large and stately homes.

It is an evergreen, well-rounded, low-spreading tree and attains a

Loquat

height of 10-25ft. Its dark green leathery leaves, about 12in long and growing from the succulent shoots, contrast strikingly with younger, grey-green, soft and downy leaves.

When grown outdoors in Britain it does best in the south-west—Cornwall, Devon and Somerset—where it has fruited successfully. It can be grown in the open against a wall in the London area, but it is shy to flower there; it does really like to be beside the seaside. Under ideal conditions a rainfall of 20-45in throughout the year suits it. Abundant moisture without waterlogging is required. Although a good summer is needed for it to flower in the open, the tree itself can resist frost, and when well hardened by cool weather it may withstand a temperature of 12°F (-11°C), although its young shoots are killed when the temperature is a little below freezing.

The loquat prefers a well-drained loam of good depth but will grow quite well on a wide variety of soils—from light sandy loam to a heavy soil. It will not do so well where there is a very marked gravelly sub-soil, an impervious clay soil, or soil containing a very high percentage of lime.

A good place for it to be grown is against the sunny back wall of a cold or slightly heated lean-to greenhouse. During the winter it should be watered moderately and then freely from April onwards. During hot weather a daily syringeing is beneficial. It can also be grown indoors as an ornamental pot plant but if left to itself it will grow quite fast, as much as 2ft in a year. Repotting should be carried out each year and by judicious pruning of the tap root it can be kept to a reasonable size.

Propagation can be from seed, budding, cuttings, grafting or layering. If grown from seed the tree develops very slowly; it will be many years before it bears fruit and it will not inherit the characteristics of the parent tree. Seed should be sown in late spring in pots containing light soil. Propagation by cuttings is usually difficult. The cuttings should be firm shoots taken in August and inserted in pots containing sandy soil which are then placed in a cool greenhouse or frame. Propagation by layering is much easier and may be commenced in the spring. The budding method is easy and economical. Rootstocks can be seedling loquat, pear or quince. When budded on to quince the tree takes on a dwarfish character and commences bearing at an earlier age. Also its fibrous root system allows easier transplanting. Loquat on quince rootstock is probably the best means of obtaining good loquat pot plants.

Young trees should be headed back at 2-2½ft so that three to five main branches are forced to develop. With grafted trees any growth from the rootstock, which will be below the union, should be removed. The loquat is by nature a compact-growing tree and requires less pruning than the deciduous fruit trees of the temperate zone. This, in fact, is the case with most evergreen fruit trees. Even so, branches must be cut back from time to time, preferably in April, so as to allow light into the centre of the tree. In older trees the dead and diseased branches must, of course, be cut out.

Flowers are produced intermittently from autumn to spring and are more profuse after a very hot summer. The flowers are yellowish white, fragrant, about half an inch broad, and they are borne in the terminal woolly panicles which are 4-8in long. They appear on the current season's growth and are borne in the apex of shoots 3-6 months old, after these have ceased growth. In some varieties of loquat the flowers are self-sterile, otherwise they are self-pollinating. The panicles usually contain 40-60 flowers but under ideal conditions there may be, at times, as many as 100. Not all the flowers will set fruit—perhaps only 10 or 12.

Thinning of fruit is practised where fruit of a larger size is required. The thinning may be of individual flowers, or whole flower panicles, or of the fruit itself. Thinning is also practised to lessen the tendency of trees to produce a large crop of small fruit one year, followed by a very small crop of large fruit the next year. The loquat is inclined to overwork itself; this should be discouraged.

The budded or grafted tree begins to bear a few fruits from the second or third year, a substantial crop in the sixth and reaches its peak when it is about 15 or 20 years old. The fruit is borne in loose clusters, and according to variety is round, oval or pyriform and 1-3in long. The colour can be pale yellow, reddish yellow, golden yellow, orange—the colours sometimes blending. The surface is somewhat downy and the skin has about the same texture as the plum, with a calyx somewhat like that of the pear. The flesh is a cream colour and juicy. The flavour is mild, sub-acid and sweet, enriched by an apple-like ester. The number of seeds may vary from two to ten but is rarely more than three or four. They are hard, brownish, shining and oblong,

Loquat

about half to three-quarters of an inch long. They separate easily from the fruit.

The fruit should be allowed to ripen on the tree to enable it to obtain its full flavour, sweetness and other qualities. Where the temperature is too high and there is insufficient water, as may happen in a warm greenhouse, the fruit remains small and may not ripen properly. On the other hand where the weather is cool and the days foggy or misty during the ripening period the fruit lacks sweetness and flavour. If the fruit is late in ripening a temperature falling to 25°F (−4°C) will kill the seed and cause the fruit to fall.

At harvesting the fruit clusters should be cut or clipped. The fruit is generally eaten fresh for dessert and very refreshing it is. It may also be used for making jelly, jam and preserves, or stewed and served as a sauce. Loquat pie made from loquats which have not fully ripened is said to be similar to cherry pie. The seeds should, however, be removed before cooking otherwise they impart a bitter flavour.

Apart from the climatic requirements for fruiting the loquat is easily cultivated and its sub-tropical appearance makes it a very pleasing small tree to have about the place.

Mandarin

Classification : *Citrus reticulata.*
Physiology : Small evergreen tree, without spines,
variable.
Origin : China or Indo-China.
History : Probably, like the orange, existed in
the East in prehistoric times; did not
reach Europe until 1805.
Recommended site : Indoors—pot cultivation.
Culinary uses : Eaten fresh for dessert; preserved in
syrup.

Citrus reticulata (mandarin) is one of the very important members of
the genus *Citrus*. It is here dealt with separately from the orange, not
because of any great difference in cultivation, but because it is a
separate species and the average person thinks of it as a different fruit.

There is little doubt that *Citrus reticulata* is a true species which has
developed separately from other *Citrus* species; if other *Citrus* species
are crossed they produce nothing like the mandarin. Clementines,
satsumas and tangerines are all considered to be mandarins and they
are all distinguished from the orange by their loose skins which almost
slip off without needing to be peeled. The true mandarin also has a
quite distinctive flavour.

The original habitat of the mandarin is thought to have been China
or Indo-China. Little is known of its history but it has probably been
cultivated by mankind as long as the orange—from the very earliest
times. There is no record of it having reached Europe until 1805.

The mandarin tree is very variable in its character but it is generally
small. Its branches are spineless and tend to be willowy and more

Mandarin

brittle than the orange. When bearing heavily the weight of the fruit may cause the branches to bend and almost touch the ground. It is a little more resistant to cold than the sweet orange and this is because at the onset of cool weather it quickly ceases growth. Among the *Citrus* trees resistance to cold in ascending order (ie least resistant first) is: pummelo, grapefruit, sweet orange, Seville orange, mandarin, kumquat, poncirus. A daily average temperature of lower than 60°F (16°C) will stop the growth of mandarin and this will cause it to be cold-resistant in comparison to other tender trees which do not quickly stop growth when cool weather commences.

The propagation and cultivation of mandarin will be dealt with here only briefly as it is broadly similar to that for orange. As is usual with the *Citrus* species (except pummelo and grapefruit) many varieties produce polyembryonic seeds. Polyembryony (see under Lime) is common in the *reticulata* species and because of this mandarins are often propagated commercially from seed. Two or three seedlings may be obtained from the one seed and if the zygotic seedlings (usually of poor growth) are removed then the remainder will be uniform trees resembling the mother tree which bore the fruit.

Given a good loam it can be grown in a 12in pot but because of the restriction of its roots it will be necessary to feed it with liquid fertiliser and to repot it every year. It needs a well-lighted greenhouse, the temperature of which should not be allowed to fall below 45°F (7°C) during the winter; early in spring it must rise to 60°F (16°C), so that growth can commence, and should reach 85°F (29°C) by midsummer.

Little pruning is required except for the removal of excessive growth. Mandarin grows fewer water sprouts than either lemon or sweet orange so there is less pruning to do in this respect.

Flowers are borne singly in the axils of leaves of growing new shoots, or in clusters in the axils of leaves of a preceding growth flush, as in the case of the sweet orange. In its natural habitat, where warm weather is more or less continuous, it bears flowers at more than one time of the year and has more than one growth flush, something like the lemon. But in the winter conditions of cool temperate climates, with poor light, it will have a single blossom time like the sweet orange.

Cross-pollination of the flowers is rarely necessary but it may increase the incidence of setting and also influence the number of seeds in the nearly seedless varieties. Satsuma varieties are seedless or nearly so, but when the flowers receive pollen from another variety they tend to produce more seeds. This also applies to seedlessness in clementines.

Fruit should be ready for picking by Christmas. In the true mandarin varieties when the fruit becomes mature the rind is rough and loose. When matured in a temperature suitable for them the segments are tender, soft, juicy, sweet and fragrant. Mandarins are lower in ascorbic acid than sweet oranges but are higher in carotinoides.

The satsuma varieties, when not properly matured, are more acid and have more of the flavour of the orange. They can be spoilt in this way if temperatures have been too low during the ripening period. In fact the flavour of all mandarin types or varieties tend to be more impaired by low temperatures than the sweet oranges.

The range of fruit and tree characters within the species is wide. There is no point in describing commercial varieties but it may be useful to define the types.

TYPES WITHIN THE SPECIES

KING MANDARIN

This is a typical but large mandarin. The rind is rather thick and rough. The flavour is pleasant when grown in a high temperature but is too acid when the temperature is low.

MEDITERRANEAN MANDARIN

Trees are thickly branched and bushy. They bear small, tight-skinned, sweet, aromatic fruit.

TANGERINE

A more upright tree. Fruits are a deep orange or orange-red colour. The fruit is sweet and aromatic or spicy.

SATSUMA

This tree tends to be dwarfish and spreading. The fruit is medium to large for a mandarin. The rind is thin, separates easily from the segments but when over-ripe is becomes puffy. It is seedless or nearly so, tender-fleshed, sweet and pleasant (when grown in a high temperature).

Mandarin

CLEMENTINE

A small Algerian tree. The fruits are small but very rich and aromatic. They develop a good flavour in temperatures too low for satsumas. The seeds from clementines are, as far as is known, all zygotic. If, therefore, you try growing clementines from seed there is no telling what sort of trees they will turn out to be.

Mango

Classification	:	*Mangifera indica.*
Physiology	:	Tropical tree growing under natural conditions 50-60ft tall.
Origin	:	East Indies, Malaya.
History	:	Cultivated in India 4,000 years ago. Recorded as having been cultivated in hot-houses in England at end of the seventeenth century. Reached West Indies and American continent in eighteenth century. Grown commercially in Florida and Mexico.
Recommended site	:	Warm greenhouse—in large container or in the border.
Culinary uses	:	Used for all dessert purposes.

There are about forty other species of *Mangifera* besides *Mangifera indica* growing in southern Asia and on the islands to the south and south-east of New Zealand and the Philippines. About thirteen of these other species are grown in a small way for their fruit. It is quite likely that at some time they have hybridized with *Mangifera indica,* the mango which is described by some as the king of tropical fruits.

The original home of the mango is believed to have been somewhere in eastern Asia and the Malayan archipelago, and it seems to have been cultivated in India for over 4,000 years. Among Hindus both the tree and foliage play a part in religious ceremony and folklore.

History has it that the Mogul emperor Akbar (1556-1605) planted an orchard of 100,000 mango trees, but long before that a Chinese traveller, Hwen T'sang, had brought the tree to the outside world.

Mango

This was between AD 632 and 640. History also has it that the cultivation of the mango under glass was attempted in Europe somewhere about 1700—quite a time ago. The following passage is quoted from *Curtis's Botanical Magazine* in 1850:

> The Mango is recorded as having been grown in the hot-houses of this country at least 160 years ago but it is only within the last 20 years that it has come to the notice as a fruit capable of being brought to perfection in England. The first and we believe the most successful attempt was made by the Earl of Powis in his garden at Walcot where he had a lofty hot-house 400 feet long and between 30 feet and 40 feet wide constructed for the cultivation of the Mango and other rare and tropical fruit but since then it has been known to grow and bear in other gardens.

It will be appreciated that for mango cultivation in England a lofty and heated greenhouse is essential. The mango is a tropical tree and under natural conditions will grow up to 60ft and will live to a good old age. Being tropical it cannot stand frost, and a hot period is necessary for the full development of its fruit. An air temperature of 26°F (−3°C) can badly damage mature trees and completely kill young ones. Although the mango seems to grow far less than guava when there is a mean summer temperature below 65°F (18°C), it is less apt to show injury to its leaves and shoots. However, in such a low temperature the ripening of the fruit is delayed considerably.

Under natural conditions the mango grows well where a good rainfall for 4 months is followed by a period of dry and rainless weather for 8 months. Rainless weather during the period of flowers and fruit ripening gives the best crops. It also grows in humid tropical regions where the rainfall is heavy throughout the year, but there the fruit production is not so good. The best regions of cultivation are undoubtedly where there is a well-marked dry season. Thus it can be deduced that humid hot-house conditions are not required continuously.

When propagating from seed it is necessary to know that there are two distinct races of mango. One race produces seed which is monoembryonic (one embryo) and the other seed which is polyembryonic (several embryos). Because of this the seedlings of some varieties may be so nearly all apometical (see under Lime) that sowing of seed is a satisfactory method of propagation. In a very general context the

188

varieties from India are monoembryonic and those from the Philippines and America are polyembryonic. The polyembryonic seed produces sprouts all of which, or all but one, will be apometical. Sometimes, however, several sprouts may appear to grow from the one seed but they are in fact shoots from only one seedling and have commenced growing from it underground. Such shoots from the one seedling may be either apometical or zygotic.

Mango seeds are rather perishable and unable to withstand much drying. Seeds which have been kept at temperatures lower than 50°F (10°C) do not germinate very well. At tropical temperatures they germinate in 3 weeks in an uneven manner. They will, however, germinate in 2 weeks and more evenly if the tough endocarp is removed before sowing. When this is done they must be sown in a sterilized compost otherwise many of them may rot. The seed should be sown not more than 1in deep, the soil being well pressed down and kept moist. When the seedlings are about 6in tall they may be transplanted to their own pots but they must be kept well watered as they are rather sensitive to root damage. They take a number of years to reach maturity.

Mango can also be propagated by cuttings taken in late summer and rooted in a propagating frame with bottom heat. In warm countries inarching is usually practised. The stock seedlings are suitable when they are about a year old and grafting is done during a period of active growth.

The mango tree is one of the most resistant to shallow and impervious soil but it develops a widely-spread root system. It must, therefore, be planted in large containers or in the greenhouse border; a well-drained compost consisting of one part peat and one part good loam is considered to be best for it. About 2 months before flowering, which is usually in July, the tree should be manured with one part manure, a half-part wood ash and a quarter-part bonemeal. After the planting very little pruning is required except to keep the tree to its required shape and a reasonable size. Tall, thinly branched trees should be cut back when young to make them branch lower down. Weak and crossing branches should be removed. Branches must be exposed to as much light as possible but it must also be remembered that every branch that is healthy is a potential fruit producer provided it is fully exposed to all the light and sunshine possible.

Mango

The grafted mango may begin to flower as early as its first year but all flowers should be removed as soon as they appear. This should be done during the first 3 years because it is desirable to build up the young tree and in any case these early flowers very seldom set fruits. The time of flowering is influenced by light and temperature. The amount of blossom is partly determined (under natural conditions) by the dryness of the atmosphere in the 3 months preceding the flowering —a dry atmosphere with plenty of light stimulates flowering. Experimentation under glasshouse conditions is necessary to establish the connection between flowering and humidity.

Mango produces its blossom mostly from the terminal buds of its shoots and very rarely from its axillary buds. The inflorescences are often in large branched panicles containing several hundred flowers which are pinkish and fragrant. These inflorescences tend to contain some imperfect flowers and in some varieties more than 5 per cent of the flowers are imperfect. Hand pollination can be advantageous.

About 5 months are required from flower to fruit. The fruit is a large drupe with a hard endocarp. The smallest are not much bigger than plums, whilst others may be 6in long and some weigh 2 or 3lb. They are yellow and red in colour, speckled with black, and usually kidney-shaped. They contain one large flattened seed surrounded by yellow to orange-coloured flesh which is juicy with a rich spicy flavour.

The fruit of the mango is a better source of vitamin A than the orange and also a fair source of vitamins B and C. Some varieties in fact are considered to be a better source of vitamin C than the orange. The fruit can be used for all kinds of dessert purposes and green mango can be used for chutney.

The best time to pick the fruit is when the green colour has almost faded but when the flesh is still firm. When harvested before they are fully ripe and kept for a few days their sweetness and general quality will improve. When possible it is better to pick the fruits with a half-inch or one inch of stalk left on them.

For anyone who has or can provide the facilities, the growing of mango offers many rewards. The Buddha, for example, was given a grove of mangoes so that he could sit peacefully in their shade and meditate. Meditation is sometimes the most refreshing and enjoyable of all occupations—the fruits of it far surpassing even those gained from gardening.

Manzanita

(BEARBERRY)

Classification	:	*Arctostaphylos* species.
Physiology	:	Small, evergreen trees or creeping, spreading shrubs. Ardent lovers of acid soils.
Origin	:	Mainly southern USA and Mexico, but one species native to Britain.
History	:	Spaniards called them 'Little Apples' but there is no record that they cultivated them. Californian species were introduced into Britain in the last century but they remain rare.
Recommended site	:	Outdoors—peaty, sunny position.
Culinary uses	:	Used like cranberries for jellies, sauces etc.

Arctostaphylos is a genus of small evergreen trees and shrubs which thrive under heathland conditions. Most of them are from warm climates and need a sunny position. These 'warm-blooded' species are generally called manzanitas. The species which is native to Britain is, of course, used to a cooler climate, and a sunny position is not quite so important. This species is usually known as bearberry.

The early Spanish pioneers in America no doubt ate the manzanitas, even though they did not cultivate them. Manzanita is, in fact, a Spanish word meaning little apple. Although some of the California species were introduced into Britain in the last century they remain rare. Certainly there has been little thought of using their fruit.

Manzanita

Manzanitas can be used in the same way as cranberries and, because of their rarity, add to the garden treasure. The berries have an agreeable taste. Those of the hardiest species are like bright red currants but the true manzanitas are brown-red in colour.

DETAILS OF SPECIES

MANZANITA (*Arctostaphylos manzanita*)

This is a native of California. It is a small shrub or tree which will grow up to 8ft tall in cooler climates. Unfortunately it does not propagate easily from seed, nor will cuttings root easily. If seeds can be obtained it might help if they are put into boiling water for about 15 seconds. The tree or shrub is rare in Britain but it may be obtainable from some nurserymen.

If you can obtain it the best time for planting is in the autumn. It should be grown in a peaty, well-drained soil in a sunny position. It must not be forgotten that the manzanitas and bearberries, in general, love an acid soil which will allow them to have a mutual and beneficial relationship with the root fungus mycorrhiza. Once planted, manzanita should be left undisturbed as it does not like having its roots interfered with.

Its pinkish white, urn-shaped flowers are produced in short terminal panicles from March to April. Pollination in Britain is often poor. The berries are one-third to half an inch in diameter and are brownish red in colour.

BIGBERRY MANZANITA (*Arctostaphylos glauca*)

This is a native of southern California and is a tree which grows to 14ft. Its bark is reddish brown. Propagation of this species from cuttings is easier than for *A. manzanita* but seed is also difficult. It needs to be planted in a warm, sunny position.

The white or pinkish flowers are produced in pendulous panicles from May to June. The berries are brownish and three-quarters of an inch in diameter. The size of the berries makes this a promising species.

PINE or GREENLEAF MANZANITA (*Arctostaphylos patula*)

A native of western North America with a habitat in open coni-

XI (left) Orange tree with blossom and first fruit. When propagated vegetatively an orange tree may begin to fruit at three years; (right) Nectarine with fruit. Note the compactness of the tree

XII Passion flower and fruit. The fruits have a hard leathery rind and suffer no harm if they fall to the ground

ferous forest. It is a spreading, much branched shrub from 3-7ft tall. Its stems have a bright red-brown bark which contrast with its evergreen, bright green leaves.

Flowers are pinkish or white, urn-shaped, and produced in corymbs or loose panicles. The berries are globose but flattened at the apex. In colour they are dark brown to almost black and one-third to half an inch in diameter.

This is one of the best manzanitas for growing in Britain; it can stand more open conditions than either *A. manzanita* or *A. glauca*.

COLUMBIA MANZANITA (*Arctostaphylos columbiana*)

This is a shrub with a more northerly range than any of the preceding. It grows from western USA as far north as British Columbia. It reaches a height of 3-5ft, has an irregular habit in its growth, and its young wood is covered with dense hairs. It propagates fairly well from cuttings.

White flowers are produced from March to May in dense drooping racemes, mainly from the ends of the previous season's growth but also from the axils of some of the leaves. The berries are bright red and are about one-third of an inch in diameter.

BEARBERRY (*Arctostaphylos uva-ursi*)

This grows in many places in the cool temperate regions of the northern hemisphere. It lives on the mountains, in sub-arctic forests, and also in pine forests. It grows wild in the northern parts of Britain, especially the Scottish Highlands, tolerating a wide range of different conditions including rock, screes, sandy banks and pine forest, and is a good rock-garden plant. It can be used to form a low evergreen ground cover. The evergreen, leathery leaves turn red in the autumn. Rose-coloured flowers are produced in small, drooping terminal clusters from April to June. The berries are globular, a quarter of an inch to one-third of an inch in diameter, scarlet in colour and shining. A pleasing plant at all times.

NEVADA BEARBERRY (*Arctostaphylos nevadensis*)

This is a mountain plant from the Sierra Nevada and is closely allied to the *A. uva-ursi*. It is a prostrate creeping shrub with scarlet berries.

193

N

Marmelos

(BAEL FRUIT; JAPANESE BITTER ORANGE)

Classification : *Aegle marmelos.*
Physiology : A deciduous, spiny tree, growing to 10ft tall.
Origin : India.
History : Grows wild in India and south-eastern Asia but the fruit is seldom eaten in those parts and certainly never cultivated.
Recommended site : Warm greenhouse—pot plant.
Culinary uses : Pulp can be used for refreshing drinks.

Aegle marmelos is the only species in the genus *Aegle* and it is closely related to *Citrus* though it is not an evergreen. It is a small deciduous tree which grows up to 10ft and its stout green stems are heavily armed with spines. But the spines are compensated for by the large white, fragrant flowers that give much pleasure in April. It seems to be a native of northern India and grows wild in many places there. Yet, despite the scarcity of food in those parts its fruit is seldom taken for food.

The marmelos tree can easily be propagated from seed sown in a warm temperature. Also cuttings of ripe wood can be taken in late summer and inserted in moist sand in a propagating frame with bottom heat. It makes a fairly good pot plant in a warm greenhouse—a good rich loamy soil is necessary. The round fruit is about 2-5in in diameter and greenish yellow in colour. The rind, smooth, hard and thin, contains a pulp with many seeds. The pulp is said to make a very refreshing drink.

Mediterranean medlar

Classification   : *Crataegus azaroles.*
Physiology   : A small, slightly spiny, deciduous tree growing 20-30ft tall.
Origin   : Western Asia; southern Europe.
History   : Tree cultivated for its fruit in eastern Mediterranean countries.
Recommended site : Outdoors—open position.
Culinary uses   : Used for jellies; eaten out of hand.

The genus *Crataegus* causes confusion because it comprises many hundreds of species, some of them so much alike that it is difficult to distinguish between the true species and the natural hybrids. About 200 of the species, shrubs and small trees, are natives of the northern hemisphere and included amongst them is the hawthorn.

They are relatives of the apple and about twenty species can be considered as offering edible fruits. The one most cultivated for its fruit is *Crataegus azaroles*, commonly known as the Mediterranean medlar. It probably originated in western Asia and from there was taken to south-eastern Europe and North Africa. It has been cultivated in England since the seventeenth century but not for its fruit.

The tree is small, only slightly spiny and grows 20-30ft tall. Although it will thrive on all kinds of soil it does not like to be in a waterlogged position and needs to be in an open, sunny place.

It can be propagated from seed though germination does not usually take place until the second year after sowing. The seed should preferably be stratified in moist sand or peat and kept in moist cold conditions to allow it to continue ripening. After this cold period there needs to be a warm period during which organisms in the soil soften

195

Mediterranean medlar

the hard outer covering of the seed. Once the young tree is big enough to be moved it should be planted in its permanent position; it does not like to be moved from place to place. The only pruning it requires is to keep it to a convenient size.

White flowers with purple anthers are produced in June in densely flowered corymbs. The fruits are abundantly produced and are of fairly large size—up to an inch in diameter. They resemble very small apples and are in fact pomes, like apples. In colour they are whitish yellow or orange and contain three to five hard seeds which are surrounded by a pulpy flesh with an apple flavour.

Although the Mediterranean medlar is the most cultivated of the species this is possibly because it was the best local species available in that area. There are, however, numerous species with worthwhile fruit from various other areas.

OTHER CRATAEGUS SPECIES WORTH CULTIVATING

CHINESE HAWBERRY (*Crataegus pinnatifida major*)

This is a native of northern China. It is a small tree which grows up to 25ft. It carries only short thorns or spines, sometimes none at all.

White flowers are produced about the end of May. In China this tree has been very widely cultivated for its fruit which was candied and strung on sticks and used to be a common sight in the markets. The fruits are about an inch in diameter, deep red in colour and spotted with tiny dots.

BLACK HAWBERRY (*Crataegus douglasii*)

A native of western North America, it is a tree which grows up to 30ft. Short thorns only are carried and sometimes none at all. White flowers are produced during May in corymbs. Fruits are glossy, purplish black or black and agreeable in taste.

SYRIAN HAWBERRY (*Crataegus tanacetifolia*)

This is a native of Syria and the surrounding countries. It grows up to 35ft and is usually unarmed. The flowers are white, fragrant, and produced in clusters in June. The fruit is yellow, touched with red, three-quarters of an inch to one inch in diameter, with an apple aroma and an apple taste.

MANZANILLA (*Crataegus pubesen stipulata*)

A native of Mexico growing on the mountains at an altitude of 3,000-9,000ft. It can withstand heavy frosts but likes a dry climate. Sometimes it is a shrub, sometimes a small tree growing to 15ft. White flowers are produced in June in corymbs.

It appears to have been cultivated for its fruits long ago in the early civilizations of the South American Indians. The fruits resemble small apples—the largest of them being nearly 2in in diameter and the average 1in—and they are yellow in colour. The flesh is mealy and not so juicy as that of a good apple.

MISSISSIPI HAWBERRY (*Crataegus coccinioides*)

A round-headed tree from the Mississippi basin, growing 15-20ft tall. It can take the form of a large shrub. White flowers with red stamens are produced in June in groups or clusters consisting of from four to seven flowers. The fruit is about five-eighths of an inch in diameter, roundish but flattened at both ends, bright red in colour and very juicy.

Medlar

Classification	:	*Mespilus germanica.*
Physiology	:	A small, much-branched, deciduous tree growing not more than 20ft high.
Origin	:	Persia.
History	:	Known to the ancient Greeks. Possibly brought to England by the Romans. Much cultivated in bygone days.
Recommended site	:	Outdoors in sunny, open position.
Culinary uses	:	Eaten raw after 'bletting'. Makes excellent jelly.

Mespilus germanica is the sole species of its genus although it is closely related to the genus *Pyrus* in which it was formerly classified. It is thought to have originated somewhere in the region of Persia from whence it spread to south-eastern Europe. It was already known to the Greeks by 300 BC.

Although it grows wild in the southern half of England where it will sometimes be found in hedgerows it is generally considered that it is not a true native but has been naturalized over the years. But if this is so it is not known when or how it was first brought to England. The Romans may have been responsible, but there is no evidence for this. For a long time it was cultivated in gardens for its fruit—but tastes change as fashions change and the easier import of foreign fruits perhaps caused it to lose favour.

The medlar tree is a slow-growing and much-branched tree. It is deciduous, and the wild tree, if not the cultivated variety, is slightly spinous. Apart from its fruit it makes an acceptable specimen tree

198

and when grown as a pyramid it looks well in the small garden.

It is possible to propagate medlar from seed sown 1in deep in the open garden in the autumn. The seed germinates fairly well but the seedlings may be spiny and seldom produce fruit as good as that from which the seed came. The best method of propagation is by budding or cleft-grafting on to seedling pear, quince, hawthorn or medlar rootstock. Budding should be done in July and grafting in April. Quince seedlings make the best rootstock when dwarf trees are required.

The medlar is in no way choosy about soil but it prefers a sunny location. It can be planted out any time from November to February. Actually it is very easy to grow and few cultivation details are necessary. Very little pruning is required except to cut out any dead and diseased wood, and to thin out a branch or two if necessary to prevent them crossing. It should be done in the winter and be as light as possible because the flowers (and fruit) are produced on the terminal ends of branches as well as on the old spurs.

The solitary white or pinkish flowers, something like wild rose flowers, are produced usually in June on short hairy stalks, and when in blossom the tree is quite attractive. The flowers are self-fertile and are followed by brown-coloured fruit with flattened open ends.

The fruits are roundish or pear-shaped and crowned with a broad hairy disc which is fringed with leafy calyx. They are not ready to be picked until late October or early November, preferably not until after the first sharp frost, and are then not ready for eating (being hard and extremely astringent) until they have been stored for a few weeks. They should be gathered on a dry day and stored calyx downwards in a cool, light place until they have almost reached the point of decay. They are then said to be 'bletted' (ie they have become soft and mellow) and have an agreeable acid taste. Fruits that have just begun to ripen but are not too soft make an excellent jelly, orange in colour and of a distinctive flavour.

If you do not want the trouble of picking and storing the fruits they can be allowed to fall to the ground and when mellow picked up and eaten.

A seventeenth-century book on astrological and herbal physic says, 'the fruit is old Saturn's, and sure a better medicine he hardly hath to strengthen the retentive faculty; therefore it stays women's longings.

Medlar

The good old man cannot endure women's minds should they run a-gadding'. If this be true about old Saturn he must, in those days, have been an old meddler!

VARIETIES OBTAINABLE

The varieties in existence are all old ones. The fruit was esteemed in the Middle Ages but there has been little development since then.

DUTCH—large, roundish fruits, $2\frac{1}{2}$in in diameter with short sepals. Greyish green until ripe, when they are brown. They ripen in October and are ready by Christmas. The tree is a good bearer and is useful for general cultivation.

NOTTINGHAM—medium-sized, pear-shaped fruit, 1in in diameter with long sepals. Yellow-brown in colour, touched with russet. They have a good flavour. The tree is less vigorous than the variety known as Dutch, and is suitable as a bush or pyramid.

ROYAL—medium-sized, round-shaped fruits, 1in in diameter. They have a good flavour and are pleasantly acid. The tree is a good bearer and makes a good small standard tree. It is a newer variety than the others.

STONELESS—small, turbinate-shaped fruits. Russet brown in colour. Moderate flavour. They keep well after harvesting.

Mombin fruit

Classification : *Spondias species.*
Physiology : Tropical trees, growing 10-60ft tall.
Origin : Tropical America; Asia.
History : Cultivated for their fruits in tropical countries. Introduced into Britain in the early eighteenth century as hot-house subjects.
Recommended site : Warm greenhouse or conservatory.
Culinary uses : For dessert—raw or cooked.

There are about ten or twelve species of *Spondias*, a few of which bear edible, plum-like fruits. They are natives of tropical Asia and America and their fruits are to be seen in the public markets of those parts. They are cultivated in some tropical countries.

Introduction to Britain was in the early eighteenth century, where of course they need hot-house treatment. They can be propagated best from cuttings of half-ripened shoots inserted in a sandy soil in a propagating frame in a temperature of 75°F (24°C). Their location needs to be a well-drained border in a greenhouse or conservatory. From March to September the temperature should be 65-75°F (18-24°C) and from September to March 50-55°F (10-13°C). The soil in which they are grown should be a sandy fibrous loam. During the time when they are in growth they should be freely watered, but only moderately when not in growth.

RECOMMENDED FRUITING SPECIES

OTAHEITE APPLE (*Spondias cytherea*)
A native of the Society Islands where it may grow to 50ft and have

a trunk diameter of 1½ft. It is dressed in bright green pinnate leaves 1ft long with 11-23 leaflets. Small greenish-white flowers form in terminal clusters. Female, male and bisexual flowers are produced on the same tree.

The fruits are globular to egg-shaped, 3-4in long and golden yellow in colour. They are thick skinned, have a large seed, but are juicy and have an apple-like spicy flavour.

YELLOW MOMBIN or HOG PLUM (*Spondias mombin*)
A West Indies species growing to 30ft. The tree has a wide crown —its few branches growing nearly horizontal. Yellow-green pinnate leaves have 9-19 leaflets. Thorn-like corky growths are produced on the bark of the tree and this is the only species of the genus with this peculiar characteristic. Fragrant yellow-white, five-petalled flowers are produced in long panicles. The egg-shaped yellow fruits are about 1in long and sub-acid to sweet. Compared with the Otaheite apple it has less pulp around the large seed.

RED or SPANISH MOMBIN (*Spondias purpurea*)
A native of tropical America where it may grow to 30ft and have a trunk about 1ft in diameter. It carries heavy, brittle branches with stout twigs. The yellow-green leaves have 9-25 leaflets. Small red or pink flowers are produced in small lateral clusters or inflorescences on the older wood. The fruits are yellow to purplish red, are up to 1¼in long and sub-acid to acid. They are an important fruit in Mexico and Central America.

MALAYAN MOMBIN (*Spondias pinnata*)
Widely cultivated in Malaysia for its fruit. It is a small tree growing 10-12ft. The egg-shaped fruits are about the size of a small mango and are produced when its leaves have been cast off.

Monstera

Classification	:	*Monstera deliciosa.*
Physiology	:	A vigorous, ornamental, evergreen climber or aroid.
Origin	:	Mexico.
History	:	Frequently cultivated as an ornamental plant but has rarely been grown for its unusual fruit.
Recommended site	:	Warm greenhouse or sun lounge.
Culinary uses	:	For dessert—eaten fresh.

The genus *Monstera* consists of about thirty species of evergreen climbers, coming mainly from South America. Amongst the species only one, *Monstera deliciosa*, offers an unusual fruit, and this, though sometimes grown as an indoor plant, is seldom grown or thought of as a fruit plant.

It is an ornamental climber with large leaves which are broad with long lobes and curiously perforated, dark green and leathery. It is also an aroid—that is, it produces aerial roots—and it is by attaching its roots to any support within its reach that it climbs.

Propagation can be from stem cuttings which have two or more segments or buds. These can be taken at any time of the year provided they are inserted in a sandy compost and in a temperature of 70-80°F (21-27°C). Seed can also be germinated under similar conditions.

It can be planted in the border of a warm greenhouse or in a pot so that it can be kept in a sun lounge or other suitable place indoors. A compost of peat, leafmould, loam and sand suits it well. During the winter months a temperature of 55-65°F (13-18°C) is required, and during the summer months it should be syringed and watered freely.

203

Monstera

The flowers are a greenish-yellow spadix with honeycomb-like markings and enclosed in a waxy white spathe. The spadix develops into a large fruit in the shape of an ear of maize but larger in size. From the time of flowering to the maturity of the fruit takes 14 months or more.

When fully mature the green colour of the fruit turns yellow and the scales which cover the surface gradually fall off. The fruit can be cut from the stem and placed in a glass of water. It ripens from the base upwards gradually and not all at the same time so that a portion can be eaten at a time as it ripens, provided it can be stored properly, preferably in a refrigerator.

The soft pulp of the fruit has a pineapple-banana odour and a sweetish pleasant taste.

Mulberry

(BLACK MULBERRY)

Classification	:	*Morus nigra.*
Physiology	:	Deciduous tree, slender but with numerous branches. Growing 20-30ft tall. Sometimes a leaning or crooked tree.
Origin	:	Persia.
History	:	Introduced into Europe by Greeks. Held in great esteem by Romans. In Britain many trees planted during reign of King James I—some still alive today.
Recommended site	:	Outdoors—in southern England open position; in north against a wall. Pot cultivation for patio, etc.
Culinary uses	:	Fresh for dessert; for tarts etc; for jam; for wine and other beverages.

Morus is a member of the Moraceae family of which the fig, breadfruit and rubber tree are also members. There are about ten species of the genus *Morus* but only two or three are usually cultivated and one in particular—*Morus nigria* or the black mulberry.

The black mulberry is believed to have come originally from Persia but it is now naturalized in those parts of Europe which have a mild climate. It was introduced into Europe by the Greeks, and the Romans later held it in great esteem. During the reign of King James I about 100,000 trees were planted in the eastern and midland counties. The mulberry is very long lived and some of these gnarled and crooked

Mulberry

old-world trees can still be seen today in the grounds of manor houses. The mulberry tree is by nature a very spreading, large-headed tree but it takes many years for it to reach this venerable form.

It can be easily propagated from seed but the seedlings take a long time to commence bearing. The best methods of cultivation are by cuttings or layering and both are easy and successful. Cuttings are taken in October or November from shoots of the current year's growth. These cuttings should be about 1in long with a heel of 2-year-old wood about 3in long. Insert them outdoors in a shady position, with two or three bud eyes showing above the ground. Roots will have formed by the following autumn and they can then be lifted and planted wherever required. Another successful method is to saw off a branch about 5ft long. The subsidiary branches on its lower end should be trimmed off leaving an 18in stem. This is inserted in the ground 18in deep where the tree is desired to grow. When this is done in October it will root and in a year or so a small fruit-bearing tree or bush will result. Layering is also easy. If this is done in summer or early autumn the branch will have rooted enough for it to be severed or weaned from the mother tree by the following autumn.

The best time to plant the mulberry tree is in spring. The soil will be warming up then and the tree likes a warm, rich, loamy soil. Unless it can be given plenty of moisture in dry weather it should not be planted on dry gravelly or chalky soils which only have a shallow loam top soil. Although the mulberry is often seen growing on lawns or in grassy parkland the best fruit is obtained where the tree is grown in cultivated soil.

The tree can be grown in various forms: as a tall standard with a 6ft stem; as a low standard on a 3ft stem; as a bush or pyramid tree. It can also be fan-trailed against a south wall and in the north of Britain it should always be grown this way. It is also a good subject for pot cultivation provided it is not allowed to dry out during the summer. A dwarf bush or pyramid can be grown in a 10in pot without any special treatment.

Standard trees require no pruning except for the removal of any dead wood and the thinning out of any branches that are causing overcrowding. This should be done during the winter. *Pyramid* trees need to have the lateral growth shortened to about six leaves in July to form spurs. The leaders, unless these are very strong growing, should not be touched and in any case only the tops of these leaders should be removed. *Wall* trees need to have the branches trained a foot apart, and in the summer all side shoots should be cut back to six leaves to form spurs. *Pot* trees need repotting each year before new growth commences. Laterals should be cut back to form short spurs and the leaders nipped where necessary.

In dry weather the mulberry tree, however it is grown, will benefit from occasional watering. Wall, bush and pot trees if they are fruiting heavily should be given a feed of weak liquid manure. When grown in the open ground the soil round about the tree should be forked over in spring and autumn.

In May the flowers form catkin-like spikes and are borne on the previous year's growth as well as on the spurs of older wood. They are greenish white, inconspicuous and unisexual. The staminate (male) flowers are in slender catkins, a half to one inch long. The pistillate (female) flowers are in shorter and thicker catkins.

After the female flowers have been fertilized they develop into an oblong, juicy berry, something like the loganberry in shape. The fruit is in fact a cluster of drupes about three-quarters of an inch to one inch long. When ripe in August and September it is purplish black in colour and has dark red juice with an agreeable acid flavour. The refreshing juice makes it a very acceptable fruit for all culinary uses —fresh for dessert, for tarts, for jam, for wine or other beverages. When not thoroughly ripe it makes very nice tarts and pies. If allowed to become very ripe during September it loses its bright crimson colour, becomes almost black and it is then pleasant when eaten fresh.

It is a fruit highly esteemed and recommended by birds. That is why dwarf pyramids are useful—they can be easily netted against birds. The fruit on the pot, wall, or dwarf bush and pyramid tree can be gathered by hand. With taller trees this is not so easy and the best way to gather the fruit from them is to spread a sheet under the branches and then give the tree a gentle shake. The ripe fruit will then fall.

Because the fruit ripens rather irregularly it is available over a fairly long period. It is surprising that the mulberry has not been grown commercially.

OTHER MULBERRIES

WHITE MULBERRY (*Morus alba*)

A native of China, it is a tree which has been much cultivated for its leaves, which provide food for the silkworm. It is a low-branched tree growing up to 30ft. Flowers appear in May in the leaf axils and at the base of new shoots. The female flowers are in catkin-like spikes one-third of an inch to one inch long; the male spikes are longer. The fruit is half an inch to one inch long, white or pinkish. Sweet and insipid.

RUSSIAN MULBERRY (*Morus alba tarica*)

This is merely a variety of *Morus alba* but is much hardier.

MONGOLIAN MULBERRY (*Morus mongolica*)

A native of Korea and China. This is a shrub-like tree growing up to 25ft. The male catkins are 1-1½in long with a bare stalk one-third of an inch long. The female catkins are shorter. The fruit is pale red and sweet.

KOREAN MULBERRY (*Morus acidosa*)

A bush or shrub-like tree whose native habitat appears to be Korea. It grows to about 10ft. Male catkins are up to 1¼in long and the female catkins only one-third as long. The fruit is dark red, juicy and sweet.

RED MULBERRY (*Morus rubra*)

A native of North America, it is the largest growing of the mulberries —up to 40ft tall. Its trunk is stout and comparatively short; its branches are spreading and comparatively few. In its homeland it is often found growing along the banks of streams. Although it was introduced to England in the seventeenth century it has never, for some reason, done very well. It does, moreover, need a rich, well watered soil.

The male catkins are about 2in long and the female catkins about 1in. The fruit is 1-1½in, cylindrical, bright red but turning almost to purplish when ripe. It is sweet, slightly sub-acid and piquant.

Nectarine

Classification	:	*Prunus persica* var. *nectarina*.
Physiology	:	A deciduous tree growing to 25ft but kept much smaller in cultivation.
Origin	:	Possibly China.
History	:	Originated as a natural 'sport' of the peach and known for at least 2,000 years. Like the peach introduced to Europe via Persia. Reached England in the sixteenth century. Today over fifty varieties of nectarine grown in USA.
Recommended site	:	Outdoors—only on a south or south-west wall. Indoors—in the glass house as a pot tree or grown in the border; in the sun lounge as a pot tree.
Culinary uses	:	Used for dessert; for preserving; for jam.

The nectarine is a natural 'sport', or mutation, of the peach (*Prunus persica*) and related therefore to the apricot, cherry and plum. Sometimes a peach tree will bear a nectarine fruit and a nectarine tree a peach fruit. This is evidence of the oneness of the peach and nectarine and the mutation which has occurred.

The peach itself is believed to have originated in China but there is no actual evidence of this except that there is a peach with a white-fleshed fruit which is indigenous to China. Where or how the yellow-fleshed variety first occurred is not known, but it came to Europe from

209

P

Nectarine

Persia. The history of the nectarine, therefore, goes back 2,000 years at least, merging into that of the peach. It came to England in the sixteenth century but, perhaps because it is not quite so hardy, it never became quite as well known as the peach. The varieties now grown are all old ones, dating back to the last century and earlier, showing that little has been done in improving them. In the USA over fifty varieties of nectarine are grown. These are mainly yellow-fleshed varieties and they are grown in the eastern states from New York to Michigan and also in the Pacific coastal region. White-fleshed varieties are grown commercially in California.

The shape of the tree and its leaf characteristics are the same as the peach. Its cultivation is also the same as for the peach, except that because it is a little less hardy its location is restricted and it is not, in England at any rate, grown in open ground to the same extent as the peach. Like the peach it can be easily propagated from seed but the resulting tree does not necessarily come true to the parent of the fruit from which the seed or stone was obtained. However, the seed or stones can be buried outdoors 2in deep and left all winter. In the spring, when germination has taken place, the seedlings can be carefully put into individual pots. By the following spring they will have become maiden trees.

The usual method of propagating nectarines is by budding chosen varieties on to seedling plum or peach rootstock during July or early August. When plum rootstock is used the variety Common Mussel produces the smallest nectarine tree; St Julien produces a medium-sized tree, and Brompton the largest tree. Plum rootstock is considered to be the best on heavy soil but peach rootstock grows fewer suckers than the plum.

Because the nectarine is less hardy than the peach it is usually, when grown outdoors, trained as a fan tree against a south- or south-west-facing wall. When you buy the tree from a nursery it may already be trained as a fan; but if you buy a maiden, or have a maiden which you have yourself grown from seed, it will be necessary to train it. For this horizontal wires spaced 6in apart are required and these should be supported by metal pegs standing out 2-3in from the wall. Sometimes nails are used to fix the tree but it is far easier to tie the tree to horizontal wires. Training will take 4 or 5 years and it can be done in the following manner.

In the first year (ie when the seedling has reached maidenhood), during March, the stem should be cut down to a height where only two buds are left. Behind the stem two canes should be tied to the wires in the form of a V. When shoots have grown from the two buds tie these lightly to the canes. During the growing period untie the canes from the wires, slightly widen the V shape and retie them. This should be done three or four times.

In the second year, during March, cut back both stems to half their length and continue to grow them along the canes, but all side shoots, except for two nearest the base of the stems, should be pinched out after two leaves have formed. Fix two more canes inside the first V to make a narrower V, then when the two shoots at the base of the existing stems begin to grow tie them to this second, narrower V. Meanwhile the first V should continue to be widened in the same manner as during the first year.

In the third year, during March, the two original stems should now be ready to be tied finally in their horizontal position along the wires. They should at this time be shortened by about a third of their length. Meanwhile the stems on the second V should be treated as were the first—pinching out all shoots except for the two nearest the base of the stems and widening the V shape during the growing period. A third V should be tied in place inside the second V, and the new or third pair of shoots tied to this new or third V.

During the fourth year, the process of training the stems and tying in new shoots should be continued. By the fifth year the fan shape should be completed.

The best time to plant a nectarine tree is in October or November. Set it about 4in away from the wall, trim any damaged roots and plant firmly, making sure that the graft union is above ground. It should be tied only loosely and temporarily to the wires until the soil has finally settled. If more than one tree is to be grown they should be planted 15ft apart. A well-drained, deep medium soil gives good results, but although (as with all stone fruits) a lime soil is preferred there should not be an excess of lime.

If the tree is to be in the glass-house but set against a wall, then its planting and training is exactly the same as when grown outdoors. When, however, it is to be grown as a pot tree it will need a richer soil: a good pot compost would consist of two parts medium loam,

211

Nectarine

one part manure or humus, one part burned earth, a little mortar rubble or sand and a good dressing of coarse bonemeal.

Towards the end of September the well-developed maiden should be carefully lifted whilst still clothed with leaves and firmly bedded in a 12in pot. It can then be trained and built up into a bush, pyramid, short standard or fan tree as required. It will take 3 or 4 years to do this. In alternate years, during September or October, it will normally be necessary to repot the tree. Old soil should be removed and replaced with new but the same pot can be kept until after 5 or 6 years, when a 15in pot will be required.

The flowers appear between February and early March so there is always danger from frost. Wall trees can be protected by hessian or other material at night but this should be removed during the day to give insects access to the flowers. The flowers are in fact self-fertile but hand-pollination will ensure a better fruit set.

The flowers are produced singly or in groups of two or three at nodes along shoots of the previous year's growth. Because it fruits on the previous year's growth it is necessary to prune the nectarine hard enough to cause plenty of new growth. However, excessive pruning will cause over-growth at the expense of the tree's fruiting capabilities. Therefore the pruning of the fan tree should be on the following lines.

During April to June replacement shoots to provide fruiting wood for the following year must be selected. This is done by allowing three shoots to remain on each current fruiting twig. One of these shoots should be at the base of the twig, one in the middle and one at the tip. The one in the middle and the one at the tip are stopped by pinching out their tips when they have made five leaves but the one at the base of the twig is allowed to grow as long as it will. When there is a choice of replacement shoots, one which faces neither towards or away from the wall should be chosen so that shoots, twigs and branches are kept in line with the wall.

When the fruit has been harvested the old shoots which have borne fruit must be cut out and the replacements tied in. A piece of twine should be tied to the base of the shoots, twisted two or three times spirally around it and then tied to the wire beyond. In this way the side shoots are trained out fanwise and into line. It is also good policy to allow two shoots to grow from the base of the main branches so that they can be kept in reserve, then if die-back (see under Apricot)

212

should cause a branch to be lost there is a young shoot to replace it and the symmetry of the tree is maintained.

With the bush tree grown in a pot the essential aims of pruning are the same: (1) removal of the wood which has fruited and its replacement by last year's new growth; (2) keeping the tree to shape. Therefore, during March, first of all remove any wood that is dead (some of this may have been caused by die-back). Then any twig which bore fruit the previous summer should be cut out, but near the base of this twig will be found a shoot which was new in the previous year and this must be left as the replacement.

When grown outdoors the tree should be given an annual summer feed of a balanced fertilizer at the rate of 4oz per square yard and, if possible, a spring mulch of manure or compost. Trees grown against a wall are always liable to suffer from lack of water so when the weather is dry it is essential to water the soil to a good depth. Also, nectarines, especially when about the size of small cherries, are liable to split if rain follows drought and the soil has been left unwatered. While the fruits are swelling they should be kept well watered.

The tree in the pot or in the glasshouse border also benefits from a mulch of manure or compost as this helps to reduce loss of moisture from the soil as well as feeding the tree at each watering. To induce growth the leafless shoots can be syringed early in the year. When in leaf in the spring the tree should be syringed daily, except on cold, dull days and when it is in blossom. Syringeing should cease when the fruit is ripening. Nectarine fruit is susceptible to sunscorch, so it may be advisable to lightly shade the roof.

Fan trees often set an excessive crop and the small fruit should therefore be thinned from time to time so as to leave about one fruit to every 9 sq in of tree. The pot tree when well developed and occupying a 12in pot can be allowed to carry up to fifteen fruit. When occupying a 15in pot it can be allowed a heavier crop.

The fruit should be checked daily for readiness for picking. Do not press it with your fingers as this bruises it. Cup your hand around the fruit and with gentle overall pressure try to ease the fruit from its twig. If it resists leave it for another day. Its richest flavour is when it is at the peak of its ripeness and is ready to fall naturally. If you desire to have it this way you can tie a piece of muslin below each fruit to catch it without damage.

Nectarine

The nectarine fruit is smaller than the peach, and whereas the peach has a velvet-like skin that of the nectarine is smooth—in fact the nectarine looks as much like a large plum as a peach. But its flesh is white, yellow or red, like that of the peach and either free-stone or cling-stone. Some people maintain that the nectarine has a unique flavour, superior to that of the peach.

VARIETIES AVAILABLE IN BRITAIN

EARLY RIVERS—large fruit; red on sunny side, greenish white on the other. Juicy, white flesh. Ripe mid-July.

LORD NAPIER—large fruit; crimson and yellow skin. Juicy, richly flavoured white flesh. Ripe early August.

HUMBOLDT—large fruit; dark red and yellow skin. Blossoms late and crops well. Ripe mid-August.

ELRUGE—medium-sized fruit; pale green with a flushed dark red skin. White flesh. Crops well. Ripe end of August.

PINEAPPLE—medium to large fruit; golden orange and red skin. Excellent flavour with slight pineapple taste. Free-stone. Best under glass—tender when outside. Ripe early September.

Olive

Classification	:	*Olea europea.*
Physiology	:	Round-headed, sub-tropical evergreen tree, growing 20-40ft tall.
Origin	:	Possibly Mediterranean region.
History	:	Cultivated at least since 3000 BC.
Recommended site	:	Greenhouse — pot cultivation or grown in the border.
Culinary uses	:	Pressed for oil or pickled.

The genus *Olea* includes about twenty species of evergreen trees and shrubs but only the common olive (*Olea europaea*) provides edible fruit. In fact there is not another species in the whole of the family Oleaceae which produces edible fruit although there are in the family such well known ornamentals as forsythia, syringa and jasmine. Privet is also a very important member of the same family.

Most of the species of the genus *Olea* are tropical. One is found growing wild in the region of the Egyptian Sudanese border and it has been suggested that this is an ancestor of the common olive. But to fruit satisfactorily the olive requires a chilling period during the winter which means that the Mediterranean region rather than southern Egypt is a more likely habitat. In fact, wild olive trees are to be found growing in the Mediterranean area, but it is not possible to argue that *these* are the true ancestors of the cultivated tree because it could well be that they have simply escaped from cultivation. Whatever its origin, the olive fruit has been known and cultivated by man for thousands of years. In those areas of civilization where climatic conditions did not suit the date only the grape and fig were held in equal esteem to the olive. Clear evidence of this can be found by

215

Olive

reference to the Bible—Judges 9:8 wherein is told the story of the trees' quest for a king to rule over them.

When the Hebrews came into the land of Canaan they found the olive growing as though it had been there from the beginning. The fruit which it bore they ate—cooked or raw—or pressed it for oil. This oil they used for all manner of things, for cooking, for lighting, for toilet, for medicine; but the best oil they used for sacred anointings.

The olive tree lives longer than any other cultivated fruit trees, with the exception of the mango. Indeed, in the Garden of Gethsemane there are now, even as there were at the time of Christ's betrayal, some very old olive trees. Gethsemane was in those days a garden or orchard of cultivated olive trees and the name is a Greek transliteration of the Hebrew word which means 'oil press'. The gnarled, ancient trees growing in the Garden today are considered to be well over 1,000 years old because it is known that a tax levy was placed on these very trees after the Arabs occupied Jerusalem in the seventh century. In the opinion of some botanists these trees could well have been growing at the time of Christ, though all the trees round the city were said to have been cut down during the siege of Jerusalem by Titus in AD 70.

In character the olive tree is round-headed and bears numerous branches which bend downwards and give it a thick bushy appearance. With very old trees the trunk, especially near the base, gives the impression of a group of trunks. Its leaves are evergreen but leathery, and have a dusty, ash-like appearance. Under natural conditions the tree grows to about 30ft.

With the loquat, feijoa, and citrange the olive tree can withstand lower temperatures than any of the other cultivated evergreen fruit trees. A healthy, well-nourished tree will make a fairly good recovery even though its wood may have suffered considerable frost damage, but it has greater difficulty in doing so when its resistance has been lowered by heavy fruit bearing in the previous season. In general a temperature below $14°F$ ($-10°C$) may cause considerable injury to a mature tree but (with the exception of juvenile trees) a temperature of $16°F$ ($-9°C$) will normally cause no harm. The flowers and young shoots are, of course, tender but the tree blossoms in summer so that no damage is done to these.

Propagation can be from seeds but unfortunately the seedlings do not come true to the parent and this method is a gamble. The seeds should be sown in gentle heat in the spring in a good seed compost. The hard shells should be very carefully cracked to help germination, which may take 4-5 months. The young seedlings should be transplanted into their individual pots when about 5in tall.

Cuttings should be 4 or 5in long and taken from strong shoots in summer. If two leaves are left at the top of these cuttings they will root fairly well if inserted in clean, sharp sand in a propagating frame, especially when bottom heat and a high humidity can be provided. By the following spring these cuttings should have developed enough root to allow them to be planted in their own pots.

The olive is more resistant to transplanting than most other evergreen trees. Although the tree will be seen growing and bearing its fruit on poor, shallow soil—and doing this better than most other fruit trees—it will in fact produce much more fruit when grown in a good soil. A good sandy loam should, therefore, be provided and it should be allowed to occupy a sunny position either in a large pot or in the greenhouse border.

After the first year, four or five shoots on the stem should be selected and the others removed. The selected shoots should be cut back to 6in, and the following year the shoots which grow from these are again thinned out and a few selected and cut back. This is done for 3 years and results in a young tree with a spreading head and branches arranged symmetrically. In succeeding years all that needs to be done is to thin out crossing branches and allow as much light as possible to get to all parts of the tree. To stop the tree from getting too big the branches may be shortened.

Although the olive tree requires a cool period during the winter to stimulate or induce good flowering (in some olive-growing areas it is considered that it requires about 2 months with an average of 50°F (10°C) temperatures should be allowed to fall below 40°F (4°C).

The creamy white flowers appear in early summer and are borne in short panicles in the axils of the leaves. The flowers are either perfect (containing both female and male parts) or male only (containing only male pollen-producing parts). The pollen, normally shed plentifully, is carried by the wind and pollination is effected by this means. (When plants shed pollen heavily it can usually be assumed that pollination is effected by wind.) During the blossoming period some humidity is required to encourage a good set of fruit. After the flowers have blossomed the shoot continues growing, with the result that the fruit may be borne some distance from the tip of the shoot.

Although the olive tree does bear fruit quite well in areas where the annual rainfall is low it will, other factors being equal, produce far better crops where the rainfall is adequate. Therefore, when the tree is grown in a pot it should never be neglected so that it suffers a shortage of water. Also, if the temperature in the greenhouse is high and the air dry, this may cause an excessive falling of immature fruit.

The fruit is an egg-or oval-shaped drupe. It varies considerably in size depending on variety—some varieties may be an inch long and half an inch wide and others no more than half an inch long. In a warm sunny climate the oil content and weight tends to be at its maximum 6-8 months after blossom time, but the fruits can be allowed to remain on the tree much longer than that if they are to be used for oil. As they ripen their colour changes from green to straw colour to rosy pink, to red, to black.

Nearly all the food value of the olive is in its oil, which has twice the energy value of sugar. The oil content in the fruit increases as the fruit develops, and in a long, warm, sunny summer where good temperatures have been maintained the oil content will be higher. When the fruits are to be used for oil they should have turned black before they are harvested. Mature fruits may, in fact, be left on the tree even if freezing temperatures occur: they can be damaged by frost but would still be suitable for oil although not for pickling.

For pickling the fruits may be gathered whilst they are still green, but this must be done carefully to avoid bruising. All raw olives have a bitter taste which is removed quite easily by placing them in a solution of 2oz sodium hydroxide per gallon of water and leaving them in this until their colour begins to change. They should then be put into fresh water daily for 2 or 3 days to remove the salt solution. After this they are put into brine.

The olive tree should not be grown solely for the fruits it may bear, but also for its symbolism of joy, happiness and peace.

Orange

Classification	:	*Citrus sinensis; C. aurantium; C. bergamia; C. medica; C. mitis.*
Physiology	:	Generally small, evergreen, slightly spiny trees growing 20-30ft tall.
Origin	:	Probably India, Siam or southern China.
History	:	Did not reach the Mediterranean area until the fourteenth century; in the sixteenth cultivation was established in South America. It reached England also in the sixteenth century and by the eighteenth the fashion for orangeries had reached its peak. Commercially grown now in Mediterranean region, tropical and sub-tropical America, South Africa and Australia.
Recommended site	:	Greenhouse or conservatory — pot cultivation.
Culinary uses	:	Sweet oranges for general dessert purposes; Seville oranges for marmalade and drinks; Citron for candied peel.

Several species of the genus *Citrus* provide fruits which are known generally as oranges—the sweet orange, the Seville, the bergamot and the citron. As their cultivation is broadly similar they are all included here under the one heading.

Orange

The sweet orange probably originated somewhere in India, Siam or southern China. There appears to be evidence that it existed in these parts in pre-historic times. The Seville orange and lemon arrived in the Mediterranean area by about AD 1100 but the sweet orange did not seem to reach there until about the fourteenth century—brought, it is thought, by Genoese or Portuguese explorers and from a different source. However, it was soon adopted and cultivated, and taken from the Mediterranean not only to the warmer climates of the New World but also further north in Europe where it was given a home in warmhouses. By the 16th century the orange had reached England.

Already in the first century AD the Romans were wintering citrus trees inside buildings, and this method of cultivation inevitably moved northwards. In 1526, at Beddington in Surrey, Sir Francis Carew had wooden huts erected over his orange trees during the winter. These trees lived for about 200 years—until they were killed off by the severe winter of 1739.

By the eighteenth century the orange tree had become a popular subject for the conservatory. Special orangeries were built for them, but without studying their actual needs. During the next century interest waned but today a revival of interest seems to be dawning. This short study is therefore intended to assist prospective and practising amateur orange growers.

Under normal conditions the tree will grow 20-30ft tall. It is an evergreen with waxy green leaves; the old are dark green and these contrast with the pale green of new leaves during growth flushes. The roots of the tree are remarkable for an absence of root hairs.

The best climate for the orange seems to be one where there are well-defined summer and winter seasons and a moderate rainfall. If temperatures are not high enough the fruits do not ripen properly and are insipid. But although warmth is required for the fruit the orange tree can develop considerable resistance to cold, in fact more than any other *Citrus* species, with the exception of the mandarin. It develops this resistance because when temperatures fall below 50°F (10°C) the tree quickly stops growth, and colder weather thereafter does not then affect it to the same degree as some of the other species.

The usual method of propagation is by budding, which is normally done in March. Rootstock of other species is frequently used to improve vigour and hardiness and increase resistance to disease. Usually there is compatability between the species and also intrageneric compatibility, for example with poncirus and kumquat. Some species are naturally more satisfactory than others as rootstock. Lemon rootstock, for example, tends to reduce the flavour of the orange fruit. Mandarin rootstock, on the other hand, does not cause any loss of flavour and the trees usually grow well. Sweet orange seedlings possess more vigour than vegetatively produced trees and these make a rootstock which causes no loss of flavour to the fruit. Poncirus rootstock will increase resistance to frost.

Cuttings, which should be of firm shoots about 5in in length, can be inserted in pots of sandy soil and put into a propagating frame in a temperature of 70-75°F (21-24°C). It is also possible to layer suitable branches in summer: they should be layered into pots filled with sandy soil.

In spring or summer seed can be sown three-quarters of an inch deep in pots filled with sandy soil. Germination takes 20-30 days. The seed may be polyembryonic or monoembryonic (see under Lime). The polyembryonic seedlings will develop into trees similar to the mother tree whereas the ultimate character of the monoembryonic seedlings— good or bad—will not be immediately known. However, there are not many varieties of the orange and to improve on them is difficult. The improvement of the orange took place perhaps in prehistoric times and in whatever way this occurred the present day standard of the species is very high. This, in effect, means that although it is difficult to obtain a new and improved variety the chance of getting a useless seedling is also less and propagation by seed is not such a gamble as it is with some fruit. When large enough the young seedlings can be put into well-drained, loamy soil in their own 3in pots. The presence of some calcium is necessary for the growth of the young orange tree.

Due to its climatic requirements it is obvious that the best place for the young plant is either in a greenhouse border or in a pot in a greenhouse or conservatory. A greenhouse suitable for the peach is considered also to be suitable for the orange. If it is to be grown in the border the soil should be a good fibrous loam, and this should be top dressed, if at all possible, with rotted stable manure or compost each year.

It must be remembered that the orange is an evergreen tree and that it should, more or less, be kept growing through the winter with

Orange

temperatures not falling below 45°F (7°C). In fact rate of growth is retarded at temperatures less than 50°F (10°C) but short periods of rest do it no harm. From March to April the temperature should be allowed to rise to 70°F (21°C), reaching a midsummer maximum of 80°F (27°C).

Ventilation is required in warm weather and if there is very strong sunlight some shading may be necessary to prevent scorching. The soil must never be allowed to become dry during the summer. The path and foliage should be syringed to simulate rain and also to help to prevent red spider trouble, but very high humidity should be avoided.

Pot cultivation offers a convenient method of growing the orange tree. A good fibrous loam to which has been added a sprinkling of bonemeal should be used. The younger the tree the better, and it should be potted firmly, making sure that the soil around the sides of the pot is well rammed down. The smallest pot that will take the roots of the young tree should be used. At 3 years old the tree will probably need an 11in pot and this will suffice for 2 or 3 years. Slight increases in the size of the pot will be required from time to time but it should be possible to keep a tree up to about 25 years in an 18in pot. After this it will be sufficient to remove about 4in or so of the top soil once a year and replace it with compost. A top dressing of well rotted manure can be piled on the top of the soil around the rim of the pot, leaving a hollow around the stem of the tree to facilitate watering.

Because the tree is being grown in a pot its roots are restricted in their search for food and it is therefore beneficial for it to be fed with a liquid manure but the nitrogen content of this should not be too high. For the same reason some of the soil around its roots will need to be replaced annually or, at least, every second year. Repotting should be done as early as possible in February. The best way to do this is to remove some of the soil around the rim of the pot and then lay the tree with the pot gently on its side. The tree is then removable with a ball of the soil around its roots.

Roots which are exposed and have been bent up against the inside of the pot should be loosened free of the soil. Any long root should be pruned back to two-thirds of its length. Before putting the tree back the pot should be well washed and dried. Fresh soil should be put into it and rammed down fairly firmly. When the tree is

222

replaced in the pot it should be at such a height that its topmost roots are just covered when the pot is filled with soil to within an inch of the top. Soil should then be put in around the side, a few inches at a time, and well rammed down with a piece of wood. When the potting is completed the top of the soil should be slightly loosened to prevent it from panning down hard.

During the summer the tree must not be so neglected that the soil in the pot dries out; on warm days it should be syringed. During the winter water is supplied only when the soil becomes dry. Temperatures similar to those mentioned for the orange tree in the greenhouse border should be maintained.

If desired the orange tree in the pot can, from time to time, be taken into your home for decoration on special occasions, but unless it is in a very light room it should not be kept there too long because it likes an airy, light environment.

In southern Europe the orange tree is sometimes grown in gardens where it is trained as an espalier, and a tree so trained bears very well. If a south-facing wall in a mild area is available it might be worth experimenting on these lines with perhaps the hardier Seville orange. Some winter protection against severe frost would, however, have to be available.

The pruning of a young orange tree should be confined to training and development of a good shape. With the young budling tree this pruning should begin soon after the scion buds have started growth. If it is left to itself it will not grow as a single stem, as deciduous trees do, but will readily start branching close to the union which would make the head of the tree too low. Low shoots, therefore, need to be removed as they appear.

After the tree has started bearing there should be no regular pruning like that done on deciduous fruit trees. Pruning usually need consist of no more than the removal of the tips only of straggling shoots in summer. If some of the branches are crowding others and preventing light from getting to the tree and fruit, these may occasionally be removed during the winter.

The young orange tree which has been propagated vegetatively (ie by budding) may begin to bear a few fruits, usually on its lower branches, when it is 3 years old, but it is slower than the lemon or grapefruit to come into maximum bearing. A seedling, if in a suitable

223

Orange

environment, may become a maiden in its eighth year, when it will bear a few fruits, and commence normal bearing in its tenth year.

The orange tree is, of course, noted for its fragrance when in blossom. Unlike the lemon tree, which may blossom almost continuously if climatic conditions are favourable, the orange tree will bear most of its flowers in the spring. The flowers form on shoots in the axils of leaves produced during the previous year. They are bisexual and usually self-compatible. Fruits may also be produced parthenocarpically.

When there is a light crop of fruit on the orange tree this tends to be of a low quality, but when all parts of the tree are bearing a good crop the best quality fruit is obtained. The time required for the fruit to mature is largely influenced by temperature but normally it will take 9-12 months. When temperatures are too low, or watering and humidity has been too high, the fruits may be insipid in taste. From observations in the USA it has been deduced that sweet oranges have a better flavour when grown at a *mean* temperature above 65°F (18°C). The size of the fruit also tends to be influenced by temperature. When the *mean* temperature is below 65°F (18°C) during the ripening period the fruit does not reach a good size.

If the crop is too heavy for the tree some of the fruit may be very small, but thinning the fruit, as is practised with the peach, does not greatly affect the size of the remaining fruit. The orange should be snipped off with secateurs; if it is pulled from the tree the rind may be broken and this allows fungus to enter.

SPECIES OF ORANGE

SWEET ORANGE (*Citrus sinensis*)

The sweet orange tree may grow 15-30ft tall and it has few or no spines. There is great variety in the size of the fruit which has a sweet pulp and only a slightly bitter rind. There are three groups of sweet orange which are as follows:

1. *Navel orange.* This is so named because of the navel-like formation at one end of the fruit which is caused by the formation of an extra set of carpels. The fruit is large with a thick rind, rich in flavour but is usually less juicy than the common orange. It is nearly seedless.

2. *Blood orange.* This has a red pigment in the pulp, either in streaks

or completely red. Usually the riper the fruit the more red pigmentation. It is often called Malta orange, for Malta and Egypt are the two main sources of the fruit.

3. *Common orange*. This is usually smaller than the navel and includes many varieties—some thin-skinned, some thick. Well known kinds are Valencia, Maroc and Jaffa. It is of considerable interest to note that in 1876 one of the Valencia varieties being grown in England by the well-known nurseryman Thomas Rivers was sent to California. It proved to be successful and was used to get orange growing established in that state. The Valencia is still very popular with the American orange growers.

SEVILLE ORANGE (*Citrus aurantium*)

This is a medium-sized tree. It is one of the hardiest of the *Citrus* species and its seedlings are frequently used as rootstock for the sweet orange.

The fruits are globular, slightly flattened at one end, 2-3in in diameter, with a deep orange-coloured, bitter rind. The flesh is very sour. The fruit is used mainly for making marmalade, or for its juice, which is diluted and used in the same way as lemon juice.

BERGAMOT ORANGE (*Citrus bergamia*)

This is very similar to the Seville but it is grown for the oil contained in the rind of the fruit. The oil is used in perfumery.

CITRON (*Citrus medica*)

This is a small, almost dwarf, tree, growing under natural conditions to no more than 8-10ft. It has short stiff branches and thick twigs. In appearance it is somewhat different to the other *Citrus* species. It is the least hardy and is susceptible to injury both from freezing and high temperatures.

The fruit is ovoid, very large, 6-8in long. The rind is lemon yellow with a rough fragrant skin and mildly acid flesh. The rind is used for candied peel. It is also a sacred fruit used in the Feast of Tabernacles, a Hebrew harvest festival; the variety normally used for this is known as Etrog.

Although citrons are classed as acid fruits there is one variety, Corsican, grown in Corsica, which has a sweet pulp.

Orange

CALAMONDIN or PANAMA ORANGE (*Citrus mitis*)

This is a small, dense, prickly tree. It is classified as a *Citrus* species although it has also been suggested that it is in fact a hybrid of the mandarin orange and the kumquat. It is, in any case, a very hardy tree and is more resistant to cold than any of the other species dealt with here.

It is often grown as a pot plant, and it fruits whilst still small—thus making a good ornamental in flower and in fruit. The fruit is smaller than the lime, being about 1½in in diameter. The flesh and rind are orange coloured. The skin is loose and the segments easily separate. It is, however, very acid but can be used for the same purposes as lemons and limes.

Oregon grape

Classification : *Mahonia nervosa*, and other *Mahonia* species.
Physiology : Dwarf, evergreen shrub growing to 2ft tall.
Origin : North America.
History : Originally included in the genus *Berberis*. Introduced into Britain from North America in the early nineteenth century. Not usually grown for its fruit.
Recommended site : Outdoors.
Culinary uses : For jam, jellies, drinks, flavouring, juices, wine.

Mahonia species were, at one time, included in the genus *Berberis*. They are now considered to be a separate genus although closely related. A very marked difference between *Mahonia* and *Berberis* is that the later has spiny branches but the former does not.

Mahonia was originally brought from America's Far West in 1806 and thence to Britain, where for some time it remained very rare. Later it was planted in game coverts and some species have now become naturalized and can hold their own with some of the native woodland shrubs. Some *Mahonia* species are planted as ornamentals but they are usually ignored as producers of edible berries.

A species still comparatively rare in Britain is *Mahonia nervosa*. The berries of this species were at one time marketed in the United States of America under the name of Oregon grapes. This name has remained and other *Mahonia* species (eg *aquifolium*) have also been

227

Oregon grape

called by it. The true Oregon grape, *Mahonia nervosa*, is a dwarf species of the genus. But although it grows no more than 2ft tall it bears evergreen leaves up to 18in long.

Propagation can be from seed sown in spring, in a frame and in a compost of sand, peat and loam. As it is a suckering shrub propagation can also be from suckers which should be taken from the mother plant in autumn or spring. Cuttings of half-ripe wood can be rooted in sandy peat under glass.

The Oregon grape is not choosy in regard to soil or location, but it will do best in a well-drained good loamy soil and in a sunny position. It is , however, hardy, and once established needs little attention.

Yellow flowers are produced in erect racemes 8in or more long. The fruits which follow are round to oblong berries, a quarter of an inch in diameter, sub-acid and dark blue to purple-blue in colour. They hang in clusters and give the impression of grapes. They can be used for jellies or jam, or to make refreshing drinks, flavouring juices, or wine.

Not only the Oregon grape but the *Mahonia* species in general offer possibilities as fruit-bearing shrubs. Some of the species which produce useful berries are listed below.

OTHER FRUIT-BEARING MAHONIA SPECIES

MAHONIA AQUIFOLIUM

This, as mentioned, is often called Oregon grape and is also from North America. It is very hardy and is widely naturalized in Britain. Although strictly an evergreen its leaves often turn scarlet in winter. It is easily propagated from seed and grows to 4ft.

Golden yellow flowers begin to appear in February but reach their peak in April or May. The flowers are in erect racemes which are crowded in a group just below the terminal bud. Each raceme is 2-3in long. The berries are produced abundantly and are black with a violet-coloured bloom.

MAHONIA PINNATA

This is from southern USA and Mexico and is, therefore, not hardy in northern climates. It grows to 10ft tall and is very similar to *M. aquifolium* but more attractive as it carries a greater profusion of flower racemes which are borne over the entire shrub. It is considered to be one of the most attractive of flowering evergreen shrubs. The berries are similar to the preceding.

MEXICAN BARBERRY (*Mahonia trifoliolata*)
This comes from Mexico and Texas. It grows to 8ft, but is not hardy and needs to be grown against a sunny wall or in a mild area. Its yellow flowers are in short corymbs. The berries are oval to round and are black with a bloom.

MAHONIA NEVINII
A native of California and rare in this country. It grows 7-8ft tall. The flowers are bright yellow and are produced, a few together, in inflorescences.

MAHONIA HAEMATOCARPA
From New Mexico and California, growing 4-10ft tall. The flowers are pale yellow and, like *M. nevinii*, are produced a few together in inflorescences. Unless it has plenty of sunshine it does not bear its berries very abundantly. The berries are blood red, globose, a quarter to a third of an inch in diameter, acidic and juicy. They are excellent for jams and jellies.

Passion fruit

(PURPLE GRANADILLA)

Classification : *Passiflora edulis.*
Physiology : Tropical evergreen vine with stems 20-30ft long.
Origin : Brazil.
History : *Passiflora* species introduced to Europe at the beginning of the seventeenth century and grown for their unique flowers. Today cultivated for their fruit in warm countries, including South Africa, Australia, New Zealand and southern USA.
Recommended site : Warm greenhouse—pot plant or border. Conservatory—pot plant.
Culinary uses : Eaten fresh with cream or sugar; for jellies; trifles; flavouring.

Over 400 species comprise the genus *Passiflora* and a number of these provide fragrant, edible fruit. Most of the species originated in South America, and Brazil in particular. Spanish Catholic missionaries saw in the unique flowers of this climber a symbol of the crucifixion and because of this the plant came to be named *Passiflora* (*passus*, suffering; *flos*, a flower).

Passiflora was soon introduced to Europe and reached England in 1629. Nowadays, in other parts of the world, some of the species are grown not only for their symbolic flowers but also for their fruits. Passion fruit vines are now cultivated commercially in South Africa, Australia, New Zealand and southern USA, and as the quest for new food and new fruit continues, the areas of cultivation will continue to spread.

Although the fruits differ according to their particular species they are all commonly called passion fruits and this causes some confusion. The species which is most widely cultivated is *Passiflora edulis* (the purple granadilla) and these notes will, therefore, be mainly concerned with this, though the others will also be described.

The purple granadilla is a woody evergreen vine or climber with stems 20-30ft in length. It climbs by means of tendrils which form in the axils of its leaves. Its leaves are large and not so attractive or graceful as the lobed leaves of some of the other species. It can be propagated fairly easily from seed. Fresh seed should be sown in the spring in a light soil and if placed in a warm atmosphere a high germination percentage will be obtained in about 2-3 weeks, but the older the seed the longer it takes to germinate. The seedlings can be transplanted when they are about 2in tall. They will show considerable variation in colour, fragrance and flavour of the fruit as well as quantity of juice.

Vines which produce uniform fruits and start bearing earlier than seedlings can be produced by vegetative means. To do this cuttings should be taken from well-matured wood in early summer. They should be of pencil thickness and have on them three to five well-developed buds. The lower leaves should be cut off, a cut made below the lowest joint, and the cutting then inserted in a very sandy soil. They will root quite well and rooted plants should be available in about 3 months.

The purple granadilla is at home in a sub-tropical climate and needs to be free from extremes of heat and cold. High temperatures cause the vines to grow luxuriously but they then set very little fruit. Frost damages the vines. Heavy yields are obtained in areas having warm and rather dry air, pollination being effected by insects. Heavy rainfall areas are not considered suitable for its cultivation.

It is apparent, therefore, that in Britain a warm greenhouse is required for its cultivation: the minimum temperature on a cold night should be 55°F (13°C) and the maximum in hot weather 85°F (29°C). The vine can be planted in a large pot or tub or in the greenhouse border. Tubs and pots are very suitable as the root restriction causes better flowering. It should be potted up in February or March. After

231

Passion fruit

potting, the atmosphere in the greenhouse should be moist and the plant kept in a shady part. The foliage may be syringed but the plant itself should be only lightly watered until it has become well rooted. It may be started off in a 7in pot and can ultimately be kept growing for years in an 18in or 24in pot provided the top soil is replaced with fresh compost each spring.

Although it is not finicky about soil and will do quite well even in a poor and dry one, it will do much better in a soil which retains some moisture and has some humus and lime. Very heavy and poorly drained soils should be avoided. The best potting compost is one which consists of two parts loam, one part peat, and one part leaf mould with a good amount of silver sand. It will benefit from manuring in the spring, before it flowers. It can be trained along wires to reach the top of the greenhouse, or if in a lean-to, it should be trained along the wall.

Pruning should be done in February or whilst the vine is dormant, and this consists of completely removing any weak growth and shortening strong canes by one-third. The fruit is borne on new shoots arising from old canes and because of this it is necessary to prune regularly to encourage new growth and to remove the old unproductive wood. A spur should be left to grow on at the base of each cane and this will replace the old cane after it has borne fruit for a year or two.

The flowers of the purple granadilla are not as attractive as those of other species of the genus. Pollination is effected under natural conditions by insects, principally the honey bee. From blossom to fruit may take about 12 weeks.

When mature the fruit attains a purple colour and it is ready for harvesting at this time. It can either be picked or allowed to drop to the ground. The fruit has a hard leathery rind and no harm is done when it falls, but if it is picked carefully when mature it will store much longer.

The fruits are round to oval in shape and about the size of a pullet's egg—though weight may vary from one-third of an ounce to two ounces or so. They contain many seeds surrounded with juicy orange-coloured pulp which, although acidic, has a very aromatic or fragrant flavour. The pulp can be used for all manner of things: it can be eaten with cream or sugar, used for jellies, for trifles, for flavouring, for icing cakes.

232

The fruit has a relatively high mineral content. It is considered by some to be a digestive stimulant. The rind is a very good source of high-quality pectin and an excellent jellying agent. Eaten with cream, the granadilla or passion fruit, whichever you prefer to call it, rivals the strawberry.

The lilikoi, or yellow granadilla (*Passiflora edulis* var. *flavicarpa*) is a yellow-fruited form of the purple granadilla, containing juicy, orange-coloured aromatic pulp. Commercially it is grown more extensively in Hawaii than elsewhere and cultivated especially for its acidic juice. The vines are said to be more vigorous than the purple granadilla. There is some difficulty with pollination because the stamens (males) permit their pollen to fall before the pistils (females) have become receptive. Hand-pollination of this variety is, therefore, necessary.

OTHER PASSIFLORA SPECIES

GIANT GRANADILLA (*Passiflora quadrangularis*)

This is another passion fruit which is grown commercially. It is slightly more tender than the purple granadilla. Temperatures should not be allowed to fall below 55°F (13°) in winter as it is used to a hot, humid climate.

It is a strong climber with very striking flowers that can be up to 4½in across, with pale pink petals, sepals green outside and white inside, and corona banded blue and purple. It is one of the most beautiful and exotic of the passion flowers.

The fruits are large, varying in length from 1-6in. They are egg-shaped or oblong, greenish yellow in colour and look something like short, thickish marrows. In the centre of the fruit, which is hollow, is a mass of purple, sweet-acid pulp with many seeds.

SWEET GRANADILLA (*Passiflora ligularis*)

A passion fruit grown in the gardens of Central America. Its habitat is the mountainous regions of Mexico and Central America at an altitude of 6,000-7,000ft. It is a vigorous climber and needs the same warm greenhouse treatment as giant granadilla.

Its fruits are slightly larger than those of the purple granadilla and are oval or slightly eliptic in form. They are orange to orange-brown

233

in colour and have a strong shell. The pulp is white and almost liquid, acidic but perfumed in taste.

MAYPOPS or MAY APPLE (*Passiflora incarnata*)

This native of south-eastern USA does not require such a warm temperature as the two previously listed species. Even so a cool greenhouse is required as temperatures should not go below 40°F (4°C) during winter. It might however be tried outside against a sunny wall in the mild parts of south-west England. As an experiment it could be trained along wires fairly close to the ground under a specially devised cloche that would allow sun and light to get to the vines. Protection against frost could be given during winter.

In its natural habitat it grows to a length of about 20ft, and although it climbs over bushes it is generally low climbing or trailing. It is an attractive vine, with three lobed leaves from 3-5in long and with fine, saw-toothed edges. The flowers are lavender and purplish blue, 3in across. The yellow fruit is 2in or more long, about the size and shape of a pullet's egg. It can be eaten for dessert; it makes an excellent jelly; and the juice can be used for drinks.

PASSIFLORA, ANTIOQUIENSIS; P. MOLLISSIMA (Sweet Calabash); *P. LAURIFOLIA* (Water Lemon)

These, and some others also provide edible passion fruits of varying quality.

PASSIFLORA CAERULA

Is often grown outdoors in England as an ornamental and produces fruit in a warm summer. This fruit is edible but not very desirable although it is said to be a good remedy for insomnia when this is caused by nervous trouble and not by physical pain. Be that as it may *Passiflora caerula* is much hardier than the other species and it may be possible to cross it with some of the others or use it as a hardy rootstock. Experimentation by budding on to selected rootstock has, for example, been carried out in South Africa.

Paw paw
(PAPAYA)

Classification	:	*Carica papaya.*
Physiology	:	Large, tropical, herbaceous palm-like plant.
Origin	:	Central America; southern Mexico.
History	:	American Indians of South America long ago knew digestive value of the fruit. Now grown commercially throughout the tropics.
Recommended site	:	Warm greenhouse.
Culinary uses	:	As a dessert; for jam, marmalade, preserves, pickles; cooked for pies, etc; used to tenderize meat.

Once upon a time paw paw was a member of the family Passiflora-ceae. It also had amongst its relations, and still does, pumpkins large and small, squashes, gourds and melons (the family Curcurbitaceae). One day, however, it was decided that paw paw's place was not really in the family Passifloraceae and it was put into its own little family, Caricaceae. Despite the fact that the family to which paw paw origin-ally belonged boasts many well known *Passiflora* beauties, this plant is neither Cinderella nor pumpkin. It has some irregular sex habits (of which more later) and is of gastronomical importance if nothing else.

The genus *Carica* consists of about thirty species, but only *Carica papaya* (paw paw) is of any real commercial importance. Centuries ago the Indians of Central America had discovered that they could eat very large quantities of food without suffering digestive upheavals provided they finished their gorge with paw paw fruit. This digestive

Paw paw

aid is due to a very powerful enzyme (papain) which is contained in the fruit.

After the discovery of America the paw paw was quickly taken to other tropical countries by Portuguese explorers and sailors. Because it can be easily propagated from seed it spread quickly throughout the tropics. It is a popular fruit today as much because of the early-bearing nature of the tree as of the mild and pleasant flavour of the fruit itself.

Although paw paw is referred to as a tree it is really a giant herbaceous perennial. It is tree-like, very much like a palm in appearance. The stem rarely has branches unless it is cut back or its growing apex is killed, although very old specimens may sometimes branch from the base and form several erect stems each with a crown of dark green foliage. The stem is succulent and hollow except at the node and increases in thickness as it gets older. Its leaves are very large, up to 2ft across and deeply divided into about seven palmate lobes which are themselves pinnately lobed.

It tolerates cool weather better than some other tropical species. Cool weather reduces the growth of the plant, but its greatest ill effect is on the fruit, and if it occurs during the ripening period the fruit will be insipid and have a pumpkin-like flavour. Temperatures below 32°F (0°C) damage the tree—and female plants are less hardy than the males.

For the paw paw sex is a very complicated matter. The plants are dioecius or almost completely so, and they have been classified according to the sex of their flowers as follows:

1. Dioecius pistillate (pure female plant). With large pistillate flowers on short peduncles in the leaf axils. The flowers have five fleshy petals.
2. Dioecius staminate (male plant). This has narrow, funnel-shaped flowers about 1in long, which are borne on long peduncles hanging from the axils of the leaves.
3. Andromondecious. This has both male and hermaphrodite flowers on long peduncles.
4. Polygamous. Two kinds: (a) female, male and hermaphrodite flowers all on the same plant and on long peduncles; (b) female, male and hermaphrodite flowers on the same plant but the hermaphrodites of two types, one with ten stamens, the other with five stamens.
5. Staminate. With male flowers on short peduncles in axils of leaves.
6. Hermaphrodite. Three kinds: (a) hermaphrodite flowers only, on

236

long peduncles; (b) hermaphrodite flowers with a few females; (c) hermaphrodite flowers with many female flowers.

None of these forms is fixed. The plant is known to change its sex during its life span—from male to hermaphrodite, to pure female. This change, however, is very gradual. In the beginning the plant may have only male flowers but after some time it may begin to bear a few hermaphrodites. After further time the hermaphrodites may predominate, then females may begin to appear; then the female flowers predominate until the hermaphrodites completely disappear and, presumably, the ascendancy of the female has been achieved!

Seed from fruit which is the result of self-pollination by hermaphrodite flowers will not be all hermaphrodite, generally two-thirds will be hermaphrodite and one-third will be female. Seed from fruit which is the result of flowers on female trees having been pollinated from flowers on hermaphrodite trees will generally be half female and half hermaphrodite, and all will be fruiting trees. Seed from fruit which is the result of flowers on a hermaphrodite tree having been pollinated from flowers on a male tree will generally be one-third female, one-third hermaphrodite and one-third male. Seed from fruit which is the result of flowers on a female tree having been pollinated by flowers from a male tree will generally be half female and half male.

Sometimes male trees will bear fruit and often this is when they are young or when they have grown old. Flowers on these male trees develop long pistils with stigmas and the fruit set is pyriform in shape (whereas that on a female tree is spherical or almost so) and hangs at the end of a very long peduncle. Hermaphrodite fruit tends to be more oblong than that produced on female trees and sometimes it is pyriform. It is usually very much smaller, about 1lb in weight, whereas that from female trees may be as much as 20lb if it is a good variety.

When seedlings are grown, and this is the usual way in which paw paw is propagated, it is not possible to distinguish between the sexes until they begin to blossom. This means that unwanted males have to be grown on and then later discarded, although there are growers in Ceylon who believe that if the unwanted males are beheaded they develop into females.

It is also possible to propagate from cuttings and by grafting, but the amount of suitable wood is extremely limited due to the tree's habit of making only a few branches. Even when the tree is cut back

237

Paw paw

to force it to branch there will still be only very few branches per tree. If seeds are washed and dried after removal from the fruit and stored in an air-tight bottle they will retain their viability for years. Seed should be sown half an inch deep and 1 in apart in a well-drained, porous compost. Germination should take 2-6 weeks but this will be governed by temperature. They are subject to damping-off. When the seedlings are 9 in high they should be transplanted into their own individual pots and then again into larger ones when about 1 month old. They are fairly fast growing.

Provided the right temperatures are available they are very easy to grow but are short lived; after about 4 years they should be replaced by new trees. It must not be forgotten, however, that female trees will need the presence of a male, but seedlings from hermaphrodite fruit will be two-thirds hermaphrodite and self-pollinating.

Paw paw should be given a good rich loam. Good drainage is essential as waterlogged conditions prove fatal. The stem is easily killed when water remains stagnant around its roots. It is, however, able to adapt itself to a variety of other conditions and can withstand more drought than the orange. It needs a good supply of nitrogen, and feeding with liquid fertilizer is beneficial. During winter a minimum temperature of 60°F (16°C) should be maintained with just sufficient watering. With high temperatures during summer it can be watered copiously and it will make full use of this water.

Paw paw is not usually pruned as it grows and fruits as a single stem, although it is often the practice with planters in Ceylon to prune the top of seedlings when they are about 5 months old. This encourages side shoots which form erect stems, each with its palm-like crown of leaves. This method is said to produce a better yield.

The time from sowing the seed until the first ripe fruit will, of course, depend on the temperature available but as a general rule it can be said to be between 12 and 18 months. Usually when the tree is about 3 or 4 years old the fruit becomes smaller and the yield less. The stems, too, begin to get too tall and sometimes break. Younger trees should then be ready to take their place.

Lack of sufficient warmth retards the ripening of the fruit. A dry warm atmosphere tends to add to the sweetness of the fruit, but excessive moisture or low temperature is detrimental, producing an insipid fruit.

238

The fruit is borne on the trunk at the base of the leaves. Its skin is smooth and green in colour, turning yellow as it ripens. Fruits are usually harvested when they are still hard and green but turning yellow. It is best picked by giving it a sharp twist with the hand or by cutting with a sharp knife. Harvested this way it can be allowed to ripen to its full flavour in a temperature of not less than 60°F (16°C) for a few days. Fruits allowed to ripen on the tree are usually much sweeter but if allowed to become fully ripe the skin may become so tender that the heavy fruit will pull itself away from the stem and cause a wound.

The flesh is deep yellow to salmon in colour and resembles the melon in appearance and consistency. Within the flesh is a cavity wherein is contained numerous dark brown seeds about the size of small peas. The flavour is sweet with a slightly musky tang but a mild, pleasant taste. It is a good source of vitamins A and C and is rich in vitamins generally. It is helpful in the digestion of meals because of the papain it contains, but the ripe fruit has little of this.

The uses of paw paw are indeed many and varied, and it is considered to be a wholesome and nutritious fruit at all stages of its development. It can be harvested green and cooked in the same way as squash but it has a better flavour; or it can be sweetened and used in the same way as apples and other fruit for pies, preserves, sauces etc. The ripe fruit can be served as a dessert. It can be sliced and served with a little sugar and whipped cream. It is also good as a crystallized fruit, or it can be served in salad with lettuce.

Paw paw milk is obtained from green, unripe but well-developed fruit. The skin of the fruit is scratched longitudinally with a sharp non-metallic instrument. Scars are made on the skin but not deep enough to cause serious wounds. To begin with only a few scars are made but these are gradually increased in size and number so that the entire skin is covered. The juice as it drips is then collected in a non-metallic bowl held under the incised fruit. Several days are allowed between two successive tappings.

The digestive properties of paw paw were long ago recognized in the tropics. American Indians rubbed the juice of the fruit over meat, or wrapped it in paw paw leaves overnight to make it tender. Paw paw fruit is said to cure constipation and piles and to put right an enlarged liver or spleen. In Hawaii parts of the plant are used as an application

239

Paw paw

for skin diseases or deep cuts. The rubbing of the fruit pulp on warts is said to make them disappear. In South Africa the cooked green fruit is used as a vegetable; and in Mauritius the leaf is smoked as a relief for asthma. In southern India the seeds, which have a spicy flavour, are said to procure an abortion if eaten by the pregnant woman; and in Java the eating of paw paw fruit is said to keep a man young and free from rheumatism!

MOUNTAIN PAW PAW (*Carica candamarcensis*)

This is the only other *Carica* species of interest. It grows in Colombia and Ecuador at altitudes of 8,000-9,000ft. It is more resistant to cold than the common paw paw but its fruit is small and tart and of use only for cooking. Attempts have been made to cross it with common paw paw but they have not been very successful.

XIII Paw paw in a West Indian garden. This is a perennial plant and can be grown in a large pot

XIV Pineapple—pot-grown:
(left) propagation can be
from the crown of the fruit;
(below) the fruit forms on the
apex of the stem

Persimmon

(KAKI; JAPANESE DATE PLUM)

Classification	:	*Diospyros kaki.*
Physiology	:	Deciduous round-headed tree growing to 40ft.
Origin	:	China.
History	:	Has been cultivated for centuries in China and Japan where there are hundreds of varieties. Now grown also in Mediterranean countries and commercially, on a limited scale, in California.
Recommended site	:	Greenhouse; outside only against a south wall in well-favoured area.
Culinary uses	:	Eaten raw for dessert. Can be used in puddings and cakes.

Diospyros is a genus of deciduous and evergreen trees originating mainly in warm countries. Some are timber trees (ebony) and others produce edible fruits.

Diospyros kaki is a small, deciduous, round-headed tree, usually growing to a height of 40-50ft. Its leaves are ovate-elliptic up to 5in long, pubescent beneath, glabrous above. The tree is dioecious (female and male flowers on different trees) or sometimes monoecious (separate female and male flowers on the same tree).

It has been cultivated for centuries in Japan and China and in those countries there are hundreds of varieties. It has been said that there are as many varieties of persimmon in Japan as there are of apples in England. In China the tree is found growing as far north as Peking

R

Persimmon

and it is also cultivated in the coldest parts of Japan. In the nineteenth century it began to be cultivated in the Mediterranean region, and is now also grown commercially in parts of California. In Britain and comparable climates it should be considered as semi-hardy and grown in the greenhouse, otherwise it will not ripen its fruit properly except in a very hot summer. A greenhouse which is suitable for peach growing will do for persimmon. It can, however, be tried against a sunny wall in a favoured area. It should then be trained as a fan tree or, if there is only a low wall, as an espalier. Any soil will suit it and it can be planted from October to February.

If persimmon is to be propagated from seed then it should be sown in pots and buried outdoors in early autumn; germination can be expected in the spring. But seedlings prove to be very variable and for this reason when propagated commercially it is usually grafted either on to its own rootstock or one of the other species.

Whatever means of propagation is used the tree should be trained to form a low head and so, when it is 2ft tall, it should be headed back. A framework of, say, four or five branches is needed and so this number of buds, conveniently placed around the stem, should be left if possible. After a well-balanced small tree has been formed little pruning is needed except for the removal of dead and unwanted branches.

Flowers appear in early summer and are yellowish white, rather inconspicuous. The fruit is about 3in in diameter, thin-skinned, of oblate shape and usually ribbed at the base. It is harvested when it is still hard but after it has reached an orange-red colour, and is clipped from the tree together with its calyx and a short piece of the stem. Ripening should be allowed to continue indoors in a warm temperature because otherwise the fruit is very astringent. The proper sweetness and flavour is only developed when the pulp has become soft. The pulp is orange or salmon-coloured and contains the elliptic flattened seed.

The fruit can be eaten raw for dessert or can be used in pies, puddings, cakes etc.

OTHER PERSIMMON FRUITS OF INTEREST

AMERICAN PERSIMMON, SIMMONS TREE, or DATE PLUM (*Diospyros virginiana*)

This is a somewhat hardier tree than the *Diospyros kaki* and is a native of south-eastern USA. It is round-headed, usually with drooping branches and can grow 50-100ft tall although it is usually much smaller. In its natural habitat it is often found in dry woodland but can thrive under very variable conditions.

The flowers are yellowish green—females on one tree, males on another. The female flowers are one-third of an inch long, solitary and with a pointed, hairy ovary. Male flowers are in small clusters. Fruits are reddish yellow or sometimes purplish, globose or oblate. They vary in size from that of a small cherry to that of a large plum 1½in in diameter.

The Red Indians readily ate these fruits but the early pioneers found them very astringent until they learned that the fruit had to be thoroughly ripe or touched by frost before being fit to eat. It is also a fact that although the tree is fairly hardy the quality of the fruit is lowered by a cool climate so that, like the kaki, it is really only suitable for a glasshouse.

DATE PLUM (*Diospyros lotus*)

A native of China and Japan, where it is often used as a rootstock for the kaki persimmon. It is a tree growing up to 45ft. The fruits are globular, about the size of cherries, changing from yellow to blue-black as they ripen, and very astringent.

ZAPOTE NEGRO (*Diospyros ebenaster*)

A native of the West Indies and Mexico. The tree grows to 50ft and has leaves 8in long. The fruits are olive green, about the size of oranges, and have chocolate brown pulp.

BUSH PERSIMMON (*Diospyros amata*)

Native of central China. Grows as a bush up to 20ft. Fruits are yellow.

Persimmon

JAKKALBESSIE (*Diospyros mespiliformis*)
Native of the Transvaal. A graceful evergreen tree growing to 70ft and carrying pendulous branches. Yellow fruits are about the size of olives.

MONKEY PLUM (*Diospyros lycioides*)
Grows in the drier parts of South Africa. It is usually evergreen and grows as a small shrub. Its small yellow flowers are fragrant. Fruits are yellow, ovoid-shaped, about half an inch long and succulent.

Pineapple

Classification	:	*Ananas comosus.*
Physiology	:	Herbaceous perennial, may become 3ft tall and have a spread of 4-5ft.
Origin	:	Brazil or Paraguay.
History	:	Cultivated in South America before arrival of Europeans. Europeans quickly spread it around the world. Introduced to Europe in 1555. Stove-houses used for its cultivation in England.
Recommended site	:	Warm greenhouse—bed or pot.
Culinary uses	:	Fresh for dessert; for juice, jelly, preserves, jam, etc.

The pineapple is one of the most important fruits and in the right habitat or location one of the easiest to grow. Its native home appears to be Brazil or Paraguay—one species, *Ananas microstachys,* grows wild there—and the people in that part of the world had cultivated it and taken it to other parts of South America before the arrival of the Europeans. 'Na-na' is said to have meant fragrance in the language of the Guarani people who lived in the area where the pineapple probably originated.

After the arrival of the Europeans pineapple cultivation spread rapidly: in 1555 it was brought to Europe and in 1605 the Portuguese were planting it extensively in part of India. Heated glasshouses known as stove-houses were erected in England for its cultivation and detailed treatises were published on its culture. As early as 1789 Abercrombie included the pineapple in his book on hot-house cultivation.

Pineapple

The early English growers found that fruits of large size, some weighing as much as 5lb and of good quality, could be grown if temperatures did not fall too low. But what caused a loss of interest in pineapple growing in this country? It was, of course, cheap and massive importation, which made the pineapple no longer a luxury to be enjoyed by the upper class.

The pineapple plant is an herbaceous perennial which may grow to 3ft tall and, at its second year of fruiting, have a spread of 4-5ft. The stem, about 1ft tall and 2in thick 14 months after planting, is thickly surrounded and hidden by long tapering leaves which are 3-5ft long and about 1½in wide. The flower inflorescence and fruit are borne at the apex of the stem.

The plant has a great resistance to drought but very little resistance to frost. It has been reported that plants in a greenhouse have withstood a temperature of 32°F (0°C) and that protected in a lathe type of house have withstood a temperature of 25°F (−4°C). But normally a temperature of 41°F (5°C) for a period of 48 hours causes injury to the fruit. High temperatures should be maintained at all times. The minimum temperature for winter should be 65°F (18°C) and for summer 90°F (32°C).

Propagation is by vegetative methods—suckers, slips or crowns being used. *Suckers* are shoots or branches arising either from the axils of the leaves or from the stem of the plant and near the ground. *Slips* are shoots or branches which grow from the fruit stem, or peduncle as it is sometimes called. *Crowns* are the clusters of short leaves which grow on the head of the fruit. Sometimes when there is a shortage of any of this propagating material a shoot or stem which has borne fruit is used, provided it has not also borne suckers. Its leaves are trimmed off and it is planted on its side, about 3in deep in the soil and allowed to sprout and form shoots. These shoots will be rather weakly but they can be used if they are later separated and planted.

Normally suckers are to be preferred. Crowns and slips take longer to bear fruit. Suckers will give a first crop in 14-18 months whereas slips and crowns usually take 2 years.

Suckers can either be planted in separate pots containing a well-drained sandy loam, or planted about 4in deep into the pineapple bed direct. Care should be taken that the heart of the sucker does not get buried. The basal leaves at the bottom of the stem should be trimmed to about 1in as this facilitates active rooting. When planted, the soil should be firmly pressed around the plant.

Slips and crowns should be turned base upwards before planting and allowed to dry; this prevents rotting of the stem after planting. Crowns can be rooted in a sandy loam when there is a good bottom heat. This is the ideal soil for the cultivation of the pineapple, and because of the necessity for bottom heat it is economical to grow them in numbers in a bed. No special kind of glasshouse is required. In hot countries pineapples are sometimes grown in shade under coconut, banana and rubber trees, and some of the early pineapple growers in Britain grew them under the grape vine; but it is better, in cool temperate climates, to keep them near the glass so that they get all the light available and continue to grow throughout autumn and winter.

Although the pineapple has shallow roots a bed as deep as practicable should be provided and the bottom should contain about 6in of brick rubble or other suitable drainage material. The plants should be set out 3-5ft apart according to their size and vigour. Always allow plenty of room between the plants so that they can spread their leaves horizontally and are not starved of light. Earth up the stems as high as the leaves will allow and keep the beds moist but not over-wet.

The successful growing of pineapple depends on good drainage which permits frequent watering with high humidity. Manuring is also essential to keep up the yield and maintain the size of the fruit. The plants should be fed with liquid manure while the fruits are developing but kept drier while the fruits are ripening.

The time between the planting and the ripening of this first crop depends on the soil, moisture content and temperatures. With good treatment they should fruit in 18 months.

A reddish-violet inflorescence is borne at the apex of the stem and there is no failure in fruitlet development. With a fruit weighing 2-3lb at its apex the stem may easily bend over and if this appears likely to happen some support should be given. At the first crop only the stem which was originally planted will bear a fruit, but by the second season one or more branches will have grown from the original stem and each will bear a fruit. Some of these second-crop branches may again bear a fruit at the time of the third crop.

The size of the fruit will, in part, be determined by the amount of leaf surface the plant possesses. Any induction of the flower while the

247

Pineapple

stem is short will tend to reduce the size of the fruit (the early growers in England soon learned this). If the house is too cool in spring, or too little water is given, or its roots are restricted in pots that are too small, the plants are apt to flower in spring, after having perhaps only been planted in the previous summer. This means that the leaf surface is small and, as a consequence, the fruit is small when it ripens.

When the fruit is cut the leaves should be injured as little as possible. Two or three new shoots will soon spring up but only one of these should be left—the others being removed and potted up for succession. As the new shoot on the old plant develops, the old leaves can be reduced until they are all removed. At the same time the roots should be given a top dressing of rich compost or manure.

From a period varying from 6 to 12 months from the time of cutting one fruit another should be ripe on the same plant. The fruit stalk should be severed with a clean cut from a sharp knife about 2in from the fruit. If the crown is removed this quickens the ripening process and reduces the time the fruit can be kept. The older part of the pineapple fruit (ie at the base) ripens earlier than the younger apical part and is always sweeter even when the fruit is fully ripe. As the fruit has no starch it therefore increases in sweetness very little once harvested, whether green or ripe. But its sweetness increases rapidly while it ripens on the plant.

VARIETIES ONCE GROWN IN ENGLAND

QUEEN

This variety is said to have been grown as early as 1658 and is still one of the most popular. The plants are small. The small fruits weigh from 2-3lb. They are golden yellow, less juicy, less acid and sweeter than most other varieties. They are now grown extensively in South Africa.

CAYENNE or KEW GIANT

This was introduced into English hot-houses about 1841. Today it still produces about 90 per cent of the world's pineapples. An average fruit of this variety in the first crop may weigh up to 6lb if the plants are in good condition and have not been forced to bear when young. The surface colour is mottled yellow and green, the flesh is pale yellow.

Pomegranate

Classification	:	*Punica granatum.*
Physiology	:	Semi-deciduous, small, roundish tree growing to 15ft.
Origin	:	Persia to Afghanistan.
History	:	Cultivated from early times. Extensively grown today in the Mediterranean area and the Middle East. Introduced to England in the sixteenth century, and to the American continent by Spanish colonists.
Recommended site	:	Warm greenhouse—pot or border.
Culinary uses	:	Eaten fresh for dessert; used for drinks.

There are two species of *Punica* and only one of these, *Punica granatum*, is grown for its fruit. It is, however, another of those fruits whose history goes back into antiquity. When the Israelites were wandering in the wilderness they yearned for the comforts of Egypt —the cool, refreshing pomegranate as well as the grape and the fig. In mythology the pomegranate is the fruit which Paris gave to Venus and from earliest times it has been a symbol of fertility.

The Romans found it growing in Carthage and it was named Punica after the old name of those parts. At a later date the Moors from North Africa planted the tree in Spain. Today it is cultivated in Morocco, Tunisia, Egypt, Spain, Israel and the Middle East generally, and in California. There are many varieties of the pomegranate and indeed as far back as the thirteenth century the Arab agriculturist, Ib'n-al-Awam, listed ten growing in southern Spain.

Pomegranate

The pomegranate was introduced into England in the sixteenth century and was growing at Syon House in 1548. Unfortunately, it needs a really high summer temperature to ripen its fruit. A humid climate also adversely affects the fruit. Even so nothing is lost in growing the tree because of the large scarlet flowers it carries.

It is a small semi-deciduous tree, though practically evergreen in sub-tropical climates and deciduous in cool temperate regions. It grows up to 15ft but because of its habit of sending up shoots or suckers it will, if untrained, take on a bush-like form. Under suitable conditions it is a vigorous grower. It can withstand frost but is injured by temperatures below 12°F (−11°C). It can stand up fairly well to drought conditions but will do better when supplied with sufficient moisture. In general it has about the same degree of hardiness as the peach tree.

Although easily propagated from seed, fruit of desirable quality is often not achieved by this method, and it is therefore better if it can be propagated vegetatively from a good quality tree. Propagation from cuttings is fairly easy but wood younger than 6 months or older than 2 years is not suitable. Cuttings, 10-12in long and about a quarter of an inch in diameter, should be taken from mature one-year-old wood and can be from suckers which grow from the base of the main shoots. Such cuttings should be taken in late spring, leaves should be removed from them and they should then be planted in a warm but shady place. Under suitable conditions root formation starts quickly.

Young trees should be transplanted in the spring, and although the adult tree can withstand considerable drought the young tree at this time should not be allowed to dry out. It will flower outdoors in a warm location and its beautiful red flowers will give much pleasure, but if fruit is desired the tree must be grown in the greenhouse, as a pot tree or in the border or, ideally, against the wall of a lean-to glasshouse. It is not fussy about soil except that it should be well drained. Manuring is beneficial in the spring.

The young pomegranate does not require much pruning except for removing the suckers and giving some shape to the tree. The young tree should be properly trained so that it has a single stem with well-distributed branches radiating from it. Because of its tendency to throw up suckers all the side shoots should be removed when the one-year-old tree is transplanted. It should also be topped when it is about 2ft high. About four or five shoots evenly distributed around the stem and starting about 1ft from the ground should be permitted to grow on; any shoots above or below these should be removed. The following year the side shoots or branches are pruned back to encourage them to develop. In about 3 years you should have built up a tree with a stocky framework, remembering that little or no fruit is borne on the interior of the tree. Any suckers which appear should be removed. These grow very vigorously without branching and usually without bearing fruit, and use up the tree's energy.

The pomegranate tree may come into maiden bearing in its fifth year but will not reach normal bearing until about the seventh. It will normally continue to crop well until it is 30 years old. The fruits are borne on spurs which grow on the mature shoots. These spurs may bear fruit for 3 or 4 years, after which they begin to lose their capacity for fruit bearing and should then be removed. Because new spurs will have to grow on mature wood thoughtless pruning must be avoided and only shoots with old, finished spurs and those crossing others should be removed. Try to let plenty of light and sunshine get to the fruiting wood.

Blossom-time should commence in late spring and may continue into the summer. At this time the pomegranate is particularly beautiful because of the large bright red flowers with which it is adorned. It carries both hermaphrodite and male flowers. The hermaphrodites will set fruit but the males, much smaller in size, are shed soon after they have opened.

With the right temperature fruits should ripen 5-7 months after the appearance of the blossom. It must again be stressed that to obtain good-quality fruit, that is with a sweet acid taste, high temperatures are required during the fruiting period. Even a temperature of 100°F (38°C) can be allowed if it is obtainable. The fruits are harvested when the rind becomes yellowish brown, and should be snipped from the stem with secateurs. Experienced growers slightly press the fruit and if it gives a sound of grains cracking inside they know that it is ready for picking.

Pomegranates will keep for some months after harvesting, especially if stored in a cool dry place. Although the rind shrinks and loses its lustrous colour the flavour does, in fact, improve by long keeping and the seed becomes more tender and edible.

Pomegranate

The fruit is about the size of an orange and is contained in a hard rind. The inside consists of a sweetish acid pulp, pinkish red in colour and enveloping many seeds. When scooped from the fruit, seed and pulp are like crystals. In Middle Eastern countries the crystals, perhaps sprinkled with rose water, are served as a table fruit. The fruit is also very much appreciated because of its cool, refreshing juice and has been used since the days of Solomon for making cooling drinks. Then, too, it has medicinal properties. In Hawaii, for instance, the fruit and the rind have been found effective as an anti-bacterial agent and in South Africa the dried rind has been used as a relief for dysentery. Mohammed gave to it spiritual properties also, for he said, 'Eat the Pomegranate—for it purges the system of envy and hatred'.

Poncirus

(HARDY ORANGE)

Classification	:	*Poncirus trifoliata.*
Physiology	:	A deciduous, thorny shrub, growing 6ft or more tall.
Origin	:	Central and southern China.
History	:	Used extensively as a rootstock for the *Citrus* species. Used as a hedge in southern Europe. Introduced into England 1850.
Recommended site	:	Outdoors in sunny position.
Culinary uses	:	For seasoning; juice can be diluted for drinks.

Poncirus trifoliata is the sole member of its genus. It has, in its history, been classed as *Citrus trifoliata* and also as *Aegle sepiaria*, and is sometimes still called by these names.

Although its fruit is of no economic importance it is included in this book because it is used as a rootstock for the *Citrus* species; because it can be hybridized with the *Citrus* species; and also because it is an 'orange' tree which can be grown outdoors in Britain.

It grows much smaller than the *Citrus* species—about 6ft, or a little taller in more favoured positions. It is thickly branched and carries many sharply pointed green spines up to 2½in long. The leaves consist of three leaflets and are, therefore, different from *Citrus*. Also, unlike *Citrus*, it is deciduous. It carries comparatively few leaves, much of their work being done by the branches and spines.

It can be propagated in the spring from seed which should be sown a quarter of an inch deep in a greenhouse or cold frame in a

Poncirus

temperature of 50°F (10°C). Poncirus seedlings are of a uniform nature and are mostly nucellar (see Lime). Cuttings can also be made from half-ripened wood in June or July and inserted in pots of sandy loam in a closed propagating frame.

In southern Europe poncirus is often used for hedging purposes and can be so used in Britain, but to obtain maximum flowers and fruit it should be planted in a sunny position. It will grow in any soil. Young trees should be planted in autumn or spring. Little pruning is necessary except in June to shorten too-vigorous growth and to give a good shape to the shrub or hedge.

Poncirus is beautiful in April and May when smothered with orange blossom. The fragrant white flowers, 2in across, are borne in the axils of the spines on the leafless branches. The fruits which follow are like small yellow oranges, 1-2in in diameter. They have hard, densely pubescent rinds that contain many oil glands. The pulp contains many fine droplets of oil. When they are first picked they give very little juice when pressed but after being kept for about 2 weeks they yield about 20 per cent juice. This juice is very acid and has a bitter flavour and a strong aroma due to oil droplets contained in it. In China the fruits are used for seasoning and flavouring. A drink can be made from the diluted juice.

Poncirus was first introduced to Britain in 1850 but, despite the fact that it is hardy and carries sweet scented 'orange' flowers, it has never attained great popularity. This may be because of its thorns—but when it is used for hedging these are an asset. In one gardening book poncirus is described as 'guaranteed boy-proof'—that is, it will rip the pants of any intruding, fruit-scrumping boy.

Apart from all this poncirus is valuable as a rootstock especially for experimentation in climates like the British. Its attributes as a rootstock can be summarized as follows: the seedlings are very uniform; it is hardier than *Citrus* rootstock; it has a dwarfing effect; it grows well in soils too wet for *Citrus* rootstock; it induces early bearing and has a tendency to increase production; it seems to have a beneficial influence on fruit flavour.

Poncirus is also of importance for hybridizing with *Citrus* species. It has, for instance, been crossed with the sweet orange. This cross has been called the citrange.

CITRANGE (*Poncirus trifoliata* x *Citrus sinensis*)

Because of its poncirus parentage this can be grown in a considerably colder climate than that suitable for the orange. It is a small semi-evergreen tree and may be considered for outdoor cultivation in the milder parts of the country.

The fruit varies in colour from yellow to orange and is from 1-4in in diameter. The flavour is sub-acid and aromatic. The juice when diluted makes a very good drink.

This is a rarely grown fruit which deserves consideration for the fruit garden.

Prickly pear

(BARBARY FIG; INDIAN FIG)

Classification   :   *Opuntia* species.

Physiology   :   Spiny, succulent plant growing 6-15ft tall.

Origin   :   Mexico; South America, southern USA.

History   :   Cultivated in America before arrival of Europeans. Said to have been brought to Europe by Christopher Columbus. Now naturalized and widely cultivated in the Mediterranean area.

Recommended site   :   Warm greenhouse or conservatory—pot or border.

Culinary uses   :   Used for dessert, jam, syrup or stewing.

Opuntia is a very large genus of succulents consisting of between 250 and 300 species. As cacti and indoor plants they are fairly familiar. Many of the species provide edible fruits which vary in shape, colour and sweetness.

Because they are very extensively grown in North African countries, where they serve the purpose of bounding fields, much like hedgerows in Britain, it is often assumed that they originated there. This is not so. They are natives of central and southern America where they were cultivated long before the arrival of the Europeans in America. There are cacti trees growing at some of the old missions in southern California which are said to be 200 years old.

XV Fruit and leaves of a tree tomato. Not only do these differ in shape from those of the ordinary tomato but the fruit has a sweeter taste

XVI Ugni, or Chilean guava. The fruit of this small semi-hardy shrub is borne in abundance

BARBARY FIG (*Opuntia ficus indica*)
The Barbary fig, as its name implies, is a naturalized succulent in the Barbary countries of North Africa where its fruit is often sold in the markets. It is said to have been taken to southern Europe from America by Christopher Columbus. This 'tree' can grow 9-15ft tall and has spreading branches with large oval prickly pads; it is, however, less prickly than some of the other *Opuntia* species.

Propagation can be from seed which should be sown in a John Innes compost. Seed of most cacti species is placed on top of the seed compost but because *Opuntia* seed is fairly large it needs to be lightly covered with some of the compost. The seed tray or pot should then be placed in a temperature of about 70°F (21°C) shaded and kept just moist. Germination is rather erratic and even though some time may pass without any sign of seedlings the seeds should not be too hastily discarded. Some seed may take a year to germinate. Vegetative propagation, on the other hand, is very easy as any part of the plant will quickly root. Pads, small or large, can be set in sharp sand in a sunny position in spring or summer. They should be sprayed occasionally until they have rooted.

Its natural habitat is in warm, dry, rocky places but contrary to usual belief it can, like many other cacti, tolerate a considerable amount of neglect. It must, however, be grown in a porous soil which should be moderately rich. A recommended compost is John Innes No 2 to which has been added a sixth part of sharp sand, grit or brick rubble.

The best time for planting and potting it is at the commencement of the growing season in spring, when temperatures are beginning to reach 60°F (16°C). Pots should be one-third filled with crocks. The soil should not be wet and some thoroughly dry soil should certainly be placed beneath and around the plant. If the roots are damaged during this transplanting it is advisable to plant it in a completely dry soil and to give no watering for a day or so. This will allow the damaged parts to heal. When it has taken root and temperatures are rising it can be given an increasing amount of water.

It requires warmth and plenty of sunshine during the summer but at the same time a well-ventilated or airy location. During the growing period water can be supplied whenever the soil begins to dry out but during autumn and winter it must be kept practically dry—

depending on the amount of warmth provided. Most species of cacti are, in fact, able to withstand temperatures much lower than they would experience in their native habitat, always provided they are not subjected to wetness during winter. Winter temperature should, preferably, be not less than 45°F (7°C) and during summer this can rise to 80°F (27°C).

Canary-yellow flowers are produced around the edges of the pads and these are followed by ovoid-shaped fruits on short peduncles, at first green but turning to a brick-red colour sometimes streaked with yellow. They are about the size of a hen's egg and are covered with very fine glochids or prickly hairs, which have to be removed before the fruits can be eaten.

The flesh is juicy and similar in colour to the outer skin. It has a pleasant taste. Although the skin looks waxy, the fruit contains no fat. The juice contains 12.8 per cent of glucose and fructose together, but no sucrose. Chopped up and served with cream, the fruits make a good dessert, or a very pleasant prickly pear syrup can be made from them. They can also be used for jam or preserve. However, if eaten to excess they can be constipating.

They contain a natural yeast known as *Saccaromyces opuntiae* which causes a ready fermentation. This yeast cannot be used with other kinds of fruit to ferment sucrose as it only ferments the natural sugars in its own juice—glucose and fructose. If any other yeast is added it is killed by *Saccaromyces opuntiae*.

Many other *Opuntia* species provide edible fruits; a few of them are dealt with below. Their cultivation is similar to that of the Barbary fig.

OTHER SPECIES BEARING EDIBLE FRUIT

DEVIL'S TONGUE (*Opuntia rafinesquii*)

Flowers are yellow, often with a reddish centre and are about 3in in diameter. Fruits are 1½-2in long and about 1in diameter. The pulp is purplish and can be eaten fresh or stewed after the bristles have been removed.

OPUNTIA UNDULATA

From Mexico. This is a 'tree' with spreading branches. It has very few spines and sometimes none at all. The fruit is large, oval, about 3-4in long, dull red in colour. The pulp is streaked with red and orange; it is very sweet but has hard seeds.

TUNA CARDONA (*Opuntia streptacantha*)

From Mexico. A 'tree', up to 15ft tall and with many spines. The flowers are large and yellow, the fruits globular, of about 2in diameter and red in colour. In Mexico it is used for a popular preserve known as Tuna Cardona.

DURAZNILLO (*Opuntia leucotricha*)

From central Mexico. A 'tree' growing up to 10ft. Its green joints are covered with very short greyish velvety hair. The flowers are deep yellow with white stamens, deep red styles and stigma with six green lobes. The fruits are round, whitish yellow and aromatic. They are commonly sold in the Mexican markets.

This succulent is easy to grow but it requires warmth.

OPUNTIA HERRFELDTII

From central Mexico. An erect, bushy, plant with a short stem growing to 3ft high. Flowers are of a sulphur yellow colour. The fruits are green, globular, about 1in in diameter, very juicy.

This also is easy to grow provided it has warmth.

OPUNTIA MEGACANTHA

From Mexico. This is a spreading, shrub-like succulent growing to 6ft. The flowers are a golden yellow colour. The oval-shaped fruits are whitish yellow. The pulp is yellow and has a vinous taste.

OPUNTIA HAEMATOCARPA

From South America. A 'tree' growing 3-12ft tall. The flowers are large and golden yellow in colour, orange-red at their centres. The fruits are violet-red with blood-red pulp.

OPUNTIA ENGELMANII

From Mexico, New Mexico, Arizona, Texas. A succulent shrub that will grow to 6ft but which has a tendency to grow prostrate. The Flowers are yellow. Fruits are sweet and with small seeds. This is a much hardier species than *haematocarpa*.

INDIAN FIG (*Opuntia opuntia; Opuntia vulgarii*)
From southern United States. This is a thick branching succulent usually prostrate in habit. The yellow flowers are 2in in diameter. The fruits are red, ovoid, 1-1½in long, fleshy and juicy. A much hardier species than any of those previously listed.

Pummelo

(SHADDOCK; GRAPE FRUIT)

Classification	:	*Citrus grandis* (*Citrus maxima*). *Citrus paradisei.*
Physiology	:	Evergreen trees growing 15-18ft tall.
Origin	:	Eastern Asia; Polynesia.
History	:	Pummelo taken to West Indies by Captain Shaddock. There appears to be no record of the grapefruit before 1750, when it was mentioned in Barbados and thought to be a better form of the pummelo or shaddock. Today it is one of the world's most important fruits.
Recommended site	:	Warm greenhouse—pot tree, or in border. Conservatory—pot tree.
Culinary uses	:	Fresh for the table; for salads; for juice, squash, syrup; for jelly.

Although grapefruit is a more important fruit than pummelo it is included under the heading of pummelo because there is doubt as to whether or not it is (1) a variant of the pummelo, (2) a hybrid between the pummelo and one of the other *Citrus* species, or (3) a separate species.

Much of the information given for the other citrus fruits (orange, lemon, mandarin, lime) is relevant to the pummelo and grapefruit and so, to avoid repetition, only matters specific to these last two fruits are dealt with here.

261

Pummelo

PUMMELO (Shaddock) (*Citrus grandis, Citrus maxima*)

As far as can be ascertained this species originated somewhere in eastern Asia. (Possibly Malaysia, spreading later to Indonesia and Polynesia). It was taken to the West Indies by a Captain Shaddock, hence the other name by which it is frequently known.

Pummelo is the most distinctive of the *Citrus* species. Its flowers and fruits are very large. It has been in cultivation much longer than the grapefruit and there are numerous varieties in Asia, from Siam to Indonesia: some trees are upright and strong-growing; others are low-spreading and dwarfish. They have nearly as much resistance to cold as the grapefruit or orange tree.

Pummelos produce only zygotic embryos (see Lime), so that if propagation is from seed there will be great variability in the offspring (hence the reason for so many varieties in different parts of the world). Usually, therefore, unless breeding for new varieties, propagation is by vegetative means.

The large flowers appear in larger clusters than in other *Citrus* species and they are borne at the apex of long shoots. The fruits are larger than the grapefruit yet they possess no more pulp as their rind is much thicker. Some varieties have pink flesh, some pale yellow and some yellowish green. It is said that after storing for some time the pulp becomes more juicy and richer in flavour, although of course the rind becomes wrinkled.

The rind makes a very nice confection known as crystallized shaddock.

GRAPEFRUIT (*Citrus paradisei*)

The grapefruit seems to have been first mentioned about 1750 in Barbados. At that time it was given the name of pomelo. The pummelo was the only similar fruit. By 1830 it had acquired the name of grapefruit in Jamaica and this name became generally accepted.

Its leaves, flowers, fruit and seeds are smaller than those of the pummelo but larger than those of the sweet orange. The rind of its fruit is thinner than that of the pummelo but thicker than those of the sweet orange. And, perhaps more telling, pummelo always produces zygotic seedlings whereas grapefruit does sometimes produce apogamic seedlings. From this it would seem that the grapefruit is quite likely to be a cross between the pummelo and the sweet orange.

Grapefruit trees are slightly less resistant to cold than sweet orange trees. Young trees are susceptible to frost but as they grow older they increase their resistance. They can be propagated either from seed or by vegetative means in the same way as the orange. The Seville orange is frequently used as a rootstock.

Less pruning is needed than for the orange tree and considerably less than for the lemon because grapefruit trees have a much greater tendency to spread low and to send up fewer water sprouts. But when branches touch the ground these can be cut away. They have a denser foliage than the orange tree and there may, therefore, be more dead wood to remove.

Flowers are borne in clusters, as on the pummelo. Pollination seldom presents any problems, providing water, nourishment and soil aeration is good. A nitrogen deficiency during blossom time or in the first months afterwards may cause some of the fruits to fall. The fruit on a well-developed, well-nourished tree hangs in clusters, but thinning rarely increases the size of the fruit. The flavour of the grapefruit is more influenced by temperature than the orange and adequate warmth to ripen the fruit quickly is required. If temperatures are too low the fruits may be on the tree 15-17 months, which means that a second crop will also be on the tree at the same time, and several months old. This may cause fruit to drop before it has reached its desired sweetness.

The fruit requires little description except to say that there are white- and pink-fleshed varieties. The fruit is rich in vitamin C and vitamin B. Its uses are well known.

Quince

Classification	:	*Cydonia oblonga.*
Physiology	:	A small, round-headed, deciduous tree, occasionally growing to 20ft.
Origin	:	Persia; Turkestan; Anatolia.
History	:	A fruit known to the Greeks and Romans; possibly introduced to Britain by the Romans. Once grew wild in Sussex. Formerly grown commercially in north-east USA.
Recommended site	:	Outdoors in moist soil—as specimen tree on lawn; or in shrubbery.
Culinary uses	:	Stewed with apples; used for jelly or marmalade; used for wine.

Cydonia is a genus of one species only; the *Chaenomeles* at one time included in the genus should not be confused with it.

The quince (*Cydonia oblonga*) is a very ancient fruit known to the Greeks and Romans who dedicated it to Venus or Aphrodite. To them it was a symbol of love, happiness and fertility and was used in marriage ceremonies. It was a fruit of great virtue and it has been suggested that this was in fact the 'forbidden fruit' of the Adam and Eve story.

The exact place of its origin is not known but it is thought to have been somewhere in the region of Persia, Turkestan and Anatolia. From these parts it made its way up through Greece. The Romans possibly brought it to England. At one time it used to grow wild in the Sussex Weald and its fruits were gathered and made into wine. Quince marmalade was also made from the fruits and this was a

264

very popular conserve. The fruit was also popular at one time in the north-eastern region of the United States but it is now neglected.

The tree is slow growing and may sometimes reach a height of 20ft. It is a round, broad-topped, umbrella-shaped tree with low branches. It carries no spines (unlike the *Chaenomeles* which were once associated with it). When in flower it is quite beautiful and it makes a nice specimen tree for the lawn or for placing in a shrubbery.

Propagation is often done by layering shoots in the autumn. It is also fairly easy to propagate from cuttings or suckers. Seeds are not considered suitable since the resulting seedlings nearly always produce only small fruit, and apart from this seeds very frequently do not ripen in cool temperate climates.

Any soil that is reasonably fertile will suit it, but a shallow soil or one that becomes dry in summer is not good as this causes the fruit to be small. Although it definitely gives a far better yield in a moist soil the danger of planting it near a stream or pond is that such locations are often frost areas. Even so it may be worth risking occasional frost danger to get a better crop from a moist area. If the tree is grown in a dry soil it should be given a good watering and an occasional feed of liquid manure during the summer. Exposure to sunshine and shelter from strong winds is desirable. Planting should be in the autumn.

No special pruning is necessary and the young tree may itself form a suitable head. If it does not, then the height at which it is headed back will depend on whether it is to be grown as a bush or as a half-standard tree. Young trees may also, for a few years, need to have their leading shoots tipped and some shoots thinned out. The natural habit of the tree is for it to be dwarfish and twiggy. Any pruning required should be done during the winter.

In May or June pink or white flowers readily form on the unpruned shoots—these flowers are solitary and at the end of the short twigs. As they are self-fertile, trees can be planted singly. The flowers are followed by pear- or apple-shaped fruits, 3in or more in diameter, and these ripen to a rich yellow colour. To develop their characteristic flavour to the full they should be allowed to stay on the tree as long as possible. A strong aroma will usually indicate the ripeness of the fruit. Usually they are ready for harvesting in October but can be allowed to stay until the first frosts begin stripping the tree of its leaves.

Quince

The fruit is still hard even when quite ripe. If unbruised it can be kept for up to 2 months when stored in a cool place. It should not, however, be stored near apples and pears because its very strong aroma may taint them; acceptable as the fragrance of the quince is with stewed fruit, it is hardly wanted with dessert apples and pears.

The quince fruit makes a very pleasing jelly of a clear orange-golden colour—very cheerful on a drab, cold-grey winter's day. Quince jam or marmalade, using the peeled and cored fruit, may be preferred to the jelly. Cotignac, a famous French preserve, is made from the fruit. Quince can be cut into slices and added to apple or pear tart (one quince to twelve apples usually and this really makes a tart). The fruit can be used for a rich and refreshing wine.

It is a great pity that the quince is not more generally grown. It beautifies the garden and enhances the cuisine.

VARIETIES AVAILABLE

PORTUGAL—not very fertile but is considered to bear the best fruit for cooking and preserving. When cooked it turns reddish. It ripens early.

BERECZKI—a vigorous tree of Serbian origin. The fruit is of good quality and tender when cooked.

CHAMPION—provides greenish yellow fruit.

APPLE-SHAPED QUINCE—an old variety and still one of the best. It is the heaviest bearer. The fruit stews very well.

VRANJA—very similar to Bereczki.

CHINESE QUINCE (*Pseudocydonia* or *Cydoni asinensis*)

This is a separate genus, consisting of only one species. Until fairly recently it was included in the genus *Chaenomeles* (see Japanese Quince). It originated in China and was introduced to England at about the end of the eighteenth century but disappeared and was reintroduced at the end of the nineteenth century from Italy where it is still commonly cultivated.

It is a small deciduous tree, sometimes remaining evergreen, and like the true quince it carries no spines. Flowers are produced in April or May, they are carmine in colour and are borne solitarily on short spurs or on the year-old wood. The fruits are egg-shaped, about 5-7in long, and when ripe attain a pale citrus yellow colour.

Although it will withstand cold it needs sun and warmth to ripen its fruit. A south-facing wall is an ideal place for it and it will bear quite well in this position.

Raspberry— black, purple, yellow

Classification	:	*Rubus* species and hybrids.
Physiology	:	Bushes growing to about 6ft.
Origin	:	North America; Asia.
History	:	Cultivated in North America, but little known in Britain and Europe where red raspberry is naturalized.
Recommended site	:	Outdoors.
Culinary uses	:	Fresh for dessert; for jams, jellies; for pies etc.

Raspberries, like blackberries, are common enough, but the British are usually familiar with only the red raspberry. Yet there are species and hybrids within the great genus *Rubus* (see Brambleberries) which produce black, purple and yellow or golden raspberries. The difference, incidentally, between a raspberry and a blackberry is that a raspberry separates from its core, whereas the core of the blackberry is an integral part of the fruit.

The red raspberry, with which we are familiar, is derived from *Rubus idaeus*, and this perhaps originated in Asia but is now naturalized in Europe. There are, however, other species originating from Asia and also America which produce raspberry-type fruits. In North America, for example, there are three worthy of mention: *Rubus strigosus*, producing red berries; *Rubus occidentalis* (Eastern Black Raspberry) and *Rubus leucodermis* (Western Black Raspberry) producing black berries. In South America there is *Rubus glaucus* (Andes Black Raspberry), and in Asia, *Rubus nivens* (Asian Black Raspberry).

Raspberry—black, purple, yellow

In the USA both *Rubus strigosus* and *Rubus occidentalis* have been widely, and for a long time, cultivated for their red and black berries respectively. The two species have also been crossed to produce purple berries. Until the beginning of this century the black raspberry was more widely cultivated than the red raspberry because its firm flesh made satisfactory dried fruit. But as canning and, later, freezing of fresh fruits came into being, the red berries became more fashionable.

Brief descriptions of some of the unusual raspberries follow.

BLACK RASPBERRY or THIMBLEBERRY (*Rubus occidentalis*)

This has strong arched canes with hooked spines and its flowers are borne in small, dense, prickly clusters. In USA it is very amenable to cultivation and is vigorous and productive. It is, however, sensitive to raspberry viruses and in Britain attempts to cultivate it commercially have not been very successful—it has been a poor cropper and the fruits have been small. Improvements should be possible by selection of seedlings.

Propagation of chosen varieties is by tip layering—in August the tip of a shoot is bent over and buried about 2in deep. The shoot readily takes root and can be separated in early spring. Leaf bud cuttings may also be used when quick propagation of a new variety in quantity is required.

Black raspberry canes should be planted 4ft apart in rows, with 6-9ft between the rows. New shoots are produced in spring and summer and these bear fruit the following year. As soon as fruiting has finished the old canes should be cut right out. The new shoots should be shortened to 12in to cause them to branch and these branches should be shortened to 8in during the winter. Sturdy canes will bear fruit more heavily than thin, lanky ones. The berries are hemispherical, small but firm. In the USA it is produced in large quantities in Michigan and New York state. Wherever it is available it is a popular fruit and is used in ice cream manufacture.

PURPLE RASPBERRY (*Rubus strigosus* x *Rubus occidentalis*)

The purple raspberry is comparatively new to Britain but has been cultivated in the USA since 1838, though even there more by amateur than commercial growers. It is a cross between two American species

269

which occurred both naturally and also under cultivation. The plants so produced are more vigorous and productive than their parents.

The purple raspberry can be propagated in the same way as the black, and should afterwards be set out at the same distances apart. The canes should be allowed to grow longer—the new shoots being cut back to about 20in and the branches to 12in.

The fruit clusters contain more berries than those of either the red or black raspberry and they are larger and juicier.

GOLDEN MAYBERRY (*Rubus palmatus* x Red Raspberry)

This plant is the result of another cross. Its history is described in 1895 by Luther Burbank the American breeder:

Some ten years ago I instructed my collector in Japan to hunt up the best wild raspberries, blackberries and strawberries that could be found. Several curious species were received the next season and among them a red and also a dingy yellow unproductive variety of *Rubus palmatus*. One of these plants, though bearing only a few of the most worthless, tasteless yellow berries I have ever seen was selected solely on account of its unusual earliness to cross with well known raspberries. Among the seedlings raised from this plant was this one and though no signs of the parent appear it can hardly be doubted that the pollen of the other parent effected some of the wonderful improvement to be seen in this new variety.

The plant reaches a height of 6-8ft and has a spreading top. Large white flowers are carried all along the branches. It is said to be one of the earliest raspberries, ripening before strawberries. The berries are large, a golden straw colour and juicy. It should be propagated and cultivated in the same way as the preceding raspberries.

GOLDEN RASPBERRY (*Rubus ellipticus*)

This is a tall, evergreen, upright plant and is covered with reddish-brown hairs. It originated in the Himalayas. It can be very conveniently used as an ornamental for pergolas in sheltered areas. The yellow fruits are about the size of the red raspberry and are said to be of good quality.

Rowanberry

Classification	:	*Sorbus aucaparia edulis.*
Physiology	:	Deciduous, slender tree growing to 40ft.
Origin	:	Northern Europe.
History	:	The tree plays a part in Scandinavian and Gaelic folklore. Fruit eaten by people of northern Europe. Planted as an ornamental throughout temperate regions.
Recommended site	:	Outdoors as ornamental.
Culinary uses	:	For jelly, jam or wine.

The rowanberry is not very different from chequers or the service berry and they do, in fact, belong to the same genus—*Sorbus*—which comprises over 100 species (see Chequers).

The rowan is a native of northern Europe and its name is said to have been derived from the Danish word 'ron' or 'rune', or the Gaelic word 'run', which can be translated as mystery or magic. The rowan tree was said to have magical powers, and in days gone by it was often planted around crofts in the Scottish Highlands as a protection against witches and evil spirits.

It is a small, slender tree growing to 40ft high. Its pinnate leaves, which come early in mid-April, consist of thirteen to seventeen leaflets. It likes plenty of light but will grow on any well-drained soil and does quite well on chalk and limestone. An open situation suits it but it can be seen growing wild in forest as well as in thicket or hedgerow. In Scotland it grows at an altitude of up to 2,000ft.

Seed may take 2 years to germinate, but otherwise it is easy to

271

Rowanberry

propagate in this way. Propagation can also be from cuttings. No special pruning is necessary except for the removal of dead wood.

The tree is well worth growing if only for its ornamental value. White or cream-white flowers are produced in corymbose clusters during May. In August, when the fruit ripens, the tree is adorned with masses of red 'berries' which are, in fact, very small pomes. The fruits have two to four compartments each containing a seed, and a very minute, brittle core. They are one-third of an inch and more in diameter, coral red to orange in colour and with yellow flesh. They have a sour but pungent taste and can be used for jam, jellies or wine making.

There are three other *Sorbus* species which may be included here with the rowan. They are called whitebeams but may be the result of natural hybridization between the rowan and the whitebeam.

WHITEBEAMS

SWEDISH WHITEBEAM (*Sorbus intermedia*)

This is a tree of southern Sweden and the Baltic countries but is now naturalized in Britain. It is of erect growth and may reach a height of 30ft. It is very resistant to town smoke and grows quite well in the heart of Glasgow.

The flowers are larger than those of the rowan. The fruits are also larger, and longer than they are broad. They are orange-red in colour and ripen in September, when they have a sweetish taste. Each fruit contains two seeds which are apomitical (see Lime). They are soon eaten by birds.

FINNISH WHITEBEAM (*Sorbus hybrida* or *Sorbus intermedia arranensis*)

This is thought to be a hybrid between the Swedish whitebeam and rowan. It has a very limited range and is found mainly in the coastal regions of Scandinavia, but excluding Denmark. Significantly it is also to be found on the Scottish island of Arran—significantly because the Vikings were frequent 'visitors' to the Western Isles and naturally deposited seed there.

The tree is small and erect, 12-13ft high. Its leaves are lobed and the lobes become larger towards the base of the leaf where they form one or two pairs of separate leaflets—an indication of hybridization between the whitebeam and the rowan, for the whitebeam has entire or simple leaves and the rowan palmate leaflets.

The flowers appear in May, and the globular fruits, half an inch in diameter and bright red in colour, ripen in mid-August. They have a bitter-sweet taste and are very suitable for jam making.

POLISH WHITEBEAM (*Sorbus mougeottii*)

This is a species from central Europe and is very similar to the Swedish whitebeam but its leaves are less deeply lobed. The edible fruits are a very attractive sealing-wax red.

T

Sea berry

(SEA BUCKTHORN)

Classification : *Hippophae rhamnoides.*
Physiology : Deciduous, spiny, much-branched shrub or small tree, growing from 3-20ft.
Origin : Western and central Asia.
History : Fruit used by local communities; plant protected in Germany during World War II because of its fruit; but not cultivated for its fruit.
Recommended site : Outdoors in full light.
Culinary uses : Used for jelly, marmalade, sauce. Medicinal value.

The genus *Hippophae* consists of three species only. They are of Eurasian origin and the species with which we are here concerned (*Hippophae rhamnoides*) although originating in Asia is now naturalized in Britain, where however it is only rarely seen growing wild —usually along the eastern coasts of Scotland and England.

Not only is it an unusual plant: it is also distinctive. Usually it grows as a bush up to 10ft tall but occasionally it takes the form of a tree and grows to 20ft. It is thickly branched and carries many spines. Leaves are narrow, greyish green on the upper surface and silvery coloured on the under surface. The leaves alone make it ornamental but it is more so in the autumn when it is generously adorned with orange-coloured berries. Unfortunately it is dioecious—that is to say the sexes are borne on separate plants—female flowers on one tree, male flowers on another. It is not possible to tell the difference between the sexes until the plants come of flowering age.

The flowers are inconspicuous, being very small and greenish without petals. They appear in May or June just before or at the same time as the leaves. The male flowers appear before the leaves and form small catkin-like spikes. The female flowers appear with the first leaves and are in short racemes. The difference between the sexes can also be seen during the winter—when the flower buds of the females are smaller than those of the males.

To obtain fruit it is necessary to grow a male in the presence of females—as many as eight females can be grown with one male. Pollination is effected by the wind but a branch from a flowering male can be taken to and shaken over a female. It can be ascertained whether the pollen of the male is right by gently tapping a branch: if it is, the yellow dust-like pollen is seen to fall.

As it is not possible to differentiate between the sexes until the plants come of flowering age it is, of course, necessary to grow on young plants which may turn out to be unwanted males. It is suggested that if plants are propagated by cuttings from females instead of propagation from seed only a minimum of male stock plants need be kept to supply cuttings to graft on to female plants to form male limbs.

Young branches may be layered in autumn or root cuttings inserted outdoors in February or March. The plant also produces suckers in large numbers and these appear in the spring, produced on rhizome-like roots, and by this method a single plant can, in 5 years, produce up to twenty new bushes within an area of 1-3sq ft. Old branches will also take root and damaged roots will produce suckers. When propagation is to be from seed this should be sown half an inch deep outdoors and during November or December. As soon as they are large enough to handle, the seedlings should be pricked out and then allowed to grow on so that ultimately the sexes can be determined.

The plant prefers to grow near the sea—on cliffs or sand dunes and it is able to establish itself on drifting sand and also to withstand salt-laden gales. It is extremely demanding in respect of light and this is why it grows where there is little competition from other bushes, for example along the sea-shore and in mountain areas. Because of this demand for light, seedlings will not grow in the shade of their parent. There is also a tendency for the lowest and innermost branches of a bush to die because they are in the shade of the highest and

Sea berry

outermost branches. Even so, despite its preference for the sea-shore and its demand for light, it does thrive quite well inland and will grow wild on gravel and sand banks. It can be grown on any ordinary soil but should be planted in a location where there is full sun or only slight shade. Planting should be done in autumn or spring. No special pruning is required.

The sea berry produces its orange-coloured fruits in large quantities and these will remain on the bush for some time because birds will not touch them. The berries are round to egg-shaped, from a quarter to three-eighths of an inch long, and are on short stalks. These berries are, in fact, very small nuts which are enclosed in orange, juicy, acid flesh. They possess an exceptionally high vitamin C content and during World War II the plant was protected by the Germans because of the value of this vitamin C.

The berries can be used for marmalade, jelly or sauce. The Tartars made a jelly from them which was served with milk or cheese, and the fisherfolk of the Gulf of Bothnia make a jelly which is served as a pleasing relish with fish.

Snowberry

Classification	:	*Chiognes hispidulum.*
Physiology	:	A creeping, evergreen shrub.
Origin	:	North America.
History	:	Not cultivated for its fruit either in USA or Canada. Introduced to Europe (Britain) in 1815 but is still very rare.
Recommended site	:	A moist, boggy spot.
Culinary uses	:	Eaten from the hand. A dessert delicacy for the table.

Chiognes hispidulum is very closely related to the *Gaultheria* species, some of which are occasionally mistaken for it. It is a native of North America, from Newfoundland to British Columbia and southwards to North Carolina. It was introduced to Britain in 1815 but is still very rare—which is a pity. Snowberry generally grows in peat bogs and mossy woodland although sometimes it is to be found in dry shady places or spreading over decaying tree stumps. It is a small creeping evergreen shrub growing close to the ground, with slender branches no more than 15-20in long. Slender stems carry forward-pointing bristles and its small leaves are a dark glossy green above and brownish underneath.

The best location for growing it is a moist, boggy, peaty spot—this can be a moist peaty sandy pocket in the rock garden. It can also be grown under other lime-hating shrubs as it does not object to shade.

Propagation can be from seed which should be sown in the autumn in a cold frame or outdoors in a sandy, peaty soil. Root offsets can also be removed in the spring or cuttings taken in April.

The small, white, bell-shaped flowers are produced on short stalks,

Snowberry

singly in the axils of the leaves. The berries which follow are white, one-third of an inch in diameter, round to oblong-shaped, and bristly. These are ready to be gathered in the autumn and they have an aromatic, delicate wintergreen flavour and are also slightly acid. They can be eaten from the hand or used as a dessert delicacy for the table. Snowberries are not produced abundantly but they are, of all the wild fruits, the most 'out of this world'.

Strawberry-raspberry

Classification	:	*Rubus illecebrosus.*
Physiology	:	Herbaceous, creeping, prickly plant growing to 1ft or more.
Origin	:	China; Japan.
History	:	Grows wild in China and Japan. Fairly rare in Europe and North America but is sometimes cultivated for its fruit.
Recommended site	:	Outdoors as ground cover plant.
Culinary uses	:	Cooked for pies; jam or syrup.

This fruit belong to the very large *Rubus* genus (see Brambleberries) but is dealt with separately because of the difference between it and most of the other species—although *Rubus rosaefolius* is so similar that it may almost be considered to be the same plant.

The strawberry-raspberry originated in China and Japan where it still grows wild. It is still fairly rare in Europe and North America although it may sometimes be found cultivated for its fruit. It is a somewhat dwarf, herbaceous, prickly plant which grows to a height of about 1ft. Because it quickly forms a dense mat and smothers any weeds, it can be considered a good ground-cover plant. Even though frost cuts it down to the ground in the winter the following spring will see a new mat of shoots pushing forth.

It may be propagated from seed but the usual method is by division of the roots in autumn. No special soil is required and the only cultivation needed is to cut the shoots down close to the ground—if this is not done by frost during autumn or winter.

Flowers are self-fertile and these are large, white and sweetly scented. The fruit is borne continuously for a long period. Bright red

279

Strawberry-raspberry

berries are borne singly, or in cluster of two or three, and in a good soil they may be of considerable size—up to 1in long.

Although sour, bitter and unpalatable if eaten out of the hand they have a pleasant flavour when cooked—rather like a mixture of strawberries and raspberries. They make a very good syrup or can be used for pies or jam.

Anyone who has a bank or other ground to cover and wishes to grow an unusual fruit should consider the strawberry-raspberry because of its ease of cultivation. Its continuous flowering and fruiting make it an ornamental plant as well as one with fruit value.

Sugarberry
(HACKBERRY)

Classification	:	*Celtis* species.
Physiology	:	Deciduous trees and shrubs.
Origin	:	North temperate zone.
History	:	Said to be the fruit of the legendary Lotus eaters. Cultivated in southern Europe. Introduced to England in the sixteenth century. Hackberry cultivated as ornamental in northern USA.
Recommended site	:	Outdoors—well-drained soil.
Culinary uses	:	For dessert and eating from the hand.

The genus *Celtis* consists of about fifty to sixty species, mainly from the northern hemisphere, and they are spiny trees related to, but more attractive than, the elms. Many of the *Celtis* species provide fruits that are eaten and enjoyed locally.

The history of at least one of the species goes back to antiquity. *Celtis australis* is said to have provided the lotus fruit of the ancients, the magical, exquisite, desirable fruit which constituted the food of the Lotophagi or Lotus eaters—the legendary people who inhabited a district of the north-east African coast. It is said that any traveller who ate the fruit or drank the wine they made from it lost all desire to return to his own country.

Propagation of all the *Celtis* species is best done from seed sown during February or March. It can be sown in seed trays in the greenhouse or outdoors during spring. The young plant should be pruned to form a shapely tree, but apart from this little subsequent pruning is necessary. A good loamy soil will suit it best but it will make do with most soils, provided these are well drained.

SPECIES OF PARTICULAR INTEREST

LOTUS BERRY (*Celtis australis*)

A native of southern Europe and the Near East it grows 50-70ft tall, has a beech-like trunk with a smooth grey bark, and is valued not only for its fruit but because of its ornamental character. This tree has been cultivated in England since the sixteenth century, but is, however, not fully hardy and in a moderate to severe frost it may be cut back to its base.

The fruit is a drupe, globular, one-third of an inch to half an inch in diameter, and borne on a very slender stalk about 1in long. It is at first reddish but turns brownish black as it ripens. It is fleshy and sweet.

CAUCASIAN SUGAR BERRY (*Celtis caucasia*)

A native of the Caucasus, Afghanistan and North India. It is a medium-sized tree and has a bushy head to it. Although very closely related to the lotus berry tree it is somewhat hardier.

The fruit is one-third of an inch in diameter on a slender stalk, yellow at first but turning brownish.

AMERICAN SUGAR BERRY (*Celtis laevigata*)

A native of southern USA and said to be very rare in cultivation. The tree grows 60-80ft tall. The fruit is egg-shaped, a quarter of an inch long, orange-red, and sweet.

HACKBERRY (*Celtis occidentalis*)

A native of North America, growing from eastern Canada to the Rocky Mountains. The tree is of variable form and size but may reach 80ft.

It produces its fruit in quantity and this, birds permitting, will hang well into the winter. The fruit is globose, a quarter of an inch to one-third of an inch long. It is at first yellow or reddish but turns a purple-black when ripe. It is a fleshy drupe with a large, round seed. It is very sweet and pleasant to the taste.

There are numerous other *Celtis* species which provide sugarberries. Those which have been described here can be used for dessert or eaten from the hand as are cherries. Before, however, these are fed to all and sundry the legend of the Lotus eaters should be remembered!

Tree tomato

Classification	:	*Cyphomandra betacea.*
Physiology	:	A very small, softwood, evergreen tree, or bush, growing from 8-12ft.
Origin	:	Peru.
History	:	Cultivated by the Indians of ancient Peru but has not attained the same importance as the ordinary tomato and not cultivated to any great extent in USA or Europe.
Recommended site	:	Greenhouse or conservatory—border or pot cultivation.
Culinary uses	:	Used for dessert, jam, preserve or stewing.

The genus *Cyphomandra* belongs to the family Solanaceae and is, therefore, related to the potato and the ordinary tomato. Only one species of *Cyphomandra* (ie *betacea*) is cultivated.

A very long time ago the agriculturally minded Indians of ancient Peru were planting this little tree for its fruit, and planting it on the mountainsides up to an altitude of 8,000ft. The plant and its fruit are not generally known in Britain, although it is fairly easy to grow in a greenhouse or conservatory as a pot plant.

It is a soft-wooded, evergreen miniature tree or bush growing to about 8 or 12ft. The leaves are very large, soft and mid-green in colour. Although only a small tree it tends to become straggly unless kept in check.

Propagation is usually from seed which readily germinates, but it can also be propagated from cuttings. The young seedlings should be

Tree tomato

transplanted to the greenhouse border or to a pot large enough to take its roots. If grown in a pot it is desirable to repot it each year until it finally occupies a large pot or tub. Because of its large, evergreen, tropical leaves it does, when grown in a pot, provide ornamental value as well as fruit. The compost in which it is grown should be a rich loam to which, if possible, should be added leaf mould and well-rotted manure.

To obtain a good yield of fruit a sunny greenhouse or conservatory where the winter temperature does not fall much below 50°F (10°C) is desirable. But although it will be killed back to its largest stems or branches by temperatures of 28°F (−2°C) it has the power to recover from such injury and new shoots will sprout lower down the stem. During the winter it should only be watered lightly but during the summer it needs abundant watering. It is, however, essential to avoid a high humidity because this may cause the stems to rot.

During April the tree should be pruned as necessary to prevent it from straggling. It is a quick grower and commences to bear fruit when only 2 years old, and it will remain productive for several years.

The fragrant purple and green flowers usually appear in spring, although under ideal conditions it flowers continuously and is a prolific bearer. The flowers are followed by red or orange-red, smooth-skinned, egg-shaped fruit, pointed at the ends. They are 2-3in long and 1½-2in wide, and hang in clusters near the ends of young shoots. At first they are a greenish purple colour but turn orange-red as they ripen. The pulp is light orange in colour and contains black seeds. They have a sweeter taste than the ordinary tomato, and are sub-acid and refreshing. They are agreeable when eaten raw for dessert but their chief use is for jams and preserves or for stewing.

An unusual fruit which ought not to be unusual.

Twinberry

(PARTRIDGE BERRY)

Classification	:	*Mitchella repens.*
Physiology	:	A slender, trailing, evergreen plant.
Origin	:	North America.
History	:	Introduced to Britain in 1761. Not cultivated either in USA or Europe for its fruit.
Recommended site	:	Outdoors—peaty position. Alpine house—pot plant.
Culinary uses	:	Eaten from the hand.

Mitchella repens, which belongs to a genus of two species only, is fairly common in the pine forests of North America. It was first discovered by the American botanist Dr John Mitchell and was named after him. It was introduced into Britain in 1761 but has never been cultivated for its fruit.

Twinberry or partridge berry is a slender, trailing, evergreen plant which grows close to the ground and spreads by taking root at its nodes. Its leaves are heart-shaped, usually about half an inch long, glossy and sometimes have white veins. Because of its mat-forming habit it makes a good ground-cover plant; it is also hardy as well as being attractive.

Propagation is normally by division of the roots in autumn or spring and it should be planted in a moist, peaty soil with plenty of leaf mould. Its location can be in a shady part of a rock garden, or under lime-hating shrubs, or it can be grown in an alpine house as a pot plant. Planting time should be autumn or spring.

The flowers occur in pairs and are either terminal or are in the

285

Twinberry

leaf axils. They are white or pinkish, fragrant and funnel-shaped. In some flowers the stamens extend beyond the corolla, and the pistil is much shorter than the tube of the flower. In others the stamens are short, and the pistil extends beyond the flower. This is just another of nature's many ways of obtaining cross-pollination.

Twinberry is unique because the flowers are produced in pairs. The twin flowers are so united at their base that the two flowers form one fruit but with the two calyxes remaining at the top.

The fruit is a globose berry, about a quarter of an inch in diameter, bright red in colour and with a spicy taste. The berries produced are not numerous and they must be considered as an unusual fruit to be eaten from the hand. They will hang on the plant all winter, or until eaten by the birds.

Ugni
(CHILEAN GUAVA)

Classification	:	*Myrtus ugni* (syn. *Eugenia ugni*).
Physiology	:	An evergreen shrub, erect growing, 4-8ft tall.
Origin	:	Chile.
History	:	Cultivated by the native inhabitants of Chile and also later by Spanish settlers. Brought to England in 1844 and thought to have good prospects as a fruit bush.
Recommended site	:	Cool greenhouse or conservatory—pot shrub. Outdoors—only in well sheltered, mild parts.
Culinary uses	:	For jelly, jam or preserves.

There are about a hundred species of the genus *Myrtus* but with the possible exception of the two species mentioned later, only *ugni* is of real interest to the pomologist.

It originated in Chile where it was known as ugni to the native peoples who readily ate its berries. The early Spanish settlers also soon began to appreciate the delicately flavoured, juicy berries and so began cultivating the plant. In 1844 it was brought to England and it was thought that because of its comparatively small growth and the delicate aroma of the fruit that it would make a very good fruit bush. In fact, trials were made for the fruit at the Grand Autumn Fruit Show of the Horticultural Society in 1857. But for some reason interest was lost, with the result that there has been no improvement in the plant as a fruit bearer.

Ugni

Ugni is a leathery leafed, evergreen shrub, rather stiff and erect in habit, and growing to a height of 4-8ft. The leaves are pointed, 1-2in long, glossy, dark green above and paler below. The leaves are not aromatic like the leaves of the common myrtle. It is only semi-hardy in Britain (but hardy in Devon and Cornwall) and should, therefore, only be grown outdoors in a mild, well-sheltered position and preferably against a wall. It is more suitable for growing in a pot or container, to be taken into a greenhouse or conservatory during winter.

Propagation is best achieved from half-ripe cuttings taken in August. If these are inserted in a sandy compost in a warm frame they will root fairly well. The following spring they can be transplanted to individual pots containing a loamy soil which should be well drained. The only pruning it requires is to keep it a suitable shape and size.

The flowers are freely produced in May and are pinkish white with many stamens. Pollination is effected by insects and fruit is borne abundantly. These are berries about the size of large peas and blue-black in colour. They have a delicate, musky flavour, are palatable, and make excellent jellies and jams.

OTHER MYRTUS SPECIES

MYRTUS LUMA (syn. *Eugenia apiculata*)

This, like ugni, comes from Chile but is a little hardier. Under suitable conditions it takes the form of a tree and grows to 20ft. Young trees beautify themselves by shedding some of their bark and revealing their creamy white under-surface which contrasts well with their mahogany brown branches.

Cultivation is the same as for ugni. The flowers are white and about five-eighths of an inch in diameter. The berries are black and sweet.

MYRTLE BERRY (*Myrtus communis*)

Today this shrub is naturalized throughout southern Europe, but in all probability it originated in western Asia, where Adam himself is thought to have originated. Certainly its history goes back to the first days of man; there is an Arab belief that when Adam was turned out of Paradise he took with him a grain of wheat, a date stone and a sprig of myrtle. In Roman mythology Venus was believed to have worn a garland of myrtle when she rose from the sea; and when satyrs tried to watch her bathing she concealed herself behind a myrtle bush.

Myrtle is said to have been introduced into England by Sir Walter Raleigh and Sir Francis Carey in 1585. However, as it was sacred to the goddess of love it is almost certain that the Romans would have introduced it. Its association with the goddess of love was no doubt the reason why, at one time, it was always included in bridal bouquets. Some of the myrtle trees growing in Britain today may owe their existence to the planting of sprigs by bridesmaids close by the door of the newly married couple's home.

The myrtle is a dense, evergreen, fragrant shrub growing to 15ft. Its stiff, glossy green leaves are very aromatic when bruised and from early times a fragrant oil has been obtained from its flowers, leaves and bark and used in perfumery. One form of myrtle which has three leaves instead of two at every joint was esteemed by the Jewish people and used in religious ceremonies and for decorating at the Feast of Tabernacles.

It can be propagated from seed sown in spring or summer in a temperature of 60-65°F (16-18°C), and kept moist and shaded. When large enough to handle, the seedlings should be transplanted into individual pots and grown on in a cool greenhouse. Also, as with ugni, cuttings can be taken in August.

In warm countries it will be found growing in dry stony places and frequently in evergreen thickets and pinewoods. In Britain it can only be grown outdoors in a mild, sheltered location. As a pot shrub it can be grown outdoors during the summer and then taken into a cool greenhouse or conservatory for the winter. It should be given a well-drained loamy soil and pruned or clipped to a suitable shape and size.

The solitary, sweet-scented flowers appear in June or July and are produced profusely. They are about three-quarters of an inch across and carried on stalks up to an inch long which grow from the axils of the leaves. Pollination is effected by insects and there is an abundance of berries.

The berries are bluish black, roundish to oblong, and half an inch in length. In Corsica these berries are gathered and used to make a very aromatic liqueur. The Romans used them to make a sauce which was eaten with wild boar.

They can also be used as a condiment and are said to be aphrodisiac!

U

Umbinza

Classification   :   *Halleria lucida.*
Physiology   :   Straggling evergreen shrub growing 4-6ft tall.
Origin   :   South Africa.
History   :   Plant used in African witchcraft and fruit eaten by native peoples.
Recommended site :   Greenhouse or conservatory—pot plant.
Culinary uses   :   Eaten from the hand or used in fresh fruit salads.

Halleria is a small genus of evergreen shrubs or small trees, which are often known as wild fuchsias or bush honeysuckles. The species provide edible berries which are gathered and eaten by natives of the areas where the shrubs grow wild.

Only one species, *Halleria lucida,* is normally available in Britain. In South Africa the Xhosa call it umbinza, and as well as it providing them with edible berries it plays a part in their folklore; when they offer a sacrifice to their ancestral spirits they burn twigs of umbinza. In Basutoland the plant is burned each spring and the ashes, after being mixed with fat, are smeared on wooden pegs which are pushed into the ground all around a village. This is done to protect the people of the village from evil spirits and bad weather.

Umbinza or *Halleria lucida,* whichever you prefer to call it, is an evergreen shrub, rather straggling in habit, which grows from 4-6ft tall. In its natural habitat it is found around the edge of forests. In cool temperate climates it needs protection as it cannot withstand frost.

It can be either propagated from seed or from soft cuttings which should be inserted in a light soil in warmth under a frame. It can then be grown in a pot in a greenhouse or conservatory. During spring and summer it will require plenty of water and it should be grown in a light but rich soil. Apart from this it needs little attention except to keep it to a convenient size and shape.

The flowers are produced in June. They are tubular in shape, red in colour, and hang in groups of a few together. These are followed by globular berries, about three-quarters of an inch in diameter. These berries are green at first, but when ripe are purple. They are extremely sweet although slightly astringent. They can be eaten from the hand or added to a fresh fruit salad to give it an exotic look.

Water chestnut; Singara nut

Classification	:	*Trapa natans*; *Trapa bispinosa*.
Physiology	:	Submerged aquatic perennials.
Origin	:	Persia, India, Egypt.
History	:	Naturalized in southern Europe. Long used as a source of food by local peoples. Now cultivated, especially in China. Introduced into Britain in the late eighteenth century.
Recommended site	:	In water tank or other container in cool or warm greenhouse.
Culinary uses.	:	For general dessert purposes.

Trapa is a genus of about thirty species of aquatic, herbaceous plants. They originated probably in Asia but are now native to North Africa (Egypt) and the warmer parts of southern Europe. Their horned fruits have long been taken for food and in Kashmir they are an important source of food for some of the communities that dwell near the lakes. In some countries, especially China, they are cultivated. During the latter part of the eighteenth century they were introduced into Britain.

The plants have two kinds of leaves—one kind floats on the water and the other is submerged. The floating leaves are angular-shaped and hairy; those which are submerged are whitish and feathery. Although they are perennials they are only short-lived and it is best to treat them as annuals.

Two species are of interest. The first should be grown in a cool greenhouse, the second in a warm greenhouse and both should have a sunny position.

WATER CHESTNUT (*Trapa natans*)
This species is native to the Upper Nile, Persia and warm parts of south-eastern Europe.

The seed should never be dried because this prevents germination. It should be stored in bottles of water in a temperature of 45-50°F (7-10°C). When required it should be transferred to a container of clean water and the temperature raised to about 60-65°F (16-18°C). Then, when germination has taken place—when very small roots become visible—the seedlings should be removed and put into a pot of very rich loam which should be submerged in water, just slightly below the surface. As leaves form and the oldest of them begin to turn yellow, carefully remove the seedlings and pot them individually into 6in pots containing rich loam. The pots should now be immersed at a depth of 9in, and gradually lowered until they are at a depth of 2ft. Water temperature should be at about 60°F (16°C).

The flowers which are produced during summer are almost hidden by the leaves. They are borne on short stalks in the centre of the rosette of floating leaves. They are small, white and insignificant. The fruit is somewhat top-shaped, or conical, about 2in in diameter and has four robust spines or horns which lie horizontally. The fruit is sometimes called water caltrop because of the similar appearance to the spiky caltrop of ancient times which was used to maim enemy soldiers and their horses. They are sweetish, rich in iron, and said to be nutritious. They can be used for dessert purposes.

SINGARA NUT (*Trapa bispinosa*)
A native of India and Ceylon and needs warmer temperatures than *T. natans* although in other respects the cultivation is the same. Its fruits have only two horns.

The seeds need to be stored in a temperature of about 55°F (13°C); 70-75°F (21-24°C) is required for germination; and when the plant is in growth the water should be at a temperature of 70°F (21°C).

Wineberry

Classification	:	*Rubus phoenicolasius.*
Physiology	:	A bushy bramble growing to 6ft.
Origin	:	China, Japan.
History	:	Introduced into Britain in 1876. Grown as an ornamental as well as a fruit bearer in temperate regions.
Recommended site	:	Outdoors.
Culinary uses	:	Fresh for dessert; or for jam, jellies or stewing.

This fruit is just another of the many provided by the great genus *Rubus* (see Brambleberries) but merits separate consideration. Although a native of the mountains of China and Japan, it is now grown in the temperate regions generally. It was introduced to British growers in 1876. Some nurserymen advertise it as an ornamental as well as a fruit bearer. It is a bushy bramble growing to a height of about 6ft and producing long, recurving, rambling canes which are covered with bright, reddish brown hairs and weak prickles. These make it a very distinctive shrub especially during the wintertime.

The wineberry is propagated by taking the young shoots or suckers that the bush produces naturally. If more than one bush is to be grown the young plants should be set out at 6ft apart. The soil should be well prepared by deep digging to make sure that the drainage is good; wineberry does not like a waterlogged soil although a partially shaded damp position is very acceptable. A good rich loam is ideal.

It can be trained along a fence or on wire trellis work where its red, bristly stems show to advantage in winter. Another method of training is to spiral it up four stakes set round it and at a distance of 3ft from its base.

294

After planting in the autumn the shoots should be well shortened to encourage plenty of growth during the first season. In the following years it should be pruned after fruiting has finished. All wood which has borne fruit should be removed and then, in March, the soft tips of the remaining shoots should be removed. Also during March a top dressing of manure is beneficial.

Pinkish white flowers are borne in summer. They are small but in dense clusters and are self-fertile. The calyx lobes envelope the growing fruits, keeping them covered until almost ripe when they open to reveal soft whitish berries which quickly ripen to a cherry-red colour. Because of the calyx covering, wineberries do not suffer very much from insects and fungi as do raspberries and loganberries.

In appearance the wineberry is something like the raspberry but more attractive because of its fresh appearance and colour. It is sweet, juicy and refreshing in taste. The berries, ready in August, all ripen at once so that the whole sprig can be cut off and served for dessert, for which purpose they are excellent. They can be eaten with cream. They are also good for jams and jellies.

Not only is wineberry a provider of unusual fruit but it has definite ornamental value in the garden. It has great attractions, and especially for children in the fruiting season!

Worcesterberry

Classification   : A *Ribes* species
Physiology   : Vigorous, spiny bush resembling gooseberry.
Origin   : Unknown.
History   : Once said to be a cross between the gooseberry and blackcurrant but now thought to be a true *Ribes* species. Rarely grown outside Britain.
Recommended site : Outdoors.
Culinary uses   : Cooked and used in the same way as the gooseberry and blackcurrant.

It is not always realized that the gooseberry and blackcurrant both belong to the genus *Ribes*. At first sight there appears little similarity between *Ribes grossularia* (gooseberry) and *Ribes nigrum* (blackcurrant) and it has, in fact, been suggested that the spiny gooseberry should form a distinct species—*Grossularia*. But the worcesterberry shows how close the currants and gooseberries are. At one time it was believed that the worcesterberry was a cross between the gooseberry and blackcurrant and it was even claimed that one parent was the Whinham Industry gooseberry and the other was the Boskop Giant blackcurrant. More recently, however, it has come to be thought of as a true *Ribes* species. Possibly it is near to the American gooseberry species, which are spiny bushes producing a half-gooseberry half-currant type of fruit. Anyway, whatever the worcesterberry is or is not, there is no proof that it is either a man-made hybrid or that it originated in North America.

In appearance the bush resembles a gooseberry bush but is perhaps a little more vigorous and a little more spiny. It likes the same kind of loamy soil, and in general its cultivation is similar.

It is quite easily propagated from cuttings which should be taken from ripe wood in October. These should be about 8in long and as straight as possible. Apart from one or two buds at the top of the cuttings all the others should be removed. The cuttings should then be planted 3in apart, in loamy soil—a slit about 7in deep having first been made in the soil, and sand or grit put along the bottom of this. They should be planted so that the top inch, with the buds, is above the soil. The soil should be trodden in firmly along the slit. They can then be left until the following October except for keeping them free of weeds and watering them during dry weather.

In the following October they can be taken from their bed and planted 6ft apart in a soil which has been deeply dug and enriched with manure or other available compost. The aim should now be to grow a bush with a short leg or stump, and all of the buds on the lowest 5in of the stem should be removed. Above this bottom 5in only four buds should be allowed to develop and the remainder of them should be cut off. During the second year the four buds will develop into branches. In subsequent years the aim of the pruning should be to keep the bush to a good shape and also to encourage a good yield of berries. In November the side shoots on the main branches should be cut back to 3 or 4in and from time to time it may be necessary to remove old wood.

The berries are borne in trusses, like blackcurrants, and hang from the undersides of the branches. They are smaller than gooseberries but larger than blackcurrants. They change from green to purplish black when ripe and sometimes can be picked as late as September. Use them in the same way as cooked gooseberries or blackcurrants.

SOME AMERICAN GOOSEBERRIES FOR COMPARISON

RIBES DIVARICATUM—a shrub or bush which grows up to 10ft. Its young wood is armed with spines up to two-thirds of an inch long. The berry is one-third of an inch in diameter, glabrous and purplish black.

RIBES ROTUNDIFOLIUM—armed with solitary spines which are

297

v

Worcesterberry

small and inconspicuous. Berries are glabrous, purple and well flavoured.

RIBES VALDIVIANUM—a much-branched shrub, growing to about 6ft. The flowers are produced in unisexual racemes. The male racemes are larger than the female and are up to 3in long and 2in wide. The berries are about one-third of an inch in diameter and are purplish black.

RIBES HIRTELLUM—sometimes called the currant gooseberry. The berries are half an inch in diameter and are purplish black.

RIBES OXYACANTHOIDES—berries are about half an inch in diameter and are reddish purple.

Zabala fruit

Classification	:	*Lardizabala biternata; Stauntonia hexaphylla:*
Physiology	:	Slightly tender, evergreen climbers.
Origin	:	Chile; Japan.
History	:	Fruit eaten in Chile and Japan. Plants introduced into Britain in the middle of the nineteenth century.
Recommended site	:	Outdoors—mild areas only, against south- or west-facing wall. Cool greenhouse or conservatory—climbing up trellis work or wires.
Culinary uses	:	For dessert.

We began this book with the akebia which is a member of the *Lardizabalaceae* family. We end it with the fruits of two other genera of the same family, for which I have coined the name Zabala.

LARDIZABALA BITERNATA

Lardizabala is a genus of two species and one only, *biternata,* is normally found in cultivation. It was introduced from Chile in the middle of the nineteenth century. With its large, leathery leaves, and flowers late in the year, it is a very distinctive climber. Although slightly tender it is vigorous in growth and may reach a height of 40ft.

Propagation is from cuttings of firm shoots, 1-2in long, inserted in pots of well-drained sandy loam in summer. The plant should be set out in September and October, or in March and April. It may be grown in a well-drained border against a south or west-facing wall in mild areas only, or against the wall of a cool greenhouse or conserva-

299

tory. It can be trained up tall trellis work, wires or pillars. The soil in which it is grown should consist of equal parts of sandy loam and peat. The only pruning it will require is the cutting away of dead and straggling shoots in April.

It produces its flowers in profusion at the end of the year. They are purple and white, and are unisexual. The females appear singly on tender stalks, the males are produced in pendulous 4in spikes. The fruits are sausage-shaped, dark purple, and up to 3in long. In Chile the fruits are much enjoyed, and are gathered and sold in the markets. As a dessert fruit they must be considered as a novelty.

STAUNTONIA HEXAPHYLLA

Stauntonia is a genus of fifteen climbing shrubs and belongs to the Burma-Formosa-Japan region. Only one species, *hexaphylla*, is cultivated in Britain and was introduced in the middle of the nineteenth century. It is a slightly tender, evergreen, climbing shrub reaching up to 10-20ft.

Propagation is by cuttings of firm young shoots inserted in sandy soil in a shady position outdoors in summer. The plant should be set out during September to October, or March to April, in deep sandy loam. Its location can be outdoors against a south wall in the south of England or in a cool greenhouse or conservatory, trained against the wall or up trellis work. Pruning, during autumn, consists of no more than cutting back by one-third any trailing shoots not required to produce fruits in the following season.

Unisexual flowers—white, tinged with violet—are produced in April. These are followed by purple-coloured fruits, resembling walnuts in shape.

It cannot be said that these zabala fruits have a great amount of flavour. However, just as each flower has its own perfume—some more pervading than others—so each fruit has its own flavour, and who is better able to appreciate their subtle variations than the man or woman who has put labour, care—even affection—into the growing of unusual fruit.

Acknowledgements

My thanks are sincerely given to those who have helped me with this book. In particular I wish to thank Mr T. H. Rivers of Thomas Rivers & Son Ltd and Mr Malcolm Muir of Ken Muir Ltd; Dr Carter Smith of Rutgers University, New Brunswick, for information on cranberry and raspberry production in the United States; and my wife Gwendolin for her co-operation, patience and help in so many ways.

Table of related fruits named in the text

Classification	Common Name	Included Under
Actinidia arguta	SIBERIAN GOOSEBERRY	Chinese gooseberry
„ *coriacea*	CHINESE EGG GOOSEBERRY	„ „
„ *kolomikta*	MANCHURIAN GOOSEBERRY	„ „
„ *purpurea*	PURPLE CHINESE GOOSEBERRY	„ „
„ *sinensis*	KIWI FRUIT	„ „
Aegle marmelos	BAEL FRUIT	Marmelos
„ „	JAPANESE BITTER ORANGE	„
Akebia lobata	AKEBIA FRUIT	Akebia fruit
„ *quinnata*	„ „	„ „
„ *trifoliata*	„ „	„ „
Alemanchier alnifolia	MOUNTAIN JUNEBERRY	Juneberry
„ *asiatica*	KOREAN JUNEBERRY	„
„ *canadensis*	JUNEBERRY	„
„ „	SHADBERRY	„
„ *florida*	FLORIDA JUNEBERRY	„
„ *oblongifolia*	SWAMP SUGAR PEAR	„
„ *ovalis*	EUROPEAN JUNEBERRY	„
„ „	SNOWY MESPILUS	„
„ *stolonifera*	QUEBEC BERRY	„
„ „ x *spicata*	—	„
Ananas comosus	PINEAPPLE	Pineapple
Annona cherimola	CHERIMOYA	Custard apple
„ *diversifolia*	LLAMA	„ „
„ *muricata*	GUANABRA	„ „
„ „	SOUR SOP	„ „
„ *squamosa*	SHARIFA	„ „
„ „	SUGAR APPLE	„ „
Arbutus unedo	TREE STRAWBERRY	Killarney strawberry
Arctostaphylos columbiana	COLUMBIA MANZANITA	Manzanita
„ *glauca*	BIGBERRY MANZANITA	„
„ *manzanita*	MANZANITA	„

Table of related fruits

Classification	Common Name	Included Under
Arctostaphylos nevadensis	NEVADA BEARBERRY	Manzanita
„ *patula*	PINE MANZANITA	„
„ „	GREEN LEAF MANZANITA	„
„ *uva-ursi*	BEARBERRY	„
Asiminia triloba	POOR MAN'S BANANA	Custard banana
Averrhoa bilimbi	BILIMBI	Carambola
„ *carambola*	CARAMBOLA	„
Berberis angulosa	HIMALAYAN BARBERRY	Barberry
„ *aristata*	PEPAL BARBERRY	„
„ *asiatica*	RAISIN BARBERRY	„
„ *buxifolia*	MAGELLAN BARBERRY	„
„ *darwinii*	DARWIN BARBERRY	„
„ *haematocarpa*	MEXICAN BARBERRY	„
„ *vulgaris*	BARBERRY	„
Billardiera longiflora	BLUE APPLEBERRY	Appleberry
„ „ *fructo albo*	WHITE APPLEBERRY	„
Carica candamarcensis	MOUNTAIN PAW PAW	Paw paw
„ *papaya*	PAPAYA	„ „
Carpobrotus edulis	HOTTENTOT FIG	Hottentot fig
Casimiroa edulis	WHITE SAPOTE	Casimiroa
Celtis australis	LOTUS BERRY	Sugar berry
„ *caucasia*	CAUCASIAN SUGAR BERRY	„ „
„ *laevigata*	AMERICAN SUGAR BERRY	„ „
„ *occidentalis*	HACKBERRY	„ „
Chaenomeles cathayensis	CHINESE QUINCE	Japanese quince
„ *japonica*	DWARF QUINCE	„ „
„ „	MAULES QUINCE	„ „
„ *lagenaria*	JAPONICA	„ „
„ *maulei*	DWARF QUINCE	„ „
„ „	MAULES QUINCE	„ „
„ *speciosa*	JAPONICA	„ „
Chiognes hispidulum	SNOWBERRY	Snowberry
Citrus aurantifolia	LIME	Lime
„ *aurantium*	SEVILLE ORANGE	Orange
„ *bergamia*	BERGAMOT ORANGE	„
„ *grandis*	SHADDOCK	Pummelo
„ *limonia*	LEMON	Lemon
„ *maxima*	SHADDOCK	Pummelo
„ *medica*	CITRON	Orange
„ *mitis*	CALAMONDIN	„
„ „	PANAMA ORANGE	„
„ *paradisei*	GRAPEFRUIT	Pummelo
„ *reticulata*	CLEMENTINE	Mandarin
„ „	MANDARIN	„
„ „	SATSUMA	„

Table of related fruits

Classification	Common Name	Included Under
Citrus reticulata	TANGERINE	Mandarin
„ *sinensis*	SWEET ORANGE	Orange
Coffea arabica	COFFEE BEAN	Coffee bean
Cornus mas	CORNELIAN CHERRY	Cornelian cherry
„ *suecica*	DWARF CORNELIAN CHERRY	„ „
Crataegus azaroles	MEDITERRANEAN MEDLAR	Mediterranean medlar
„ *coccinioides*	MISSISSIPI HAWBERRY	„ „
„ *douglasii*	BLACK HAWBERRY	„ „
„ *pinnatifida major*	CHINESE HAWBERRY	„ „
„ *pubesen stipulata*	MANZANILLA	„ „
„ *tanacetifolia*	SYRIAN HAWBERRY	„ „
Cydonia oblonga	QUINCE	Quince
Cyphomandra betacea	TREE TOMATO	Tree tomato
Diospyros amata	BUSH PERSIMMON	Persimmon
„ *ebenaster*	ZAPOTE NEGRO	„
„ *kaki*	KAKI	„
„ *lycioides*	JAPANESE DATE PLUM	„
	MONKEY PLUM	„
„ *mespiliformis*	JAKKALBESSIE	„
„ *virginiana*	AMERICAN PERSIMMON	„
„ „	DATE PLUM	„
	SIMMONS TREE	„
Elaeagnus angustifolia	OLEASTER	Goumi
„ „	RUSSIAN OLIVE	„
„ „	WILD OLIVE	„
„ *argentea*	SILVER BERRY	„
„ *commutata*	„ „	„
„ *edulis*	GOUMI	„
„ *multiflora*	„	„
„ *orientalis*	TREZIBOND DATE	„
Empetrum hermaphroditiem	MOUNTAIN CROWBERRY	Crowberry
„ *nigrum*	BLACK CROWBERRY	„
„ var. *purpureum*	PURPLE CROWBERRY	„
„ *rubra*	SOUTH AMERICAN CROWBERRY	„
Eriobotrya japonica	JAPANESE MEDLAR	Loquat
„ „	JAPANESE PLUM	
Eugenia apiculata	MYRTUS LUMA	Ugni
„ *cordatum*	WATER BERRY	Brazilian cherry
„ *curanii*	JAVA PLUM	„ „
„ *jambos*	ROSE APPLE	„ „
„ *malaccensis*	MALAYA APPLE	„ „
„ *ugni*	CHILEAN GUAVA	Ugni
„ *uniflora*	PITANGA CHERRY	Brazilian cherry
„ „	SURINAM CHERRY	„ „

Table of related fruits

Classification	Common Name	Included Under
Euphoria longana	LONGAN	Litchee
Feijoa sellowina	PINEAPPLE GUAVA	Feijoa
Ficus caprica	FIG	Fig
Fortunella japonica	MARUMI KUMQUAT	Kumquat
„ *margarita*	NAGAMI KUMQUAT	„
Fragaria vesca sempervirens	ALPINE STRAWBERRY	Alpine strawberry
Fuchsia corymbiflora	FUCHSIA BERRY	Fuchsia berry
„ *exorticata*	„ „	„ „
Gaultheria miquelina	MIQUEL BERRY	Checkerberry
„ *ovatifolia*	MOUNTAIN CHECKERBERRY	„
„ *procumbens*	BOXBERRY	„
„ „	PARTRIDGE BERRY	„
„ „	TEA BERRY	„
„ *shallon*	SHALLON BERRY	„
Gaylussacia baccata	BLACK HUCKLEBERRY	Huckleberry
„ *brachycera*	BOX HUCKLEBERRY	„
„ *dumosa*	DWARF HUCKLEBERRY	„
„ *frondosa*	DANGLEBERRY	„
„ „	TANGLEBERRY	„
„ *resinosa*	BLACK HUCKLEBERRY	„
„ *ursina*	BEAR HUCKLEBERRY	„
Halleria lucida	UMBINZA	Umbinza
Hippophae rhamnoides	SEA BUCKTHORN	Sea berry
Lardizabala biternata	ZABALA FRUIT	Zabala fruit
Litchi chinensis	LYCHEE	Litchee
„ „	LYCHEE	„
Mahonia aquifolium	—	Oregon grape
„ *haematocarpa*	—	„ „
„ *nervosa*	OREGON GRAPE	„ „
„ *nevinii*	—	„ „
„ *pinnata*	—	„ „
„ *trifoliolata*	MEXICAN BARBERRY	„ „
Malpighia glabra	ACEROLAS	Barbados cherry
Mangifera indica	MANGO	Mango
Mespilus germanica	MEDLAR	Medlar
Mitchella repens	PARTRIDGE BERRY	Twinberry
Monstera deliciosa	MONSTERA	Monstera
Morus acidosa	KOREAN MULBERRY	Mulberry
„ *alba*	WHITE MULBERRY	„
„ „ *tarica*	RUSSIAN MULBERRY	„
„ *mongolica*	MONGOLIAN MULBERRY	„
„ *nigra*	BLACK MULBERRY	„
„ *rubra*	RED MULBERRY	„
Myrtus communis	MYRTLE BERRY	Ugni
„ *luma*	MYRTUS LUMA	„

305

Table of related fruits

Classification	Common Name	Included Under
Myrtus ugni	CHILEAN GUAVA	
Musa cavendishii	CANARY BANANA	Banana
„ „	CAVENDISH BANANA	
Olea europea	OLIVE	Olive
Opuntia engelmanii	—	Prickly pear
„ *ficus indica*	BARBARY FIG	„ „
„ *herrfeldtii*	—	„ „
„ *leuchotricha*	DURAZNILLO	„ „
„ *megacantha*	—	„ „
„ *opuntia*	INDIAN FIG	„ „
„ *rafinesquii*	DEVIL'S TONGUE	„ „
„ *streptacantha*	TUNA CARDONA	„ „
„ *undulata*	—	„ „
„ *vulgarii*	INDIAN FIG	
Owenia acidula	AUSTRALIAN NATIVE NECTARINE	Desert plum
„ „	EMU APPLE	„ „
„ „	MOOLEY APPLE	„ „
„ „	RANCOORAN	„ „
„ „	WARRONGAN	„ „
„ „	BULLOO	„ „
„ „	DILLY BOOLEN	„ „
Passiflora antioquiensis	—	Passion fruit
„ *caerula*	—	„ „
„ *edulis*	PURPLE GRANADILLA	„ „
„ „ var. *flavicarpa*	LILIKOI	„ „
„ „ „	YELLOW GRANADILLA	„ „
„ *incarnata*	MAY APPLE	„ „
„ „	MAYPOPS	„ „
„ *laurifolia*	WATER LEMON	„ „
„ *ligularis*	SWEET GRANADILLA	„ „
„ *mollissima*	SWEET CALABASH	„ „
„ *quadrangularis*	GIANT GRANADILLA	„ „
Persea americana	AVOCADO PEAR	Avocado pear
„ *gratissima*	„ „	„ „
Physalis ixocarpa	JAMBERBERRY	Cape gooseberry
„ „	TOMATILLO	„ „
„ *peruviana*	PERUVIAN CHERRY	„ „
„ *pruinosa*	GROUND CHERRY	„ „
Poncirus trifoliata	HARDY ORANGE	Poncirus
„ „ x *Citrus sinensis*	CITRANGE	„
Prunus armenaica	APRICOT	Apricot
„ *amygdalus*	ALMOND	Almond
„ *cerasifera*	MYROBALAN	Cherry plum

Classification	Common Name	Included Under
Prunus dasycarpa	BLACK APRICOT	Apricot
„ *persica*	NECTARINE	Nectarine
var. *nectarina*		
Pseudocydonia	LARGE CHINESE QUINCE	Quince
Psidium cattleianum	CATTLEY GUAVA	Guava
„ „	STRAWBERRY GUAVA	„
„ *friedrichsthalianum*	CAS	„
„ *guayava*	GUAVA	„
Ribes —	WORCESTER BERRY	Worcesterberry
„ *divaricatum*	—	„
„ *hirtellum*	CURRANT GOOSEBERRY	„
„ *oxyacanthoides*	—	„
„ *rotundifolium*	—	„
„ *valdivianum*	—	„
Rosa pomifera	WOLLY DOD'S ROSE	Applerose
„ *rugosa*	APPLEROSE	„
Rubus allegheniensis	MOUNTAIN BLACKBERRY	Brambleberry
„ *canadensis*	CANADIAN BLACKBERRY	„
„ *chamaemorus*	AVRONS	Cloudberry
„ „	MAROSHKA	„
„ „	MOLTEBEERE	„
„ *illecebrosus*	STRAWBERRY—RASPBERRY	Strawberry-raspberry
„ *laciniatus*	OREGON EVERGREEN BLACKBERRY	Brambleberry
„ *leucodermis*	WESTERN BLACK RASPBERRY	Raspberry
„ *millspaughii*	THORNLESS BLACKBERRY	Brambleberry
„ *nivens*	ASIAN BLACK RASPBERRY	Raspberry
„ *occidentalis*	EASTERN BLACK RASPBERRY	„
„ „	THIMBLEBERRY	„
„ *palmatus* x	GOLDEN MAYBERRY	„
„ *phoenicolasius*	WINEBERRY	Wineberry
„ *procumbens*	FIELD DEWBERRY	Brambleberry
„ *prucerus*	HIMALAYAN GIANT BLACKBERRY	Strawberry-raspberry
„ *rosaefolius*	STRAWBERRY—RASPBERRY	Raspberry
„ *strigosa* x *occidentalis*	PURPLE RASPBERRY	Brambleberry
„ *trivialis*	SOUTHERN DEWBERRY	„
„ *vitifolius*	WESTERN DEWBERRY	„
Rubus hybrid	BOYSENBERRY	„
„ „	KING'S ACE BERRY	„
„ „	LAXTON BERRY	„
„ „	LOWBERRY	„
„ „	NECTAR BERRY	„
„ „	PHENOMENAL BERRY	„
„ „	VEITCHBERRY	„

Table of related fruits

Classification	Common Name	Included Under
Sambucus canadensis	AMERICAN ELDERBERRY	Elderberry
„ *caerula*	WESTERN ELDERBERRY	„
„ *callicarpa*	CALIFORNIAN ELDERBERRY	„
„ *glauca*	BLUE ELDERBERRY	„
„ *nigra*	ELDERBERRY	„
„ *nigra fructo-lutea*	YELLOW ELDERBERRY	„
„ *pubens*	WHITE ELDERBERRY	„
leucocarpa		
„ „ *zanthocarpa*	GOLDEN ELDERBERRY	„
„ *racemosa*	RED ELDERBERRY	„
Sheperdia argentea	NEBRASKA CURRANT	Buffalo berry
„ *canadensis*	CANADIAN BUFFALO BERRY	„ „
Sorbus aria	WHITEBEAM	
„ *aucaparia edulis*	ROWANBERRY	
„ *domestica*	SERVICE BERRY	Chequers
„ *hybrida*	FINNISH WHITEBEAM	Rowanberry
„ *intermedia*	SWEDISH WHITEBEAM	„
„ „ *arranensis*	FINNISH WHITEBEAM	„
„ *latifolia*	FONTAINBLEU	Chequers
„ *mougeottii*	POLISH WHITEBEAM	Rowanberry
„ *torminalis*	SERVICE BERRY	Chequers
Spondias cytherea	OTAHEITE APPLE	Mombin fruit
„ *mombin*	HOG PLUM	„ „
„ „	YELLOW MOMBIN	„ „
„ *pinnata*	MALAYAN MOMBIN	„ „
„ *purpurea*	RED MOMBIN	„ „
„ „	SPANISH MOMBIN	„ „
Stauntonia hexaphylla	STAUNTONIA	Zabala fruit
Trapa bispinosa	SINGARA NUT	Water chestnut
„ *natans*	WATER CHESTNUT	„ „
Vaccinium ashei	RABBIT EYE BLUEBERRY	Blueberry
„ *atrococcum*	BLACK HIGH BUSH BLUEBERRY	„
„ *caepitosum*	DWARF BLUEBERRY	„
„ *canadensis*	CANADIAN BLUEBERRY	„
„ *corymbosum*	HIGH BUSH BLUEBERRY	„
„ „	SWAMP BLUEBERRY	„
„ *erythrocarpum*	SOUTHERN CRANBERRY	Cranberry
„ *hirsutum*	HAIRY BLUEBERRY	Blueberry
„ *macrocarpon*	AMERICAN CRANBERRY	Cranberry
„ *melanocarpum*	GEORGIA BLUEBERRY	Blueberry
„ *membranaceum*	MOUNTAIN BLACKBERRY	„
„ *myrtillus*	BILBERRY	Bilberry
„ „	BLAEBERRY	„
„ „	WHINBERRY	„

Table of related fruits

Classification	Common Name	Included Under
Vaccinium myrtillus	WHORTLEBERRY	Bilberry
,, *ovatum*	WESTERN BLUEBERRY	Blueberry
,, *oxycoccos*	SMALL CRANBERRY	Cranberry
,, ,,	MARSH WHORTLEBERRY	,,
,, ,, *macrocarpus*	CRANBERRY	,,
,, *pennsylvanicum*	LOW BUSH BLUEBERRY	Blueberry
	SWEET BLUEBERRY	,,
,, ,, *angustifolium*	DWARF MOUNTAIN BLUEBERRY	,,
,, ,, *nigrum*	—	,,
,, *uglinosum*	GREAT BILBERRY	Bilberry
,, ,,	BOG WHORTLEBERRY	,,
,, *vacillans*	DRY-LAND BLUEBERRY	Blueberry
,, *virgatum*	SOUTHERN HIGH BUSH BLUEBERRY	,,
,, *vitis idaea*	COWBERRY	Cranberry
,, ,, ,,	MOUNTAIN CRANBERRY	,,
,, ,, ,,	RED WHORTLEBERRY	,,
Viburnum alnifolium	HOBBLEBERRY	Guelderberry
,, *lentago*	WILD RAISIN	,,
,, ,,	SHEEPBERRY	,,
,, *nudum*	—	,,
,, *opulus*	HIGH BUSH CRANBERRY	,,
,, ,, *americanum*	,, ,, ,,	,,
,, ,, *luteum*	—	,,
,, *prunifolium*	STAGBERRY	,,
,, *trilobum*	HIGH BUSH CRANBERRY	,,
Vitis vinifera	GRAPE	Grape
Yucca baccata	DATE FRUIT	Eve's date
Zizyphus jujube	CHINESE JUJUBE	Jujube
,, ,,	CHINESE DATE	,,
,, *mauritanius*	INDIAN JUJUBE	,,
,, *rotundifolia*	—	,,
,, *sativa*	CHINESE JUJUBE	,,
,, ,,	CHINESE DATE	
,, *spina christi*	ARABIAN JUJUBE	